FAMILY
AND
WORK

Recent Titles in
Contributions in Family Studies

A Coat of Many Colors: Jewish Subcommunities in the United States
ABRAHAM D. LAVENDER, EDITOR

Passing: The Vision of Death in America
CHARLES O. JACKSON, EDITOR

Cross-Cultural Perspectives of Mate-Selection and Marriage
GEORGE KURIAN, EDITOR

A Social History of American Family Sociology, 1865–1940
RONALD L. HOWARD, EDITED BY JOHN MOGEY

Women in the Family and in the Economy: An International
Comparative Survey
GEORGE KURIAN AND RATNA GHOSH, EDITORS

Revolutions in Americans' Lives: A Demographic Perspective on the History
of Americans, Their Families, and Their Society
ROBERT V. WELLS

Three Different Worlds: Women, Men, and Children in an
Industrializing Community
FRANCES ABRAHAMER ROTHSTEIN

FAMILY
AND
WORK

COMPARATIVE
CONVERGENCES

Edited by
MERLIN B. BRINKERHOFF

Contributions in Family Studies, Number 8

GREENWOOD PRESS
Westport, Connecticut · London, England

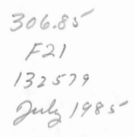

Library of Congress Cataloging in Publication Data

Main entry under title:

Family and work.

(Contributions in family studies, ISSN 0147-1023 ;
no. 8)

Results of a colloquium held at the University of
Calgary.

Companion vol. to: Work, organizations, and society.
Bibliography: p.
Includes index.

1. Family—Congresses. 2. Employment (Economic
theory)—Congresses. I. Brinkerhoff, Merlin B.
II. University of Calgary. III. Series.
HQ728.F3117   1984   306.8′5   83-10721
ISBN 0-313-23703-4 (lib. bdg.)

Library of Congress Catalog Card Number: 83-10721
ISBN: 0-313-23703-4
ISSN: 0147-1023

First published in 1984

Greenwood Press
A division of Congressional Information Service, Inc.
88 Post Road West, Westport, Connecticut 06881

Printed in the United States of America

10 9 8 7 6 5 4 3 2 1

Contents

Figures and Tables

FAMILY
AND
WORK

1

The Family-Work System: From Micro- to Macro-Comparisons

MERLIN B. BRINKERHOFF

Many social scientists, especially North Americans, have fallen into the trap of overspecialization. Specialization is endemic in post-industrial societies, even within academia. One consequence of overspecialization is that the broad, holistic view is often lost, or at least neglected.

The chapters in this two-volume set, *Family and Work: Comparative Convergences* and *Work, Organizations, and Society: Comparative Convergences*, attempt to avoid this pitfall by adhering to a general theme that examines the interdependence of the family and work systems from a comparative perspective. Special attention is given to the organizational environment within which work and family activities take place. Overspecialization may be avoided, at least in part, through this more holistic approach.

These volumes came out of a colloquium held recently at the University of Calgary. Several criteria were considered when inviting this select group of scholars to present papers at the conference. The contributors were chosen, in part, because of their published research on the sociology of family or work and their ostensive commitment to comparative studies. We desired a good mix of theoretical and empirical papers, qualitative and quantitative approaches, and micro- and macro-analyses. Of course, participants were encouraged to present new, original ideas and/or data that would fit into the general theme.

Another prerequisite for inclusion was willingness to complete and distribute the papers *prior* to the colloquium, in order to provide ample opportunity for the discussants to prepare meaningful responses. Consequently, the commentaries (also included in this volume) are for the most part significant scholarly contributions too. Some are highly critical of theoretical assumptions; others examine methodological considerations. All raise questions that pertain to the papers on which they are based and that are of interest to students of such issues. As would be expected, not all the contributors agree with all the comments about their papers, but the many stimulating queries serve to provoke substantial discussion and reexamination of important ideas.

This volume, *Family and Work: Comparative Convergences*, contains only those papers and discussants' comments that deal directly with the family and work interrelationships. To appreciate the broader theme of the colloquium, the reader is invited to examine the companion volume, *Work, Organizations, and Society: Comparative Convergences*, which places these interrelationships in an environmental context external to the family. Throughout the present volume, there are allusions to the symposium's overall theme, but the emphasis in this volume is confined to family and work; the companion volume will concentrate on the organizational/societal environment.

This introductory chapter has three objectives: to examine briefly some selected propositions that link family and work systems; to explore the meaning, purpose, and strengths of comparative studies in sociology; and to outline some important components of the sociocultural and organizational environment where family and work activities occur.

The Interdependence of Family and Work Systems

In this introduction we do not investigate all the complexities of systems theory (for examples of systems theory, see Aldous, 1978; Buckley, 1967; Hall, 1979; Hill, 1971; Katz and Kahn, 1978; and Parsons, 1951), nor do we examine all the intricacies of the family and work systems taken independently or jointly. Our modest objective is merely to demonstrate that these two systems are not separate and cannot be studied in isolation. Traditionally, family and work have constituted separate sub-disciplines in sociology (Bahr, 1982; Gray, 1979; Pleck, 1977, 1978); over the last couple of decades, however, an increasing number of scholars have begun to consider these interrelationships. Much of the added interest in the interaction of these two systems has been generated by the burgeoning field of sex roles, or (perhaps more appropriately termed) gender relations. We will return to this impact later.

It is well documented that in pre-industrial societies the kinship unit usually acted as the producers of goods and services. Most familial members were producers in some fashion. With the advent of industrialization, the nuclear family came to be characterized by a division of labor in which the husband and father continued as producer, in an economic system external to the family, while the wife and mother maintained hearth and home. Some have argued that the male's role is "instrumental" while the female's role has become "expressive," or that of nurturer (e.g. Parsons, 1960). In post-industrial society this sharp separation of roles by sex has begun to break down. There is greater and greater emphasis on equality, joint decision-making, joint activities, and cooperation in the occupational world (e.g. Rapoport and Rapoport, 1969). In short, in pre-industrial times the family unit served as both producer and consumer, whereas contemporarily the family consumes as a unit but produces in separate, disjunctive roles that are external to the family. This is not to suggest that there are not substantial effects of one system upon the other. (For additional insights into the complex interrelationships among industrialization, modernization, or stage of development and familial occupational roles, see for example, Beneria and Sen, 1981; Boserup, 1970; Boulding, 1976; Cancian, Goodman, and Smith, 1978; Carlos and Sellers, 1972; Stewart, Lykes, and LaFrance, 1982; and Youssef, 1976.)

At this point, we must state that "work system" refers to those occupational activities external to the family. We know that much work is undertaken within the family (e.g., housework, child work, yard work), but we prefer to restrict the term to paid, extra-familial work that occurs in the marketplace.

Kamerman (1979:632) argues that "separation of work and home—or work life and family life—has been identified as one of the most significant characteristics of industrialized societies." The separation she refers to is in terms of activities and location; each system continues to have significant impact upon the other. Where the family supplies occupants for positions in the work system, the occupational roles influence the way in which they are able to carry out their family roles (Rodgers, 1973). Aldous (1978:35) eloquently outlines some of the obvious implications of the transaction between family and job:

It's [the job's] time and energy demands on men, women, and adolescents which determine meal and leisure time schedules as well as needs for childcare facilities. Lack of job security creates the financial problems that underlie marital and parent-child conflict in working and lower-class families (Rubin, 1976). Large corporations regularly shift their middle-management personnel to plant sites about the country and reportedly promote those men whose wives conform to corporation standards of entertaining and getting along with people (Whyte, 1951). . . . Professionals and men who manage may find their occupational roles more salient than their family roles. In these cases, families are coopted to serve career interests, and wife-mothers must assume major responsibility for the family. If employed wives have to leave stimulating jobs because of the priority of the husband's occupational success, the competing occupational demands can strain marital ties.

In a manner similar to Aldous, much of the literature seems to illustrate disproportionately the ways in which work affects family and not vice versa; that is, the effects often appear unidirectional. This is undoubtedly due in part to the "overwhelming dominance of work on family life" (Kamerman, 1979:633). We argue that there is a reciprocal interdependence—family concerns also influence work. Selected examples could include the wife's roles as social secretary and receptionist for the husband's work-related duties; the family's attitude about geographical mobility when the worker faces a transfer; the cross-pressures that both work and families experience when both demand loyalties and commitment (Rodgers, 1973); family strains, tensions, and crises that influence occupational role performance and subsequently mobility; and so on. Currently one of the major effects of the family on work is the increasing tendency for married women to enter the labor force. For example, selected lower-status occupations, such as white-collar clerical workers, increasingly are being filled by women (Lowe, 1980). We would posit that part of the reason for the relative neglect of examining the family system's direct impact upon the work system involves the vast heterogeneity characteristic of the work system.

The linkages between work and family can be examined at two different conceptual levels: that of the individual couple, or the micro-level, and that of the macro-societal level. Where the chapter by Hyman Rodman and Constantina Safilios-Rothschild in this volume adheres more to the former, Marta Tienda's work exemplifies the latter. Pleck (1977, 1978), for example, refers to the micro-level analysis as the work-family role system. The positions of husband and wife are linked by family roles. The husband's work interfaces with his family role, the wife's family role, and possibly his wife's work role. By slightly modifying Pleck (1977:418), we can diagram the work-family system and observe that there are six two-way linkages, each of a reciprocal nature (see Figure 1–1). Because each of these positions has multiple roles, the complex interdependencies are greatly magnified.

Figure 1-1

Linkages Between the Positions in the Work-Family Role System[1]

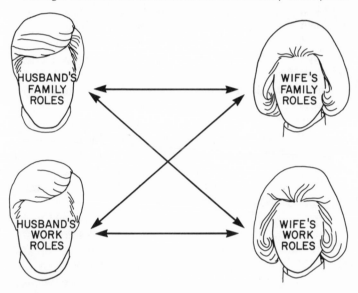

[1]Adapted, in part, from Pleck (1977:418)

By adding children to the system, as Tienda's chapter does, the network becomes even more intricate.

Consistent with systems theory, there is a body of central concepts which should be noted: (1) *interdependence* of units within the work-family system (e.g., the husband's work role has direct impact on the wife's work status); (2) *boundary maintenance* and the degree of "openness" characteristic of the work-family system (the system is a semi-open one, where wives leave the work system at the birth of their first child to reenter it after the children commence school); (3) the work-family system as an *adaptive* system (interactions within are characterized by tensions and conflicts that demand adaptation); and (4) the work-family system as a *task* performance group (tasks involve physical maintenance of members, including economic exchanges, socialization of family members, social control of members, maintenance of morale and motivation, and the reproduction of members).

More than two decades ago, Dyer (1956) recognized the reciprocal influences of family and work and argued that they were mediated through the father's work role. Today the wife's or mother's work role has taken on much greater significance. (Particular attention should be paid to Eugen Lupri's comments on "bringing women back in," found in this volume.) An increasing number of wives are entering and remaining in the work force. It has become more and more difficult for young couples to survive financially without both partners participating in the marketplace (e.g., Amsden, 1980; Ferber, 1982; Wilson, 1982). They are caught in a "life cycle squeeze" (Oppenheimer, 1974). The tendency for women to stop working at the birth of the first child and return after the children enter school is rapidly diminishing (Lupri and Mills, 1982). A "major problem of working women is managing childbearing and child rearing *while remaining in the labor force*" (Kamerman, 1979:647, emphasis added). Women work today not only because of economic need but also for self-fulfillment, enjoyment, and other non-pecuniary reasons.

Over the past decade considerable attention has been paid to dual-career couples and the adaptations that have been necessary (e.g., Aldous, 1981; Frankel, Manogue, and Paludi, 1982; Holmstrom, 1972; Michel, 1971; Rapoport and Rapoport, 1976). Probably the major problem pinpointed by most social scientists is the "role overload" suffered by couples where both partners work full-time. In the event of role overload, the wife is often expected to be the adaptive one, because her work role is usually considered lower status. Family emergencies, such as a sick child, are usually handled by the wife's juggling her occupational responsibilities, not by the husband. Data suggest that employed wives often find themselves faced with two full-time jobs, one at home and the other in the marketplace, and they receive little help and support from their husbands (Berk, 1980; Meissner et al., 1975; Miller and Garrison, 1982; Nickols and Metzen, 1982).

Not only does the family system adjust to dual careers, but the occupational structure also must adapt. Some countries and work organizations have instituted policies to ameliorate the situation described above. Paid maternity leaves, subsidized day-care centers, flexible work time, and work-sharing patterns are a few examples of innovative adaptations (Jiménez-Butragueño, 1982; Kamerman, 1979; Safilios-Rothschild, 1974, 1976). As women increasingly enter and remain in the work world, other occupational and familial adaptations will be forthcoming. Policy changes have also been necessary to handle child labor considerations (e.g., Goddard and White, 1982; Standing, 1982).

In sum, we argue that the family and work systems are interdependent in many ways. The chapters in this volume explore examples of only a few selected linkages. In addition, they provide illustrations of family and work interdependencies in non-North American societies, namely, Trinidad and Peru. Why should this be important? That is, why investigate families from a comparative perspective?

Comparative Studies: What and Why?

Following a symposium on comparative social research held at Indiana University, Hill (1973:457) confessed, in his overview, that he experienced "considerable uncertainty as to both the meaning of 'comparative' and the professional self-identity of the 'comparativist.' " He then proceeded to demonstrate empirically (based on the papers presented at the symposium) the wide range of substantive interests, theoretical positions, and methodological strategies that were claimed to be comparative. Our own colloquium on family and work systems, intended to be comparative, also covers a wide spectrum. Although we will not define exactly what is meant by comparative sociology, some brief discussion of its varied meanings and usefulness may help us appreciate more fully the contributions in this volume.

Early sociologists, including Herbert Spencer, Auguste Comte, Émile Durkheim, and Lester F. Ward, among others, contended that "sociology is comparative." Females are compared with males, young with old, Christians with Muslims, liberals with conservatives, and so on. The objectives of sociology—to describe, explain, and predict behavior—can be accomplished only by comparison. Sociology is inherently comparative; following Grimshaw (1973) and Warwick and Osherson (1973), however, we prefer to give "comparative sociology" a more specific definition. Less ambiguous terms employed as synonyms include "cross-societal," "cross-national," and "cross-system" (Tomasson, 1978). Grimshaw (1973:18) suggests that comparative sociology involves "attempts to explain similarities or differences in social behavior through references in structured social relationships and the testing of limits on generalizations of propositions derived *through research in different* societies" (emphasis added). Warwick and Osherson (1973:8) use the concept "comparative method to refer to social scientific analyses involving observations in more than one social system, or in the same social system at more than one point in time." The latter refers to historical analysis by sociologists (e.g., Elder, 1981; Scott and Tilly, 1975; Smelser, 1976).

Some scholars would suggest that these conceptualizations are too constraining. Indeed, most of the chapters that make up this volume do not fit the definitions proposed by either Grimshaw or Warwick and Osherson. Tomasson (1978:2) notes that "single case studies of 'other' societies predominate" among those usually considered to be comparative. Area studies are often conducted on a single society, and the findings then contrasted, either explicitly or implicitly, with a better-known society such as the United States. Hyman Rodman's chapter on Trinidad and Marta Tienda's on Peru are examples of comparative work adopting this "case study definition."

The nomenclature "comparative" has also been applied to works that appear as loose examples or illustrations. They are not based on hard data. Rodman and Safilios-Rothschild's chapter "Weak Links" is of this sort. They write of parallel phenomena in various societies in an attempt to illustrate generalizations. Payne (1973:13) asserts that "comparative sociology is *not about illustrations* drawn from various countries *unless such data are used specifically to generate theory*" (emphasis added). Rodman and Safilios-Rothschild's contribution is both rich with illustrative materials from diverse countries and fertile with propositions that may lead to theory. For additional discussion of the comparative concept, see the introduction to Chapter 8, which is an annotated bibliography of selected comparative treatises.

Comparative sociology, more stringently defined as a methodological orientation, is not practiced much, but it appears that a rebirth may be on the horizon. Recently there have been renewed interests in historical studies and in "world" sociology, both of which tend to be comparative. If our intellectual forefathers were strongly committed to comparative works, why did they decrease? In short, why are they not more popular today? Tomasson (1978) and Rokkan (1964) both state that sociologists abandoned the comparative enterprise because they had to enhance their methodological status among their fellow academics. They turned to "hard-headed empiricism." The comparative method did not easily lend itself to the rigorous specialization referred to at the beginning of this chapter. Hence it fell into disuse. Comparative sociology is not uncomplicated; it is replete with problems and challenges. Warwick and Osherson (1973:11–49) list four basic problems that the comparativist confronts: (1) conceptual equivalence across social systems, (2) measurement equivalence, (3) linguistic equivalence, and (4) sampling issues. (For further discussions of assorted related problems, see also Armer and Grimshaw, 1973; Brislin, Lonner, and Thorndike, 1973; Marsh, 1967; Przeworski and Teune, 1970; Rokkan, 1968; and Smelser, 1976). In addition to these problems, comparativists often find themselves in a strange culture, communicating in a foreign language and attempting to collaborate with foreign social scientists who have a very different image of social science research. With the many attendant difficulties, why advocate the comparative method? How will this approach help us understand family and work systems better? The literature contains several related responses to this query which can be synthesized into a single, general objective. The social scientist's goal is to discover empirical generalizations that have wide, even universal, applicability. In other words, we are attempting to discover patterns of behavior that will hold for many different groups. The difficulty is that many theoretical concepts and their interrelationships are culture-specific. They have been theoretically posited and empirically examined in only one location, often the United States. By investigating our theoretical propositions in more than one sociocultural setting, we are better prepared to assess the degree of universality. For example, in research on family and work systems comparing Mexico and Canada, Brinkerhoff (1982) discovered that Mexican women do not tend to leave the labor force at the birth of their child to reenter it after the child begins school to the extent their Canadian counterparts do. This finding forces us to reexamine certain theoretical linkages within family life-cycle theory. What are the social conditions under which women remain at work even when they have preschool children? In short, comparative studies are essential in order to establish universals; they provide better, or more complete, tests of our propositions.

Research methodology is often defined as the "control of variance" (Kerlinger, 1973, 1979; Smelser, 1976). We attempt to maximize the amount of variation on our "causal" or explanatory variables in order to assess their differential impact on the explained variables. By examining propositions in different societal contexts, we are able to increase the amount of variation on the variables. Naturally, the assumptions underlying the choice of research sites to compare (societies, nation-states, cultures, historical periods) must be based on factors that are related to the theoretical problem under investigation.

In this section we propose to justify why social organization must be considered while treating the family-work system (e.g., Marsden, 1982). To do this we will discuss in only a paragraph or two the following five concepts: organizations and environments, careers, socialization, technology, and organizational participation. Of course, there are many other ways in which the family-work system is affected by—and affects—organizations which cannot be discussed within this brief introductory chapter. Examples from the literature will be cited. Let us commence by considering the organizational environment as it is infused with sociocultural factors.

Not only does the specific organization for which one works exert influences on one's behaviors, but other organizations in the community, nation-state, and world also form part of the environment affecting one's roles in the work organization and the family. A given organization interacts with other organizations that control resources; hence, interorganizational analysis can be employed to clarify social relationships that lead to production, distribution, and consumption of goods and services. Aldrich (1979:21) points out the importance of "the community and societal context within which organizational change occurs. Social movements, changes in societal values, cross-societal diffusion of innovations, and the incorporation of peripheral areas into the world capitalist system (Wallerstein, 1974), have had major impacts on the production of new types of organizations and the transformation of old ones." The Aldrich-Wallerstein argument is of major importance when considering a system's and subsystem's approach to family and work. Wallerstein (1974, 1979) contends that an analysis must be at the world system level, where others examine only nation-states. By way of contrast, Tienda's chapter in this volume focuses on the importance of ecological regions within a single nation-state, Peru, while Rodman analyzes the individual worker within the family system. All levels of analyses are quite appropriate but answer different questions. The important point is that the various systems and subsystems constitute part of the environment for other systems and subsystems. They are linked together to form a complex network. Figure 1–2 vastly oversimplifies the realities of the situation, since the number of organizations and sociocultural influences are manifold. However, it does serve to sensitize us to some of the structures and processes that impinge upon the family-work role system. Consistent with "open-systems theory," one must remember that the enclosures (as described in both the box [representing the sociocultural environment] and the circle [symbolizing the formal work organization]) around the systems and subsystems are semi-permeable, that is, they are not fixed or closed boundaries.

Olsen (1978) observes that organizations are linked in two basic ways. First, individuals are members of more than one group. Second, the organizations themselves crosscut and overlap one another in their interactions. Olsen (1978:74) provides a simple but effective example:

Figure 1–2

Socio-Cultural Environment, Work Organizations and Roles in the Family-Work System

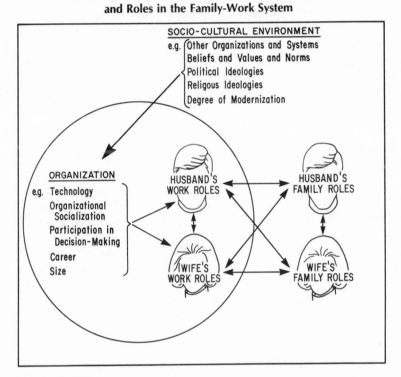

A business concern influences many families through the work schedules and pay rates of its employees; many friendship cliques and committees are formed within the business; this organization must deal with labor unions, a chamber of commerce and other associations; it pays taxes to the local community as well as to the federal government; the manner in which it is organized may contribute to the formation of "working" and "management" social classes; it plays an active part in maintaining the economic network of the society; it may rely heavily on business contracts from the national government, and in times of crisis it is called upon to help defend the society by carrying its burden of the national defense effort.

Families often serve as the glue to bond organizations together into complex networks. A few extremely wealthy families, for example, often control major organizations. Interlocking boards of corporate directors are often kinship linked. Aldrich (1979:335) summarizes several studies that illustrate this and concludes, "Kinship ties are certainly an extremely stable basis for interorganizational relations, as long as family members retain control of their organizations." Of course, families do not have to own the means of production to interface with organizations.

Families are also directly linked to work organizations through their members' occupations and careers (Figure 1–2). Thompson (1967:104) describes these linkages: "Social systems are always structured, and in the society geared to complex organizations, economic activities are clustered into *occupations*. Individuals are sorted and prepared for them and are taught to fashion *careers*, either within an occupation or in some combination of them." Occupations and careers, then, are typically found *within* complex organizations. Careers may be broadly conceptualized as a set of organizational expectations someone must meet at selected contingency points or time periods. For this reason, Van Maanen (1976:67) prefers the concept *organizational socialization* rather than occupational socialization. Organizational socialization focuses attention on the dominant setting and on the values, norms, and behaviors one is expected to acquire in order to participate in the organization (also Walker, Tausky, and Oliver, 1982). Organizational socialization continues throughout one's career, but the process is more prominent early in one's work history (Steinberg et al., 1981). Socialization also occurs prior to entering the organization; families, schools, churches, and other institutions aid in the process. Characteristics of the community in which the organization exists enter into the socialization process. If the process is to make the new recruit into a useful member of the organization, community norms must also be internalized (Van Maanen, 1976). The norms and values in the dominant culture begin to prepare one for the occupational role. In short, the *sociocultural environment* usually infuses *norms* and *values* consistent with those of the organization. The family performs a major role in this socialization process.

There are situations where organizations are entirely new to a geographical area (e.g., entirely new forms of an organization, or when a developing nation adopts overnight a new organization in its entirety from one of the post-industrial societies) when specific skills, norms, and values will by necessity be taught in cooperation with formal organizations such as schools. No longer do existing organizations, kinship relations, ethnic ties, or other systems adequately provide this service. These "new organizations" require the "intermeshing of new roles

and a new structure of relations . . . with a high cost in time and resources'' (Aldrich, 1979:184; Bendix, 1956; Brim and Wheeler, 1966;
Moore, 1969; Stinchcombe, 1965).

Organizations provide the contexts for *careers* for their workers. The
career concept has many implications for the theme of this volume—
the interdependence of family and work. Kanter (1977), in her research monograph on an industrial supply corporation, enumerates many
of these. For example, organizations have a hierarchical structure that
demands considerable "overwork," travel, evenings away, and so on,
to the neglect of wife and family, if one is to be a successful "climber."
Organizations even institute policies that involve the wives of career-
ists (e.g., offering educational programs or parallel meetings during
conferences) and often evaluate the wives along with their employed
husbands. This is especially true for those embarked on careers in up-
per levels of management. Mortimer, Hall, and Hill (1978) hypothesize that the central attributes of the husband's work role limit his family activities and consequently limit the wife's opportunities for
occupational participation (also Brinkerhoff, 1980). They refer to this
as a "two-person career," because the man requires his wife's full-
time support while he attempts to progress up the organizational hierarchy. If a man is strongly career-oriented, the corporation demands
loyalty and dedication with implications that spill over into the other
components of the family-work system. (The above few paragraphs require some qualifications, because not all occupations or careers are
found in organizations, e.g., nearly 10 percent of those employed in
Canada, are *outside* organizations.) Hence, there are individual careers, occupational careers, and organizational careers.

Technology is another organizational characteristic that merits mention. As suggested earlier, the nature of technology has changed considerably throughout the industrializing stages. It varies vastly across
nation-states as well as by region within. Westley and Westley (1971:48)
describe how technology constitutes part of the social environment: "It
can be argued that the differences in craftsmanship or unit production,
mass production, and continuous process production, which are only
stages on a continuum of technical efficiency, are, in human terms,
differences so great as to constitute diversified social environments, to
foster various attitudes toward fellow workers, management, unions,
and the society at large, and to change the meaning of work and leisure." To focus on technology is to focus on "turbulent change." One
of the greatest changes to which man must adapt is the changing world
of work. "What seems to characterize the age of automation and mass

consumption is a state of 'fluidity,' in which a man may expect in his own lifetime to change his job, to be retrained, to change his social and geographic environment, his friends, his community, his standard of living, even his beliefs and values, not once but perhaps many times" (Westley and Westley, 1971:43). Of course, technological change can be the source of organizational problems as well as individual problems (Dubin, 1976).

When considering technological change in the context of this volume, one must also note that such change has influenced the occupational structure. For example, within the tertiary sector of the economy many new occupations have arisen. Many of these new jobs are of a white-collar type that has facilitated the entry of women into the labor force. No single factor has been more important than technological change in affecting the family-work system because it has provided opportunities for women to work. Even within a single industry, work has different meanings for the person on the assembly line, the clerk, the engineer, and the manager. Technology is highly related to work stress and pressures (McLean, 1979).

Another important characteristic of organizations pertains to the degree of *participation* workers have in the *decision-making process*. Some contend that this participation is related directly to feelings of alienation. Work stress, pressures, and alienation have direct impact on relationships in the family system. Worker participation and job flexibility are organizational techniques that are postulated to reduce alienation and stress.

Kanter (1977:250) summarizes our argument about the importance of the organization and environment:

Work is not an isolated relationship between actor and activity. What happens to people in the course of their work is determined by the larger setting in which it takes place, and that setting, in contemporary society, is likely to be an organization. Jobs and the relations of people to them cannot be understood without reference to the organized systems in which the contemporary division of labor operates. Understanding organizations and how they function is the key to discovering the ways in which people manage their work experiences. . . . Thus, analysis of a job alone is not enough, without considering where it takes place. . . . The nature of the *total system* is important in determining the relationship of any individual worker to her or her work (emphasis added).

To complete Kanter's observation, one must consider the family as an important part of the "total system." Furthermore, as we have contended throughout this chapter, any analysis of the family-work system is strengthened by considering it in comparative perspective.

The Interdependence of Family and Economic Roles: A Preview at the Micro-level

This final section will provide a brief synopsis of the chapters and the "comments" in this volume. The intent here is not to be exhaustive but to integrate the materials selectively, we hope whetting your appetites for your own careful sojourn through the provocative chapters.

In Chapter 2, Pierre L. van den Berghe presents a sociobiological paradigm that he maintains has universal applicability and can be employed comparatively. Van den Berghe's commitment to the sociobiological view of family and work is a refreshing approach that is not entirely inconsistent with the system's perspective advocated in our earlier remarks. Hall (1979:20) agrees that the "biological components of social interaction may be neglected" and develops the argument that the "concept of family systems offers an integrated approach." Both van den Berghe and Hall would concur with our earlier comments that overspecialization and compartmentalization have led us to ask many of the wrong questions. Van den Berghe's analogy of the ant illustrates the changes that have occurred in the family-work system during industrialization.

An underlying assumption central to the writings of both van den Berghe and Tienda is that of an economic model of man. A cost-benefit analysis underlies their formulations. Humans work in order to acquire resources to enable them to reproduce, to raise families. There is, however, considerable evidence to counter this assertion. Many people work for various kinds of intrinsic rewards, and not merely to survive and reproduce. For example, people are increasingly remaining childless by choice. Because of time and space limitations, van den Berghe's contribution is terse. The reader may wish to turn to van den Berghe's (1979) book for a fuller treatment. For the compartmentalists who choose to ignore sociobiology, van den Berghe furnishes exciting notions and invites them to read more deeply, to investigate those ideas that he can only gloss here. In Chapter 2, van den Berghe, as a comparativist, has provided us with a model of family and work which is not culture-bound or time-bound. He illustrates its utility at various times in history. You are challenged to ferret out those propositions that may be universals.

A thought-provoking, constructive critique of van den Berghe's paradigm by Augustine Brannigan is also found in Chapter 1. Brannigan's lively response to van den Berghe contests not only selected assumptions of the sociobiological model but also "methods of proof." Brannigan chooses not to focus on common criticisms of sociobiology (e.g., the denial of free will, generalizing from bacteria and ants to human behaviors), but instead treats matters of theory construction. He suggests that the theory is non-falsifiable and that it commits the fallacy of affirming the consequent. Brannigan questions the "narrative" as a method of proof. Sociobiologists assume what others take as problematic, that social behavior is genetically (genotypically) based. In terms of our theme, family and work, Brannigan agrees with van den Berghe that "we work to survive, to reproduce, and to provision our offspring." Yes, we work to keep from going hungry, but there is considerable *cultural variation* in how we work and why we work, as well as in what we eat. These social behaviors are not genotypically determined. Brannigan does not completely dismiss van den Berghe's sociobiological model, but he does see it as having *limited* utility. You, the readers, are invited to examine both positions to decide for yourselves.

Chapter 3, "Weak Links in Men's Worker-Earner Roles" by Hyman Rodman and Constantina Safilios-Rothschild, points out how cultural variation affects "how we work to survive." The authors argue that families are organized in ways that facilitate men's performance of their work roles in order to support their families. It is the *male's worker-earner role* that connects the work subsystem to the family subsystem to form the family-work system presented earlier in the present chapter. (However, we do not want to confine the "system" to male work roles.) Rodman and Safilios-Rothschild demonstrate well the interdependence of family and work. Where the roles are "damaged," the system must adapt. The authors delineate four special situations where the worker-earner role may be damaged and adjustment required: (1) in young families where the male's earning power is limited; (2) in lower-class families where unemployment and underemployment persist; (3) in cases of illness and disability; and (4) in the case of old age.

The "weak links" model has two assumptions: (1) "the husband-father is expected to be the major earner in the family, and (2) the husband-father's failure to fulfill this role adequately is defined as a personal failure." The authors point out that the universal applicability of the model is restricted because the assumptions do not always hold in various sociocultural environments. Perhaps the two assumptions are not totally necessary when examining "weak links" in the worker-earner roles. For example, the worker-earner may well be the female-mother in present times (see, e.g., the discussion by Eugen Lupri that follows Chapter 3), or the role may be filled *jointly by both spouses* as the model in the introductory portion of the chapter suggests. Of course, in many cases the female-mother may be performing this role because of the "damaged" worker-earner role of the male. She works as an adaptation to unemployment or underemployment of her spouse. Regardless, Chapter 3 sensitizes us to the importance of cultural variations surrounding the worker-earner role.

Lupri's major criticism of the "weak links" model is that the female also performs the work role. He suggests that women's roles as workers may be much more than mere adaptations to males' damaged roles. Women are more permanently in the labor force than the model suggests. Furthermore, wives work because of various motivations that go beyond their economic needs. Lupri would extend the model to "bring women back in" as worker-earners. Of course, Rodman and Safilios-Rothschild recognize "women as earners" in both the introductory and concluding portions of their chapter, but they choose to focus more on the male as worker-earner.

In spite of substantial social change, women continue to be linked more to the family, and men more to the work system. As change continues to propel females toward employment in the marketplace, one naturally ponders how institutions other than the family may be called on to assist the damaged workers-earners. Will government cooperate more fully in providing funds for day-care centers, paid maternity leaves, and the like? Will economic institutions adapt by providing increased job-sharing possibilities, flex-time, more equitable pay for female labor? Will religious institutions cooperate in their positions vis-à-vis the changing norms and values that accompany working mothers, single-parent families, and so forth? Such questions illustrate the importance of persistent adaptation in our family-work system and its environment.

Marta Tienda's paper on family labor supply in Peru, in Chapter 4, implicitly incorporates some of the ideas of Rodman and Safilios-Rothschild. For example, Tienda argues that where occupational differentiation is low the utilization of workers will be low, which will result in the need for more workers to compensate for high unemployment and underemployment. In such cases (damaged worker-earner roles), additional family members will be called on to work for pay outside the family. Tienda does not confine her arguments to women entering the labor force; she also incorporates children as helpers. Tienda's chapter is therefore also unique in its attempt to conceptualize and measure family labor supply. Children as well as women may help when the male worker-earner role is damaged. (For additional discussions of children's work, see Ennew, 1982; Davin, 1982; and White and Brinkerhoff, 1981.) It must be remembered that Tienda's concept of "work" is formally defined. Some of the findings might be different had she employed primary data and could examine more thoroughly employment in cottage industry, agricultural activities, and family business. The magnitude of family labor supply, especially in developing areas such as Latin America, is undoubtedly gravely underreported in official statistics (e.g., Arizpe, 1977; Beneria, 1981; Gonzalez-Salazar, 1976; Wilkie and Reich, 1977).

Tienda's chapter provides an excellent example of the environment's influence on the work-family system. By dividing Peru into three ecological zones, she demonstrates the importance of the organization of production on family labor supply. Tienda's chapter should be reconsidered in light of Robert Marsh's chapter on modernization in the companion volume entitled *Work, Organizations, and Society: Comparative Convergences*. The three ecological areas can be conceptualized as different levels of development. Again, this factor affects the family-work system considerably. Tienda's chapter also presents data on social-demographic characteristics (e.g., education of head of household), household composition (e.g., extended type, family size), and ecological aspects (e.g., natural zones, urban) as they influence the family labor supply. Much of her analysis neatly fits into the model that the damaged worker-earner role leads to an adaptation in which various family members must enter the work system. Moreover, her chapter supports our sensitizing model (Figure 1-2) as she investigates some of the sociocultural and organizational factors that influence the family-work system.

Joseph E. DiSanto argues that Tienda's utilization of the family labor supply concept is ambiguous. He suggests that she confuses it with the distinctly different concept "division of labor." Although DiSanto is critical of Tienda's "operational definitions"—measurement procedures—she should get full marks for her attempts to work with some very complex, important variables.

Where Tienda's chapter, based on secondary survey data from Peru, is highly quantitative, Hyman Rodman's ethnographic description of the family-work system in Trinidad, reported in Chapter 5, is qualitative. Rodman's case study is comparative in the sense that we can compare aspects of our own families and societies with the Trinidadians. Specifically, Rodman provides a description of the weak links in the worker-earner roles of the lower-class Trinidad family. He examines three forms of marital relationships: friending, living, and married.

James S. Frideres' comments on Rodman's Trinidad case study conclude that it is too economically based and that the culture surrounding this matrifocal society deserves greater attention. For example, Frideres asks if the mother has economic control under this matrifocal structure. He appears to be questioning the age-old problem of "conceptual equivalence," which we raised as a problem of doing comparative research earlier in this chapter. Frideres argues that Rodman, approaching Trinidad from the North American culture, does not take matrifocality into account adequately. In addition, Frideres asserts that Rodman should consider historical factors as they related to values. For the purposes of this colloquium, however, the Trinidad ethnographic sketch serves to provide a rich illustration of the family-work system.

In Chapter 6, Ronald Angel and Marta Tienda hypothesize that extended-family patterns may result from adaptations to the "damaged role" reported by Rodman and Safilios-Rothschild. To test their propositions, they compare non-Hispanic whites, blacks, and those with Mexican, Puerto Rican, Central/South American, and other Spanish origins. From a complex analysis, they conclude that race and culture, and *not* poverty, account for co-residences. Female-headed households are also much more likely to have extended-family patterns, that is, non-nuclear members who reside together. Richard Wanner questions, and rightly, the causal ordering between poverty and extended family; however, there can be little doubt that race and ethnicity precede extended-family formation in temporal ordering. In terms of the schema in this introductory chapter, Angel and Tienda's chapter incorporates the sociocultural dimension, demographic characteristics, and both spouses' work roles as they interact to influence the family-work system.

Chapter 7, by Pierre L. van den Berghe, is an overview of the chapters that make up this volume. There was no discussant. As van den Berghe points out, the authors treat a broad range of subtopics, all of which are directly relevant to the general theme of family and work roles in comparative perspective. Van den Berghe attempts to impose his sociobiological framework on these chapters to provide a coherent whole.

The sociobiological paradigm, as presented in van den Berghe's overview found in Chapter 7, concentrates on several concepts. Maximization of inclusive fitness, altruism, nepotism, sociality, reproduction of the species, and parental investment are the major theoretical notions treated in this chapter. Van den Berghe admits, "without shame," that the sociobiological model is reductionistic. He argues that one must start at the very "lowest level of analysis" to explain as much variation as possible before proceeding to the next higher level. In addition, the nature of the data varies tremendously. Rodman's data are qualitative, ethnographic field observations that may be more interpretable by the sociobiologist, at least by van den Berghe. This suggests, as Brannigan did in Chapter 2, that such qualitative field work provides information for the narrative as a "method of proof." Tienda, by comparison, would agree with van den Berghe's goal of "the explanation of variance," but she would define it very differently. The narrative, based mainly on qualitative observations, does not suffice to explain variance.

Van den Berghe effectively integrates Rodman's Trinidad chapter into his sociobiological paradigm by focusing on parental investment, nepotism, and kin selection. In this matrifocal society the male invests less biologically and socially; consequently, since his contribution to the offspring is less, he is more inclined to depart from the pair bond. This explains Rodman's patterns of "friending," "living," and "married." Although van den Berghe is critical of Tienda's use of secondary, aggregate data, he fits her chapter into his framework. He argues that the extended family is a function of nepotism and reciprocity and that any study of occupational patterns requires us to study kin.

In summary, the contributions in this volume are wide-ranging. They must be, in order to begin to scratch the surface of an area with as many complex, interrelated facets as family and work. Van den Berghe has done *yeoman's duty* in his integrative overview. Where sociobiology serves to bring together "some" aspects of "some" of the chapters into a meaningful whole, the model posed in this introductory chapter might be similarly useful. Finally, we contend that it should be possible to fuse both models, the sociobiological paradigm and the family-work open systems framework. Our readers are challenged to consider this.

Chapter 8 is a highly selective annotated bibliography that should prove useful to researchers and teachers in the general area of family and work. For the most part, the sources cited or alluded to in this introductory chapter have not been incorporated into the annotated bibliography. Whereas some of the sources in this introduction are not comparative, others could have been included. The present chapter might be considered a bibliographic essay and might serve as a companion to the annotated bibliography found in Chapter 8.

You are invited to examine in detail the arguments that link family and work roles. The authors suggest many propositions that might be fruitfully tested and present comparative data and examples. The chapters range from mainly theoretical to mostly analytical, from ethnographic descriptions to multivariate statistical findings. In spite of their differences, they all lead to the conclusion that family and work roles are highly interdependent and must be examined conjointly.

References

Aldous, Joan
  1978   Family Careers: Developmental Change in Families. New York: John Wiley and Sons.
  1981   Dual-Earner Families. Special Issue of the Journal of Family Issues 2(2).
Aldrich, Howard E.
  1979   Organizations and Environments. Englewood Cliffs, N.J.: Prentice-Hall.
Amsden, Alice H. (ed.)
  1980   The Economics of Women and Work. Middlesex, Eng.: Penguin Books.
Arizpe, Lourdes
  1977   "Women in the informal labor sector: The case of Mexico City." Signs: Journal of Women in Culture and Society 3:25–37.
Armer, Michael, and Allen D. Grimshaw (eds.)
  1973   Comparative Social Research: Methodological Problems and Strategies. New York: John Wiley and Sons.
Bahr, Stephen J.
  1982   "The economics of family life: An overview." Journal of Family Issues 3:139–146.
Bendix, Reinhard
  1956   Work and Authority in Industry. New York: John Wiley and Sons.
Beneria, Lourdes
  1981   "Conceptualizing the labor force: The underestimation of women's economic activities." The Journal of Development Studies 17:10–28.

Beneria, Lourdes, and Gita Sen
1981   "Accumulation, reproduction, and women's role in economic development: Boserup revisited." Signs: Journal of Women in Culture and Society 7:279–298.

Berk, Sarah Fenstermaker (ed.)
1980   Women and Household Labor. Beverly Hills, Calif.: Sage Publications.

Boserup, Ester
1970   Woman's Role in Economic Development. London: George Allen and Unwin.

Boulding, Elise
1976   "Familial constraints on women's work roles." Signs: Journal of Women in Culture and Society 1(3):95–117.

Brim, Orville G., and Stanton Wheeler
1966   Socialization After Childhood: Two Essays. New York: John Wiley and Sons.

Brinkerhoff, Merlin B.
1980   "Women, their work and families: Some continuities in studies of social constraints." Paper presented at Canadian Sociology and Anthropology Association Annual Meetings, Montreal, Quebec.

1982   "Familial constraints on women's work: A comparative analysis." Journal of Comparative Family Studies 13:307–328.

Brislin, Richard W., Walter J. Lonner, and Robert M. Thorndike
1973   Cross-cultural Research Methods. New York: John Wiley and Sons.

Buckley, Walter
1967   Sociology and Modern Systems Theory. Englewood Cliffs, N.J.: Prentice-Hall.

Cancian, Francesca M., Louis Wolf Goodman, and Peter H. Smith
1978   "Capitalism, industrialization, and kinship in Latin America: Major issues." Journal of Family History 3(4):319–336.

Carlos, Manuel L., and Lois Sellers
1972   "Family, kinship structure, and modernization in Latin America." Latin American Research Review 7(2):95–124.

Davin, Anna
1982   "Child labor, the working-class family, and domestic ideology in 19th century Britain." Development and Change 13:633–652.

Dubin, Robert
1976   "Work in modern society." Pp. 5–35 in Robert Dubin (ed.), Handbook of Work, Organization, and Society. Chicago: Rand McNally and Company.

Dyer, William G.
1956   "The interlocking of work and family social systems among lower occupational families." Social Forces 34:230–233.

Elder, Glen H., Jr.
1981   "History and the family: The discovery of complexity." Journal of Marriage and the Family 43:489–520.
Ennew, Judith
1982   "Family structure, unemployment, and child labor in Jamaica." Development and Change 13:551–564.
Ferber, Marianne A.
1982   "Labor-market participation of young married women: Causes and effects." Journal of Marriage and the Family 44:457–468.
Frankel, Judith, Mary Ann Manogue, and Michelle Paludi
1982   "The employed mother: A new social norm?" International Journal of Women's Studies 5:274–281.
Goddard, Victoria, and Benjamin White
1982   "Child workers and capitalist development: An introductory note and bibliography." Development and Change 13:465–478.
Gonzalez-Salazar, Gloria
1976   "Participation of women in the Mexican labor force." Pp. 183–201 in June Nash and Helen Icken Safa (eds.), Sex and Class in Latin America. New York: Praeger Publishers.
Gray, A.
1979   "The working class family as an economic unit." Sociological Review Monograph 28:186–213.
Grimshaw, Allen D.
1973   "Comparative sociology: In what ways different from other sociologies?" Pp. 3–48 in Michael Armer and Allen D. Grimshaw (eds.), Comparative Social Research: Methodological Problems and Strategies. New York: John Wiley and Sons.
Hall, C. Margaret
1979   "Family systems: A developing trend in family theory." The Sociology of the Family: New Directions for Britain, Sociological Review Monograph 28:19–31.
Hill, Reuben
1971   "Modern systems theory and the family." Social Information 10:7–26.
Hill, Richard J.
1973   "In retrospect: A brief analysis of the confessions of comparativists." Pp. 457–465 in Michael Armer and Allen D. Grimshaw (eds.), Comparative Social Research: Methodological Problems and Strategies. New York: John Wiley and Sons.
Holmstrom, Lynda Lytle
1972   The Two-Career Family. Cambridge, Mass.: Schenkman Publishing Company.
Jiménez-Butragueño, María de los Ángeles
1982   "Protective legislation and equal opportunity and treatment for women in Spain." International Labour Review 121:185–198.

Kamerman, Sheila B.
1979   "Work and family in industrialized societies." Signs: Journal of Women in Culture and Society 4:632–650.

Kanter, Rosabeth Moss
1977   Men and Women of the Corporation. New York: Basic Books.

Katz, Daniel, and Robert Kahn
1978   The Social Psychology of Organizations (2nd ed.). New York: John Wiley and Sons.

Kerlinger, Fred N.
1973   Foundations of Behavioral Research (2nd ed.). New York: Holt, Rinehart and Winston.

1979   Behavioral Research: A Conceptual Approach. New York: Holt, Rinehart and Winston.

Lowe, Graham S.
1980   "Women, work, and the office: The feminization of clerical occupations in Canada, 1901–1931." Canadian Journal of Sociology 5:361–381.

Lupri, Eugen, and Donald L. Mills
1982   "The changing roles of Canadian women in family and work: An overview." Pp. 43–77 in Eugen Lupri (ed.), The Changing Positions of Women in Family and Society: A Cross-Cultural Comparison. Leiden: E.J. Brill.

Marsden, Lorna R.
1982   "The relationship between the labor force employment of women and the changing social organization in Canada." Pp. 65–76 in A. Hoiberg (ed.), Women and the World of Work. New York: Plenum Publishing Corporation.

Marsh, Robert M.
1967   Comparative Sociology: A Codification of Cross-societal Analysis. New York: Harcourt, Brace and World.

McLean, Alan A.
1979   Work Stress. Reading, Mass.: Addison-Wesley Publishing Company.

Meissner, Martin, Elizabeth Humphreys, Scott Meis, and Jack Scheu
1975   "No exit for wives: Sexual division of labor and the cumulation of household demands." Canadian Review of Sociology and Anthropology 12:424–439.

Michel, Andree (ed.)
1971   Family Issues of Employed Women in Europe and America. Leiden: E. J. Brill.

Miller, Joanne, and Howard H. Garrison
1982   "Sex roles: The division of labor at home and in the workplace." Annual Review of Sociology 8:237–262.

Moore, Wilbert E.
1969   "Occupational socialization." Pp. 861–883 in David A. Goslin
        (ed.), Handbook of Socialization Theory and Research. Chicago:
        Rand McNally and Company.

Mortimer, Jaylan, Richard Hall, and Reuben Hill
1978   "Husbands' occupational attributes as constraints on wives' em-
        ployment." Sociology of Work and Occupations 5:285–313.

Nickols, Sharon Y., and Edward J. Metzen
1982   "Impact of wife's employment upon husband's housework." Journal
        of Family Issues 3:199–216.

Olsen, Marvin E.
1978   The Process of Social Organization (2nd ed.). New York: Holt,
        Rinehart and Winston.

Oppenheimer, Valerie Kincade
1974   "The life-cycle squeeze: The interaction of men's occupational and
        family life cycles." Demography 11:227–245.

Parsons, Talcott
1951   The Social System. Glencoe, Ill.: The Free Press.
1960   "The American family: Its relation to personality and to the social
        structure." Pp. 3–33 in Talcott Parsons and Robert F. Bales (eds.),
        Family Socialization and Interaction Process. New York: The Free
        Press.

Payne, Geoff
1973   "Comparative sociology: Some problems of theory and method."
        British Journal of Sociology 24:13–29.

Pleck, John
1977   "The work-family role system." Social Problems 24:417–427.
1978   "Men's family work: Three perspectives and new data." The Family
        Coordinator 28:481–488.

Przeworski, Adam, and Henry Teune
1970   The Logic of Comparative Inquiry. New York: John Wiley and
        Sons.

Rapoport, Rhona, and Robert N. Rapoport
1969   "The dual career family: A variant pattern and social change."
        Human Relations 22:3–30.
1976   Dual-career Families Re-examined. New York: Harper and Row.

Rodgers, Roy H.
1973   Family Interaction and Transaction: The Developmental Ap-
        proach. Englewood Cliffs, N.J.: Prentice-Hall.

Rokkan, Stein
1964   "International cooperation in political sociology: Current efforts
        and future possibilities." Pp. 5–18 in Erik Allardt and Yrjo Lit-
        tunen (eds.), Cleavages, Ideologies, and Party Systems. Helsinki:
        The Academic Bookstore.

1968   Comparative Research Across Cultures and Nations. The Hague: Mouton.

Rubin, Lillian B.
1976   Worlds of Pain: Life in the Working-class Family. New York: Basic Books.

Safilios-Rothschild, Constantina
1974   Women and Social Policy. Englewood Cliffs, N.J.: Prentice-Hall.
1976   "Dual linkages between the occupational and family systems: A macrosociological analysis." Signs: Journal of Women in Culture and Society 1:51–60.

Scott, Joan W., and Louise A. Tilly
1975   "Women's work and the family in nineteenth-century Europe." Comparative Studies in Society and History 17:36–64.

Smelser, Neil J.
1976   Comparative Methods in the Social Sciences. Englewood Cliffs, N.J.: Prentice-Hall.

Standing, Guy
1982   "State policy and child labor: Accumulation versus legitimation." Development and Change 13:611–632.

Steinberg, Laurence D., Ellen Greenberger, Alan Vaux, and Mary Ruggiero
1981   "Early work experience: Effects on adolescent occupational socialization." Youth and Society 12:403–421.

Stewart, Abigail J., M. Brinton Lykes, and Marianne LaFrance
1982   "Educated women's career patterns: Separating social and developmental changes." The Journal of Social Issues 38:97–118.

Stinchcombe, Arthur L.
1965   "Social structure and organizations." Pp. 142–193 in James G. March (ed.), Handbook of Organizations. Chicago: Rand McNally and Company.

Thompson, James D.
1967   Organizations in Action: Social Science Bases of Administrative Theory. New York: McGraw-Hill Book Company.

Tomasson, Richard F.
1978   "Introduction: Comparative sociology—the state of the art." Comparative Studies in Sociology 1:1–15.

van den Berghe, Pierre L.
1979   Human Family Systems. New York: Elsevier.

Van Maanen, John.
1976   "Breaking in: Socialization to work." Pp. 67–130 in Robert Dubin (ed.), Handbook of Work, Organization, and Society. Chicago: Rand McNally College Publishing Company.

Walker, Jon E., Curt Tausky, and Donna Oliver
1982   "Men and women at work: Similarities and differences in work values within occupational groupings." Journal of Vocational Behavior 21:17–36.

Wallerstein, Immanuel
   1974   The Modern World System: Capitalist Agriculture and the Origins
            of the European World-Economy in the Sixteenth Century. New
            York: Academic Press.
   1979   The Capitalist World-Economy. Cambridge, Eng.: Cambridge
            University Press.
Warwick, Donald P., and Samuel Osherson
   1973   "Comparative analysis in the social sciences." Pp. 3–41 in Don-
            ald P. Warwick and Samuel Osherson (eds.), Comparative Re-
            search Methods. Englewood Cliffs, N.J.: Prentice-Hall.
Westley, William A., and Margaret W. Westley
   1971   The Emerging Worker: Equality and Conflict in the Mass Con-
            sumption Society. Montreal and London: McGill-Queens Univer-
            sity Press.
White, Lynn K., and David B. Brinkerhoff
   1981   "Children's work in the family: Its significance and meaning."
            Journal of Marriage and the Family 43:789–800.
Whyte, William H.
   1951   "Corporation and the wife." Fortune 44:109–111.
Wilkie, James, and Peter Reich (eds.)
   1977   Statistical Abstract of Latin America. Los Angeles: University of
            California.
Wilson, Susannah Jane Foster
   1982   Women, the Family, and the Economy. Toronto: McGraw-Hill
            Ryerson.
Youssef, Nadia Haggag
   1976   Women and Work in Developing Societies. Westport, Conn.:
            Greenwood Press.

2

Family and Work: A Sociobiological View

PIERRE L. VAN DEN BERGHE

Nearly a century ago, Friedrich Engels (1942) boldly stated the central importance of work and the family, or better, of production and reproduction as the twin material bases of human existence. In the preface to the first edition of *The Origin of the Family, Private Property, and the State*, originally published in 1884, he wrote:

According to the materialist conception, the determining factor in history is, in the final instance, the production and reproduction of immediate life. This again, is of a twofold character: on the one side, the production of the means of existence, of food, clothing and shelter and the tools necessary for that production; on the other side, the production of human beings themselves, the propagation of the species. The social organization under which the people of a particular historical epoch and a particular country live is determined by both kinds of production.

Unfortunately, Engels himself did not follow up on the biological implications of his statement, and subsequent generations of social scientists, both Marxist and non-Marxist, largely ignored or trivialized the biological underpinnings of human behavior and sociality. They overwhelmingly divorced the study of production from that of reproduction, relegating the latter to either demographic nose counting or to the specialized fields of "the family," or "kinship and marriage," in both sociology and anthropology. Demographers are an almost totally atheoretical lot, largely because they have, for the most part, remained ignorant of, and impervious to, the exciting advances of the last decades in the fields of population genetics and ecology. When sociologists speak of ecology, they mean, however much they deny it, the spatial distribution of people. The highest level of abstraction achieved in demography scarcely transcends empirical generalization or primitive cost-benefit analysis. The "demographic transition" is an example of the former, and demographic accounts of migration, of the latter. That theoretical bankruptcy is concealed behind a fanciful methodological facade but is nonetheless quite real.

The sociology of "family and marriage" has the saving grace of not hiding behind a speciously rigorous methodological apparatus, but it is theoretically vacuous as well. It consists, for the most part, of bad ethnography of North American societies, occasionally spiced for exotic effect, with borrowings from anthropology. It has taken the biology of human mating and reproduction for granted, and then proceeded to describe ongoing systems of kinship and marriage as if humans were merely disembodied carriers of rules, norms, values, and so on. Anthropologists have done substantially the same, albeit in a conceptually far more sophisticated way, because they worked from a vastly greater data basis.

Work, too, has been studied, principally by economists and sociologists, as a disembodied specialty only tangentially related to the biological underpinnings of our existence. Thus, labor economists are concerned about such demographic factors as age distribution, marital status, and fertility insofar as they affect the supply of labor, but the biology of work is almost entirely extraneous to their theoretical models based on supply and demand, seen as determined principally by wages. As for sociologists, they have studied work from a variety of perspectives: Marxist class analysis, the sociology of occupations, complex organizations, the division of labor, and so on. What these perspectives have shared was, likewise, a disregard for human biology (beyond the survival requirements, which were taken for granted) and an isolation of work from family institutions. In respect to the latter, brief statements are made to the effect that, as societies become more complex, differentiated, urbanized, industrialized, and so on, family institutions and work become increasingly separated. This conclusion is then accepted as a good enough reason for the students of each topic to ignore the other.

Naturally, such a blanket characterization is somewhat of an overstatement, and, at least within anthropology, there seems to be a revival of the Marxist or, more broadly, materialist, tradition of putting production and reproduction together again (Goody, 1976; Meillassoux, 1977). If I may, however, focus my strictures on sociology, I would suggest that one of the main reasons for the obvious intellectual stagnation of that discipline has been its nearly total isolation from the biological sciences for at least half a century.

In the specific area which concerns us here—family and work—we are led to ask the wrong questions and to formulate problems the wrong way around. For example, we often tend to regard the family as an archaic residue which interferes with modern systems of production. Women, we suggest, are deprived by motherhood of the privilege of entering the labor force. Attachment to kin introduces friction in the mobility of labor. Inheritance of status within families reduces social mobility. Nepotism interferes with efficiency of production. Familistic sentiments run counter to economic rationality. The population explosion impedes economic development in the Third World. "Excessive" fertility reduces the standard of living. Children are "dependents" and by implication burdens, and so on.

In short, much sociology, both of the Right and of the Left, has been pro-work and anti-family, pro-production and anti-reproduction. In these respects it merely reflected common elements of capitalist and socialist ideology. The revival of feminism during the 1970's further increased the stridency of what might be dubbed the "sterile worker" or "ant" ethic. To create, to produce, to work, to abort, to contracept, and to adopt are good. To loaf, to "waste time," to procreate, to re-produce, to conceive are bad. As I shall suggest later, there are interesting reasons why this "ant" ideology should be so assiduously peddled in industrial countries, both capitalist and socialist. But, prevalent though it has become in contemporary industrial societies, the ant ethic has not been favored in the vast majority of the world's societies during all but the last 100 years or so of human history. Nearly all cultures have been strongly pro-natalist and anti-work. The "lazy" native surrounded by a swarm of children whom we so like to stigmatize because he epitomizes the anti-ant, and whom we would so much like to sterilize and put to work, represents, I would suggest, human normalcy. It is we, in industrial societies, who are reversing our priorities, and making ends of means, because we have created such highly abnormal conditions for ourselves.

Indeed, let us look at ourselves biologically. The ultimate currency of success in biological terms is, of course, reproduction. Natural selection operates through differential reproduction. Behavior conducive to successful reproduction and to successful nurturing of offspring to reproductive age is biologically selected for, since organisms that behave that way leave more copies of their genes in the successive gen-

erations than organisms that behave otherwise. An organism can enhance its fitness through its own direct reproduction, or, vicariously,
by assisting its kin in being reproductive. The "inclusive fitness" of
an organism is, therefore, measured in terms of its own reproductive
success and that of its kin, discounted by degree of relationship. For
example, if I have four children (each of whom has half of my genetic
material), and six nephews (each of whom shares one fourth of his
genes with me), my total fitness is 3.5; in the next generation, there
are the equivalent of 3.5 selves, the two contributed by my four children, plus the 1.5 made up by my six nephews.

The human family is the form of social organization that enables us
to be reproductively successful in the special way for which our species evolved. We produce few offspring on whom we lavish an enormous amount of care for a long period of maturation, but we suffer
low mortality rates. We are what biologists call "K selectionists," as
distinguished from the prolific, low parental care, high mortality strategy of "r selectionists." We form fairly stable pair-bonds because a
stable, cooperative relationship between the parents contributes to the
fitness of the offspring (and therefore of the parents as well). We developed a sexual division of labor around the gathering-and-hunting
economy which was that of our hominid ancestors for several million
years. We care not only for our immediate relatives in the nuclear family,
but also for our more distant ones, because they too share genes with
us and therefore contribute to our inclusive fitness. We use the pair-
bond to form systems of exchange and alliance not only between individuals, but between extended kin groups to widen the scope of our
cooperative arrangements, and we often preferentially marry kinsmen
(such as cross-cousins) further to reinforce our networks of consanguineal and affinal ties.

In short, the complex networks of kin and marriage ties formed in
every human society are always the nub of human sociality. This is
somewhat less overwhelmingly the case in the more complex, industrial societies that evolved in the last 200 years than in simpler, especially stateless and classless, societies. Nevertheless, we continue to
behave nepotistically even in industrial societies. While our kin and
affinal ties no longer encompass *most* of our relationships as they did
in earlier times, they still account for a large chunk of our most important, intimate, solid, and longest-lasting human bonds. Even in our
congested megalapolises, we continue to play our genes' game of replicating themselves (Dawkins, 1976) by cooperating with our spouses
to raise children and by being nice to our relatives. A number of stud-

ies have shown the continued importance of extended kin ties even in the most highly urbanized environments (Young and Willmott, 1957).

Unfortunately, it would take us too far afield to present in detail the evolutionary theory which underlies the sociobiology of the human family. Basic sociobiological theory is now widely available in a variety of books accessible to laymen (Barash, 1977; Daly and Wilson, 1978; Dawkins, 1976; Wilson, 1975). As for human applications of sociobiology, the field is literally bursting with publications (Alexander, 1975; Barash, 1977; Barkow, 1978; Chagnon and Irons, 1979; Greene, 1978; Hartung, 1976; Trivers, 1971; van den Berghe and Barash, 1977; Wilson, 1978). As my latest book (van den Berghe, 1979) endeavors to document in some detail, a sociobiological approach to the human family is indispensable to understanding not only the pan-human characteristics of our behavior, but also much of the structural and cultural variability in human systems of kinship and marriage. This is not to say that either culture or the environment is unimportant, but rather that culture is our species' way of adapting to our changing environment (including that part of it which is of our own making, i.e., our sociocultural environment).

Culture is the human way of being evolutionarily, i.e., reproductively, successful. Our complex brains make us a very special kind of animal: we are partially self-conscious, rational animals communicating through symbolic language and transmitting that vast store of information and rules of conduct we call culture. But we remain nonetheless organisms which, consciously or unconsciously, behave in the selfish furtherance of their individual interests. In biological terms, we are programmed, both genetically and culturally, to behave in fitness-maximizing ways.

Our genetic programs are quite open, distal, and flexible, and therefore, we do exhibit a wide range of cultural variability. But that variability itself is only partially arbitrary and fortuitous. It is a fortuitous accident of birth, for example, whether we speak English, Gujarati, or Kiswahili. All human languages are equally suitable to the transmission of information; hence, it matters little which one we learn. (There are, of course, differences in the practical usefulness of various languages, but linguistic inequality results not from the intrinsic qualities of languages but from the relative number, wealth, and power of their speakers).

However, much culture, including kinship structure (rules of endogamy, exogamy, and preferential marriage; rules of descent, of residence, and of inheritance; extent of monogamy, polygyny, and po-

lyandry; degree of inbreeding; and so on), is an ecological adaptation
to a natural environment (Harris, 1979). There is no question that the
proximate cultural mechanisms whereby we adapt so as to be reproductively successful have only a very *distant* and *indirect* linkage to
our genes. Still, we tend to behave, very much like other organisms,
in a way that maximizes individual inclusive fitness; our cultural arrangements are largely codified ways of behaving in fitness-maximizing ways.

So much for the family side of the problem. Now let us look at work.
Work, in the broad sense, is any activity which contributes, directly
or indirectly, to the sustenance of an organism. That sustenance must,
of course, include its reproductive effort, otherwise the biological cycle is aborted. In the last analysis, work involves the expenditure of
energy for the conversion of environmental resources into the replen-
ishment of that energy plus a surplus for the reproductive effort. Unless the energy budget is in the black, the effort is futile, and in the
long run, fatal. In that broad sense, all living things "work"; indeed,
we readily recognize work in bees, ants, birds, beavers, and other animals whose foraging or nest-building activities are analogous to ours,
though we would have a difficult time recognizing "work" in a plant.

Clearly then, like other animals, we work to survive, to reproduce,
and to provision our offspring. All the other things for which we work
are really frills which have only become possible for more than a tiny
minority in the last hundred or so years of human history. Oftentimes,
we lose sight of the fact that we work to raise a family because the
chain of events between work and sustenance is a very long one. Thus,
I am now writing this at home in longhand to be typed later by an
unrelated female. Months from now, I shall read from the typescript
to an audience of foreigners, 1,000 kilometers away. In exchange I
hope to receive a piece of paper which I will take back 1,000 kilometers and bring to a large building, where I shall trade it against other
pieces of paper which my wife in turn could swap for about two weeks'
supply of food and clothing for herself, my three sons, and me.

In the above example, the chain of causation between the work and
the subsistence of my family is long enough that I have to make a conscious effort to recall it. Actually, my family would survive without
it, so I am really working for frills. In this particular case, the frill is
financing part of a 20,000 kilometer trip to Paris to attend an international symposium on attention structure in primates. The energetic balance of the two transactions to me and my family will actually be very
close to zero, but, as my mother, my sister, and various nieces, aunts,

and cousins conveniently live in Paris, I have enough of a nepotistic interest in the second trip to make it worth my while to dissipate in it the benefits of the first trip. So, indirectly, I am still working for my family, and thus ultimately for the propagation of my genes. Parenthetically, it should be noted that the energetic balance of all this travelling to the eco-system which supports me will be heavily negative. In effect, I am parasitizing my habitat, and, in unison with approximately four billion of my conspecifics, I shall continue to do so with abandon. We shall return to the long-range implications of this ruthless selfishness for which our genes have programmed us.

As we all know, a number of drastic developments transformed the nature of human work. Generally, as technology improved, the carrying capacity of the habitat in human life expanded drastically, at the cost of more labor-intensive and habitat-impoverishing exploitation techniques. The first great leap forward (or backward, depending on one's perspective) was the Neolithic Revolution of 10,000 to 12,000 years ago with extensive swidden horticulture. Then came the rise of large, powerfully centralized states made possible by intensive agriculture with irrigation, the plow, and so on. Finally, we had the Industrial Revolution. Each increase in productive technology was instantaneously converted into reproductive success. The human population expanded to fill new niches, and multiplied manifold, at the expense of most other life forms, except a limited number of domesticated plant and animal species.

Many other things happened together with population growth. With agriculture and livestock-raising, a surplus could be produced, which in the simpler, tropical, horticultural societies was also converted into reproductive success through increased polygyny (often subject to "bride wealth" payments). For the several thousand years that it took humanity to fill to capacity its new agricultural and pastoralist niches, labor became the limiting factor of production as never before. In hunting-and-gathering societies, population was held down by ecological pressures such as availability of water, climate, migration of game, and so on. The land could support only as many people as managed to survive the worst season of the year, or the worst years in cycles of drought or disease. Available labor was grossly under-utilized for much of the year, as the ability to secure additional food by additional work was often severely limited. With agriculture and animal husbandry, much more food could be produced and stored much more reliably, but this required much more work. Forests had to be cleared; soil turned over, fertilized, and irrigated; crops seeded, weeded, and harvested; herds pastured, protected, milked, and cared for. With more fields and more livestock, more mouths could be fed, but this required yet more work. More work could produce more wealth with which to acquire more wives who could both work and produce children who, in turn, could produce yet more. The pro-natalist ethic was now reinforced by a work ethic. Through hard work one could become even more reproductively successful. The hard worker joined the *pater familias* and the *alma mater* in the cast of good characters. "Work hard and multiply" became the double moral injunction.

The next major step in this escalating process was the rise of the state and of the parasitic ruling class that came with the state. Through organized violence, peasants and slaves could be parted with their surplus production, and through the parasitic exploitation of labor, the ruling classes could not only maximize their reproductive success, but also begin to accumulate luxuries and frills not directly convertible into reproduction. The product of labor could now be alienated from the producer, who therefore had to work doubly hard, for now he had to support not only his own reproductive effort, but that of his rapacious masters. His incentive to work was reinforced not only by the threat of punishment, but also by the work ethic, preferably with recompense in the hereafter. The more his work was exploited, the more the peasant or the slave was told how virtuous and noble hard work was. The slogan on the gates of the Nazi concentration camps proclaimed: *Arbeit macht frei!* (Work is liberating!)

With the Industrial Revolution, another productivity threshold was crossed, and another population explosion followed, one that still ripples through the Third World as it now belatedly enters the industrial age. During the nineteenth century, and still today in the Third World, industrialization brought misery and hard work to the toiling masses, but by the twentieth century, productivity gradually rose to the point that, in the richer countries, work could buy frills not only for the ruling class, but also for wider and wider segments of the population. At least in a few privileged countries, productivity seemed, at last, to outstrip reproductivity. Work, which by now was becoming second nature to people brainwashed by the work ethic, was finally making attainable rewards other than the joys of reproduction, indeed, rewards from the enjoyment of which reproduction detracted, or even rewards which reproduction made unattainable.

Now that work created a multitude of goods and services making life increasingly worth living, it is not surprising that man began to overcome his reproductive imperative. Take a highly self-conscious, selfish, hedonistic creature, give it the option of unprecedented luxury and enjoyment if it curtails its reproduction, and throw in a reliable technology of birth control that enables it to indulge to the fullest in sexual recreation without reproductive consequences. Is it any wonder that fertility is declining in the affluent countries?

Indeed, we may be experiencing one of the most profound revolutions in human history, a revolution against our own genes. Our genes programmed us to behave selfishly because, by so doing, we played the genes' game of replicating themselves. In Dawkins' (1976) felicitous phrase, an organism is a "survival machine" for genes, much as a chicken is an egg's way of making another egg. But we are self-conscious organisms with a capacity to agonize over our destiny, to revolt at our inevitable death, and to regard ourselves as more important than the sum of our genes. Separate reliably the enjoyment of sex from its reproductive end, and you give people the capacity to fool their genes, and to play their own hedonistic game for their own selfish ends.

To this brave new world corresponds the new ethic which I called the "ant ethic." The new imperative is no longer "work to reproduce," but "work, work, work." The virtuous thing to do now, we are told, is to use contraceptives, to practice abortion, to engage in homosexuality, to support Zero Population Growth, to adopt children instead of producing our own, or, as a supreme test of morality, to run to the neighborhood clinic for a vasectomy or tubal ligation. To be sure, there are still some reactionary, recalcitrant male chauvinists and brainwashed housewives who perversely reject the ant ethic. Research suggests that, by the test of deliberate, lifelong childlessness, these reactionaries still number some 95 percent of the population (Veevers, 1973, 1975), but things may change.

The moral basis for the ant ethic, we are told, is the "tragedy of the commons." If we continue to exploit selfishly Spaceship Earth's limited resources in order to maximize individual fitness, we shall surely face collective extinction, we are told. This is undoubtedly correct. Humanity has been courting eco-catastrophe for a long time. We have caused a serious deterioration of our planet's resources for several thousand years. It is said that, in Roman times, a squirrel could travel from the Straits of Gibralter to Jerusalem without touching the ground. Let it try now, and it would die of thirst on the outskirts of Tangiers. Furthermore, the pace of the deterioration is steadily escalating. In the long run, of course, as Lord Keynes remarked, we are all dead. This is true not only of ourselves as individual organisms, but also of the

ability of our planet to sustain *any* life form. Through unbridled resource exploitation, we can accelerate our demise as a species, but our
ability to prevent the sun from cooling down is quite limited. Yet, if
we are to succeed in the more modest aim of decelerating the pace of
our collective self-destruction, the ant ethic is not good enough. It is
not enough to curb our reproduction. This, we are already beginning
to do, not, I believe, because we are moral and altruistic, but for the
profoundly selfish reasons I just suggested. The next order of business
is to develop an anti-work, anti-consumption, anti-productivity ethic,
and to extoll leisure, laziness, contemplation, meditation, and welfare
chiselling. The "counter-culture" of the last decade heralds perhaps
that ethical wave of the future.

The moral of my story is that I should not have written this chapter.
Having written it, I should not have taken a plane to attend a symposium on family and work in Calgary. And having perpetrated that im-
pardonable sin, I should forego my trip to Paris to visit my mother.
But then I know that I am an incurable reactionary and a ruthlessly
selfish, immoral person: I love my mother, I have three children, and
I did not get a vasectomy. My wife is even beginning to sink to the
senile depravity of wanting grandchildren—just a few mind you, but
still her very own little one-quarter selves. If all my neighbors believe
in Zero Population Growth, abortion, homosexuality, and vasectomy,
all power to them. My grandchildren will have more room to play on
the commons.

References

Alexander, Richard D.
　1975　　"The search for a general theory of behavior." Behavioral Sci-
　　　　　ence 20:77–100.
Barash, David P.
　1977　　Sociobiology and Behavior. New York: Elsevier.
Barkow, Jerome H.
　1978　　"Culture and sociobiology." American Anthropologist 80:5–20.
Chagnon, Napoleon, and William Irons (eds.)
　1979　　Evolutionary Biology and Human Social Behavior. North Sci-
　　　　　tuate, Mass.: Duxbury Press.
Daly, Martin, and Margo Wilson
　1978　　Sex, Evolution, and Behavior. North Scituate, Mass.: Duxbury
　　　　　Press.

Dawkins, Richard
   1976   The Selfish Gene. London: Oxford University Press.
Engels, Friedrich
   1942   The Origin of the Family, Private Property, and the State. New York: International Publishers. (First published in 1884).
Goody, Jack
   1976   Production and Reproduction. London: Cambridge University Press.
Greene, Penelope
   1978   "Promiscuity, paternity, and culture." American Ethnologist 5:151–159.
Harris, Marvin
   1979   Cultural Materialism. New York: Random House.
Hartung, John
   1976   "On natural selection and the inheritance of wealth." Current Anthropology 17:607–622.
Meillassoux, Claude
   1977   Feemes, Greniers et Capitaux. Paris: Maspero.
Trivers, Robert L.
   1971   "The evolution of reciprocal altruism." Quarterly Review of Biology 46:35–57.
van den Berghe, Pierre L.
   1979   Human Family Systems. New York: Elsevier.
van den Berghe, Pierre L., and David Barash
   1977   "Inclusive fitness and human family structure." American Anthropologist 79:809–823.
Veevers, Jean E.
   1973   "Voluntary childlessness." The Family Coordinator, April, 199–206.
   1975   "The moral careers of voluntarily childless wives." The Family Coordinator, October, 473–488.
Wilson, Edward O.
   1975   Sociobiology: The New Synthesis. Cambridge, Mass.: Harvard University Press.
   1978   On Human Nature. Cambridge, Mass.: Harvard University Press.
Young, Michael, and Peter Willmott
   1957   Family and Kinship in East London. London: Routledge and Kegan Paul.

Comments—Sociobiology: Much Ado About Nothing?

AUGUSTINE BRANNIGAN

In his *Culture and Sociobiology*, Jerome Barkow (1978:5–19) prefaces his remarks with the question "Are you reading this article to maximize your inclusive fitness?" Presumably sociobiology is so encompassing a form of explanation that it includes even the social activities of doing science. Consequently, as a critic of sociobiology I feel compelled to point out that I am not proposing these observations to seduce the reader and thereby to maximize my genetic fitness in future cohorts or generations; rather, I am trying to maximize the inclusive fitness of my *ideas* within the profession. If the task is to maximize one's genetic fitness, it would make more sense to try to get into someone else's jeans, rather than merely to talk about "them." What I propose to do here is quite basic: I would like to state my impressions of what constitutes a sociobiological explanation, I will spell out some issues I take with these explanations, and I will relate these to Dr. van den Berghe's chapter.[1]

What is a sociobiological explanation? While most students of sociology would like to equate sociobiology with a simple reduction of behaviour to genetically controlled instincts, this is not at all the case. Nor is sociobiology a biological explanation of social behaviour which relies on the familiar recommendation about the decisive relevance of both nature and nurture in the determination of behaviour. What sociobiology *is* concerned with is the development of accounts of *social* behaviours—and especially (to date) altruism—through the use of population genetics models. Social behaviours, like altruism, were until recently something of an anomaly in the context of natural selection.

How can the man who is always willing to lay down his life for others ever find his *genes* being perpetuated in the population? If natural selection is operating on these individuals, presumably they should be eradicated over time—provided this phenotypic behaviour has a discrete genotypic basis—in other words, altruism which endangers ego's life will tend to undermine ego's "fitness" or reproductive success. This is where sociobiology becomes ingenious. Sociobiologists argue that selection processes operate not only at the level of the individual but also at the level of kin, that is, the genetically related groups. The altruistic animal whose phenotypic generosity is *shared* genotypically by the kin group may in fact ensure the *fitness* of the kin population if self-sacrifice *saves* the group more lives than it costs. Consequently, the spontaneous alarm call of the marmot may endanger one or two individuals in the flanks of a colony, but this will ensure the fitness of the entire group in the long run, provided that the altruistic behaviour has a genotypic foundation *and* that its *phenotypic* behaviour is ecologically adaptive (Barash, 1977:115). The altruism of soldier ants or bees who selflessly throw themselves against invading wasps or other predators is indisputably based in discrete genotypic "wiring" or "programming." The same mechanism has been successfully related to altruism in "higher" species—including the altruistic warning behaviour of marmots—and the model has been posited as a form of explanation for numerous other *social* behaviours. Indeed, Wilson (1977:4) claims that "sociobiology is the systematic study of the biological basis of *all* social behaviour," and in fact the model has been developed by David Hull (1978) to explain the altruistic activities of scientists in a piece waggishly published in *Animal Behaviour*.[2]

However, it should be pointed out that while kin-level selection is the primary mode of explanation in this area, it is not the only one. Robert Trivers (1971) has argued that members of the same species could evolve a system of "reciprocal altruism" with very distantly related individuals. Reciprocal altruism involves helping very distantly related animals where the altruism expanded is *coincidentally* mutual and where at small cost to each individual the altruism ultimately aids the inclusive fitness of both stocks of animals. Consider the case in which ego saves the life of a drowning man. If ego's chances of drowning are calculated at 5 percent, while they are 50 percent for the drowning man, in ego's evolutionary perspective it makes sense to save alter, if alter can at a later date save ego's life (though as Sahlins [1977] has shrewdly noted, one probably should not put too much stock in the ability of a man who can't swim to rescue one from drowning later).

But again the model of selection is applied to explain the existence of an anomaly for natural selection, and once again the phenotypic altruism is related to the genotypic "selfishness" of the act. It is selected for (a) because it is genotypically based and (b) because it maximizes the fitness of the target populations.

Criticisms of Sociobiology

There appear to be as many criticisms of sociobiology as there are critics. Numerous unfair charges have been made regarding the nascent racism of sociobiology, its conservatism regarding the sexual division of labour in family and work settings, its denial of free will, and its unsubstantiated generalizations from the behaviour of bacteria and ants to human societies (e.g., Reed, 1978; Osler, 1980; Allen, 1975). Indeed, science journalists like Nicholas Wade (1976) have documented and decried the vicious personal attacks on the founder of sociobiology, Edward Wilson. Rather than detail these criticisms, I prefer to address an issue of theory construction in this area which concerns the entire *style* of explanation. Numerous writers have argued that sociobiology is unscientific because it is empirically unfalsifiable—"there is no possible behaviour which, if it existed, would falsify the theory"—for example, in explaining kinship structures and matrilocal versus patrilocal residence patterns, sociobiology describes the inclusive fitness of both arrangements with the same theory (Osler, 1980). Other critics point to the logical problem of "affirming the consequent" in the definition of inclusive fitness: any altruistic action is directed either to one's kin or to strangers. If directed to kin, this is adaptive because of kin selection; if directed to strangers, this is adaptive in terms of reciprocal altruism.[3] *Any* altruistic act is deemed adaptive, and this adaptiveness is used to explain why it occurs. Why? It has been selected for; therefore, if it exists it must be adaptive.

Both these criticisms miss something of the style of the explanation. Sociobiology explanations—like simple natural selection models—do "appear" to be unfalsifiable and/or tautological and/or appear to affirm the consequent because they rely in every particular illustration on a narrative form of explanation.[4] In other words, while we are prepared to accept the general statement that every species and its attributes exist as a result of natural selection, in every particular instance we are forced to develop a *narrative* that reasons how *x* could have evolved to its present form.[5] For example, how did birds begin to fly?

Well, "in the beginning" some proto-dinosaurs evolved feathers to regulate their body temperature (like the ostrich). Their wings were selected as a mode of adaptation which when used like a cape provided an increased ability to control body temperature and hence to survive in more varied temperatures (therefore this affected their ecological niche). The wings still had residual claws at the joints which these birds used to capture food, and in the pursuit of this food they discovered they had already evolved an airfoil. *Voilà* flight (Desmond, 1975:167ff.). This is what I mean by a narrative explanation: The narrative is an instantiation of a general law or principle which spells out all the various historical conditions necessary to account for the particular organ or species or habit which is under examination. Charles Darwin's (1859) *Origin of Species* is filled with numerous narrative accounts that illustrate how the *general* theory could work in peculiar and particular cases. For example, his account of the selection of the eye is one of the most notable illustrations of this form of argument.[6] Sociobiology also relies on similar narratives to demonstrate how a particular habit/behaviour could become targeted by selective pressures and could evolve into a genotypically based behaviour favoured for its adaptability. However, in the case of sociobiology (versus simple natural selection) the habit is selected at the level of the kin group, not the individual, and the behaviours identified for special treatment have struck us as intuitively problematic for a selection model explanation (especially altruism). Hence we reconstruct an account such as the following: "First, there were all kinds of marmots, some who did and others who did not give the warning cry collectively. As time progressed, predators successfully picked off the silent (phenotypically selfish) stocks while the altruistic stocks managed to survive as a whole through the self-sacrifice of the few. That's why marmots give warning calls today."

Such accounts torment critics to no end. They appear to be self-serving, unfalsifiable, and circular illustrations that merely restate in the particular instance what is presumed by the general case. Critics have argued that these accounts are like Rudyard Kipling's "just so" stories—like why the rhino has wrinkled skin or how the leopard got its spots (Gould, 1978). The sociobiologist, like the storyteller, is able to invent all the details of pre-history to give his account the ring of a "likely story." This problem, however, is not new in evolutionary theory, nor is it wrong. Darwin's narratives drove more than one critic around the bend. Here is a good illustration from Fleeming Jenkin's 1867 review of *The Origin of Species* (Hull, 1973:319). Jenkin pointed out that the problem with Darwin's theory begins when a disbeliever tries to point out the difficulty of believing that some odd habit or complicated organ can have been useful before fully developed. The believer who is at liberty to invent any imaginary circumstances, will very generally be able to conceive some series of transmutations answering his wants.

He can invent trains of ancestors of whose existence there is no evidence; he can marshal hosts of equally imaginary foes; he can call up continents, floods, and peculiar atmospheres, he can dry up oceans, split islands, and parcel out eternity at will; surely with these advantages he must be a *dull* fellow if he cannot scheme some series of animals and circumstances explaining our assumed difficulty quite naturally.

Likewise, the sociobiologist can evoke any number of constructions to show how some inherently *social* activity, whether it be helping out one's kin or—helping a group of strangers (or any other social activity such as nepotism, racism, or human optimism, or "male sexual infidelity" and "female coyness," homosexuality, sharing of scientific ideas or any stage of the division of labor in any civilization, or the relationship between work and reproduction)—could be easily marshalled under the umbrella of population genetic models, that is, how any *social* activity can be explained by a genetical model.

While we *might* feel we are being had—inasmuch as we cannot identify a single social behaviour that stumps the sociobiologists—we should not on this ground alone distrust the theory; after all, if Wilson *is* correct, all social behaviour can be explained by population genetics—and the sociobiological accounts have the ring of likely stories, not because they are *post hoc* reconstructions or because they are tautological, but because they are *true*, and while falsifiable have *not* been falsified.

There is, however, something that does unsettle the confidence of even the sympathetic critic. Darwin's problems were predominantly *morphological*: "How did this or that *anatomical structure* evolve?" Without dispute these structures were controlled by a biological code, a genotype. While he could naturally posit that some phenotypic structure was controlled by a genotype, in sociobiology this assumption is not without its problems. In other words, Darwin could argue that *if* a structure was controlled by the "germ material" and *if* the structure gave the animal adaptability, those populations with it would tend to expand, while those without it (other things being equal) would tend toward extinction. The first premise—that the anatomical structure is controlled by the germ cells or genes—is unproblematic. The only alternative hypothesis in his day was natural theology, which held that biological structures like the eye are controlled not by germ cells but by the hand of God. This could not be entertained seriously by scientists because it did not lend itself to material research. Nonetheless, some scientists objected to the theory purely on religious grounds. For Darwin, however, the real issue was the claim that nature would select from among the variable forms the fittest. However, with sociobiology the premise that *if* social behaviours are genetically controlled they are a target for kin selection is not so straightforward: sociobiologists *assume* the very premise that all the critics put at issue. That is, while they stress the *consequence* that sociality *might* be a function of kin selection, the argument is controversial not for its conclusion but for its premise: the conditional (if it is genetically based) has become an article of faith, at least for the purposes of research. And that research tends to consist of the invention of narratives to work out *how* particular social behaviours could be selected, while the premise of the genotypic bases of these behaviours is treated as a foregone conclusion. That's what I shall deal with now.

Darwin's premise about the biological basis of anatomy was unproblematic because there were no viable alternatives for this premise. Can the same be said for sociobiology? Are social behaviours such as homosexuality or male infidelity rooted ultimately in biology? Most critics argue, "Of course not. These are *learned* behaviours." But at this point the sociobiologist becomes a truly slippery (i.e., adaptive) fish: the process of learning—and consequently the cultural forms that are collectively defined and widely appropriated—are deemed to be biologically based. That there is no strict correspondence between the phenotype (e.g., capitalism, badminton, smoking) and the genotype is unproblematic for the sociobiologist inasmuch as there is never any strict correspondence between these two things. For example, the phylogenetically distinctive songs of birds emerge ontogenetically only after the birds witness other members of their species performing (Marler and Tamura, 1964). Without this environmental experience, the bird will perform only a rudimentary version of the tune. Likewise, the green color of plants will emerge only in the presence of light. Consequently, genotypes may limit the scope of phenotypical behaviour, but they do not determine (or overdetermine) that behaviour, and the goodness of fit becomes more tenuous among the mammals and most tenuous among the primates.

One implication of this is that social learning theories of human interaction, as well as normative order explanations and interactionist perspectives and so forth, are not alternative accounts to sociobiology; they merely stress *phenotypic* variation as opposed to stressing the fact that variation itself is programmed genotypically. The problem raised here is obvious: the looseness of fit between genes and behaviour is so great that we could place in suspended judgement the explanatory value of simple biology. Otherwise we will be pressed to explain all the variation over the course of human history as well as the variation between cultures with a *constant*, that is, biology. Consequently, we can safely relegate biological facts to a *necessary condition status* in the explanation of any social action, while directing our attention to social facts. In other words, biology is true but inconsequential for the understanding of any *particular* social behaviour in man.[7]

The alternative to this is to show how specific *social* behaviours are *strongly* controlled by genetics as opposed to *loosely* made possible by the general human ability to learn culture. At the present time, this has not yet been done. In fact, when Barash (1977) extrapolates the findings of animal studies to man he prefaces his speculations with the caveat that he is going to play "Let's Pretend." This is not to say that sociobiology *will not* deliver, or *cannot* deliver, but merely that it has not delivered demonstrations that social behaviours in man are strongly determined by genetics.

The last issue is important. If sociobiology cannot show the strong basis for the determination of social behaviours and social structures by genotypes, we shall be hard pressed to illustrate how some social *pheno*type could be selected for, and hence how it could maximize the inclusive fitness of the social *geno*types. For example, it we want to explain the Good Samaritan phenomenon in terms of a population genetics model like reciprocal altruism, it makes a great deal of difference whether the altruism is involved in a specifically genotype-based disposition—as opposed to a disposition grounded in the general reinforcement of experience called learning. In the former case, the genotype controls the behaviour fairly directly, while in the latter case the genotype controls merely the ability to learn. If the genotype has this fairly direct control of behaviour, then we can easily appreciate the value of population genetics models to explain how the behaviour could become stabilized in a population. On the other hand, if the behaviour is based in the genotypes that control the general area of learning (which may subsume all culture), then the adaptive value of the behaviour (if it has any to speak of) will target *learning* ability, but not learned altruism per se.

Consequently, population genetics might be illuminating in understanding how *learning* gets selected for, but not how altruism (or any particular mode of learned adaptation) gets stabilized. In other words, this type of social behaviour can be explained by a sociobiological model only to the extent that the behaviour does have a discrete genotypic basis. Otherwise, the strongest claim of the sociobiologist will be only that culture *ultimately* has a biological foundation (in other words, it may be important generally, but this is not very helpful in any particular instance of social research). On the other hand, this argument does not deny that altruism could get stabilized in a tradition (via learning), but we do not need population models to understand how this could occur.

In sum, we face a dilemma. On the one hand, hard-core sociobiology might be a powerful tool if it could show the specific genotypic basis of social behaviour. But it hasn't. On the other hand, the weak argument that reduces all social and cultural behaviour to biologically controlled learning explains everything in general but nothing in particular—and this model does not even require a *socio*biological model; selection at the *individual* level (as opposed to the kin level) would be sufficient.

The Sociobiology of Family and Work

First I should spell out the key idea that I hear Dr. van den Berghe arguing in his chapter. The basic thesis is that "we work to survive, to reproduce, and to provision our offspring." If we restate this thesis to remove the teleological implication, we get: Those who work have a selective advantage in terms of their *own* immediate survival (vs. those who don't work), they have a reproductive advantage (over those who don't work), and they reinforce this advantage by provisioning their offspring (vs. those who don't work).

The question is: Is the disposition to work inherited? Is it genotypically based? Yes and no: Yes, we have a biological disposition against going hungry, and certain species have genetically fixed foraging patterns and strict dietary limitations in what they can digest. But there is enormous latitude in how species can satisfy their respective appetites. Species that have evolved the ability to adapt by means of learned cultural arrangements are able to exploit numerous types of food and shelter to ensure their immediate survival and their ability to reproduce.

Dr van den Berghe has provided us with a narrative account of the enormous changes in our modes of adaptation over the course of human history from Neolithic times to the present. It appears clear that modern work arrangements, thanks to new technologies, have expanded enormously the *fitness* of the entire species; that is, the new methods of ''work'' (i.e., providing food and shelter), have increased the fertility of historical man (vs. prehistoric man). However, I think we would have great difficulty showing that the success of the species could be traced to changes in man's *biological* makeup during this period. Consequently, if we tried to explain new work arrangements in a truly sociobiological fashion, we would be faced with explaining a variable with a constant.

The reproductive success of the species probably *can* be explained by an *evolutionary* model in which selection pressures work at the level of the cultural group; cultural groups that showed the greatest adaptability (via learned techniques) were given a reproductive advantage over those that did not. While this may be true—and I would be the last to deny it—it does not constitute a sociobiological explanation. No assumptions have to be made about the specific genotypes that control hunger and work. It appears that *culture*, not biology, controls our work arrangements—which in turn influence our fertility (though, as Dr. van den Berghe has observed, even fertility can be controlled by culture). But none of this requires the population genetic models that characterize true sociobiology.

This is not to deny that hard-core sociobiology has relevance in understanding work and fertility in the course of human history. It does. For example, it is argued that the foundations of agriculture and its success in the Old World are tied to a *genetical* transformation. Before 8000 B.C., nomads gathered the seeds of grasses for food. At about 8000 B.C. there occurred a genetic crossing of wild wheat and natural goat grass, producing an accidental fertile hybrid, emmer, consisting of the 14 chromosomes of goat grass and the 14 chromosomes of wild wheat. Emmer was much plumper and probably much more nutritious than wild wheat. As though this wasn't fortune enough for the species, there occurred a further accidental crossing of emmer with another natural goat grass, which resulted in the basic 42-chromosome bread wheat we know today. It should be pointed out, however, that this new hybrid was too heavy to be spread by the wind. It had to be planted by hand. In other words, the spread of bread wheat along with the revolution in agriculture were probably the result of a strange form of *reciprocal altruism*: humans spread the wheat, thereby maximizing its fitness, while reciprocally the wheat maximized the fitness of the *cultural* groups who farmed it (Bronowski, 1973). That accidental event was repeated intentionally by selective breeding of other plants and animals. In these cases we have a strange case of reciprocal altruism inasmuch as it does rely on genetical transformation, but only for one species (our food species). Nonetheless, the *fitness* of both parties is improved, though again the fitness here means the fitness of certain *cultural* groups—not genetic populations. So while one can see the limited utility of sociobiology, it would be a mistake to hang either all our species' woes or all its successes on its biology, and hence we would be mistaken as analysts to seek the key to explanation of human societies in genetical models like sociobiology.

Notes

1. Van den Berghe has written a number of articles that lay out the utility of the sociobiological approach in more detail. This chapter is only a provisional application of the model. For more detailed discussions of the approach, see van den Berghe, 1974, 1978a, 1978b.

2. It should be pointed out that Hull uses the *model* of altruism to explain why scientists share their ideas; he adopts not the reductionism of sociobiology but the general *form* of the argument that altruism shown to others may serve the goals of the individual scientist. Hence scientists share ideas because it is in their own individual interests to do so. Hull (1980) has also written an overview of the sociobiology movement from the perspective of the sociology of science.

3. I disagree with this objection. One can hardly identify a significant natural law that does *not* in every empirical instance affirm the consequent. Affirming the consequent is a fallacy only when it is used to discover a new law. However, the law of natural selection is hardly new. Its extension to social phenomena is inductively sound, though not logically derived.

4. There is an enormous amount of literature on the explanatory value of historical narratives in social history. Hull (1975) has discussed the issue in terms of the explanations of *natural* history found in geophysics, paleontology, and evolutionary biology.

5. According to Goudge (1961), although evolutionary explanations are often formulated as narrative accounts, they nonetheless have a sufficient conditionship form. In other words, the particular sequence of events in the chain of developments surrounding, for example, the origin of amphibians from fish, or apes that walked upright, or flying reptiles constitutes a set of conditions sufficient to produce each of these events as a result. Yet as Hull (1975) has pointed out, the terms of these laws are not transhistorical; they are particular historical conditions acting on *historical* species. This is very much the case in *social* histories. Hull argues that the success of biological narration is linked to the identification of crucial central units or subjects for narrative, i.e., "species."

A different view of narratives is found in Ruse (1971). He dismisses the relevance of narratives and their sufficiency. He claims that the historical conditions of any species are subsumed by the covering law of selective pressure.

Narratives are irrelevant. However, the covering law model of scientific laws seems to be different from the situation in physics. Historical instances of physical laws are clearly instantiations of general if not universal relationships. For example, the law that "the period of a single pendulum is proportional to the square root of its length" could be observed in the clock tower of Big Ben as well as in a hanging at the old gallows of the Don Jail. In both cases, the swinging bodies would conform to the law, though allowances would have to be made for artifacts peculiar to the arrangement. However, the problem with such laws of physics is that all concrete pendulums are only exemplifications of abstract or ideal relationships. Consequently, the physicist chalks up the differences between the ideal and the actual simply to being artifacts, for every pendulum is governed by this nomic relationship between periodicity and length. So if some particular historical pendulum becomes problematic, it is a problem for the engineer or the artisan, not the physicist. The physicist is not about to find a new permutation to the law; he would find, if anything, a *new* law. In this respect the physicist and the evolutionist are in different enterprises. Though the evolutionist employs and seeks basic laws, each historical exemplification is of interest in that, among other things, it furnishes linkages between existing and/or extinct populations. In such an enterprise, the historical descriptions are part and parcel of the discoveries, as opposed to mere "applications" or exemplifications (like the balls dropped from the Tower of Pisa). The evolutionist has general laws as well as historical populations, as well as narrative explanations that furnish sufficient accounts of the link between the former and the latter. In this respect, his work is not like that of the physicist but like that of the cosmologist, geophysicist, or geologist: it is simultaneously historical and descriptive, as well as nomological and "required."

6. See Chapter 6, "Difficulties of the Theory," for Darwin's (1859) discussion of "organs of extreme perfection and complication." Darwin argues that even the human eye could have arisen by the forces of natural selection working on minute variations over time. This discussion appears to have been directed to William Paley's early intuitionist arguments in *Natural Theology*, where Paley pointed to the complexity and perfection of the eye as *prima facie* evidence of God's handiwork.

7. Similar opinions have been advanced against all natural selection theory. Ludwig von Bertalanffy (Gould, 1978:530) suggested that the theory would collapse because it purported to explain *too much*.

References

Allen, Elizabeth, et al.
    1975   "Against sociobiology." New York Review of Books, Nov. 13, 182–186.

Barash, David P.
  1977   Sociobiology and Behavior. New York: Elsevier.
Barkow, Jerome
  1978   "Culture and sociobiology." American Anthropologist 80:5–19.
Bronowski, J.
  1973   The Ascent of Man. London: BBC Books. (Esp. 65–68).
Darwin, Charles
  1859   The Origin of Species. London: Murray.
Desmond, Adrian J.
  1975   Hot Blooded Dinosaurs. London: Futura Books.
Goudge, T. A.
  1961   The Ascent of Life. Toronto: University of Toronto Press.
Gould, Stephen J.
  1978   "Sociobiology: The art of storytelling." New Scientist 16:530–
          533.
Hull, David L.
  1973   Darwin and His Critics, Cambridge, Mass.: Harvard University
          Press.
  1975   "Central subjects and historical narratives." History and Theory
          14:253–274.
  1978   "Altruism in science: A sociobiological model of co-operative be-
          haviour among scientists." Animal Behaviour 26:685–697.
  1980   "Sociobiology: Another new synthesis." Pp. 77–98 in George W.
          Barlow and James Silverberg (eds.), Sociobiology: Beyond Na-
          ture/Nurture? Boulder, Colo.: Westview Press.
Jenkin, Fleeming
  1973   "Review of the Origin of Species." Pp. 307–344 in David L. Hull
          (ed.), Darwin and His Critics. Cambridge, Mass.: Harvard Uni-
          versity Press.
Marler, P., and M. Tamura
  1964   "Culturally transmitted patterns of vocal behavior of sparrows."
          Science 146:1483–1486.
Osler, Margaret J.
  1980   "Sex, science, and values: A critique of sociobiological accounts
          of sex differences." Unpublished manuscript.
Quadagno, Jill S.
  1979   "Paradigms in evolutionary theory: The sociobiological model of
          natural selection." American Sociological Review 44:100–109.
Reed, Evelyn
  1978   Sexism and Science. New York: Pathfinders Press.
Ruse, Michael
  1971   "Narrative explanation and the theory of evolution." Canadian
          Journal of Philosophy 1:59–74.

Sahlins, Marshal
   1977   The Use and Abuse of Biology. London: Tavistock Publications.
Trivers, Robert L.
   1971   "The evolution of reciprocal altruism." Quarterly Review of
             Biology 46:35–47.
van den Berghe, Pierre L.
   1974   "Bringing beasts back in." American Sociological Review 39:777–
             788.
   1978a   "Bridging the paradigms: Sociobiology and the social sciences."
             Society 15(6):42–49.
   1978b   "Sociobiology: A new paradigm for the behavioural sciences."
             Social Science Quarterly 59:326–332.
Wade, Nicholas
   1976   "Sociobiology: Troubled birth for new discipline." Science
             191:1151–1155.
Wilson, Edward O.
   1977   Sociobiology: A New Synthesis. Cambridge, Mass.: Harvard Uni-
             versity Press.

3

Weak Links in Men's Worker-Earner Roles: A Descriptive Model

HYMAN RODMAN AND CONSTANTINA SAFILIOS-ROTHSCHILD

Abstract

The worker-earner role is a joint role in which a person's earning capacity in an occupation contributes to the support of a family. Because of strong expectations that men play an important role as worker-earners, a variety of consequences stem from situations in which men's worker-earner roles are damaged. This chapter develops a descriptive model of the worker-earner role by analyzing the impact of, and adaptation to, four different situations in which men's ability to perform the role is impaired: (1) the life cycle squeeze; (2) lower-class family status; (3) disability; and (4) old age.

Introduction

In a simple society, where each person's family role and work role are integrated, the support provided by kinship groups tends to be strong, so that illness, unemployment, and old age do not become social prob-

The authors thank the William T. Grant Foundation for funds to complete this chapter, originally a paper presented at the Colloquium on Family and Work Roles in Comparative Perspective held in Calgary, Alberta, Canada, on March 13–14, 1980. They also thank Saralyn Blanton Griffith, Max Learner, and Patricia Voydanoff for their assistance. After the Colloquium, a revision of the paper was published in Helen Lopata and Joseph Pleck (eds.), Research in the Interweave of Social Roles, Volume 3: Family and Jobs (Greenwich, Conn.: JAI Press, 1983). It is being reprinted here by permission of the authors, editors, and JAI Press, Inc.

lems. In more complex societies, where work roles are differentiated from family roles, illness, unemployment, and old age represent potential problems. This has been the case especially in societies characterized by nuclear families in which the man was expected to be the primary breadwinner.

It is commonplace to look at the links between the work world and the family world, and to investigate their mutual influences. We have formalized one aspect of these links between work and family by introducing the concept of the worker-earner role as a joint role that places a person in both worlds simultaneously (Rodman and Safilios-Rothschild, 1968). As a worker a person is also an earner for the family. Within a family that is not an independent economic unit, someone must go to work for the "income" to buy the resources needed by the family. We refer to the worker-earner role as the role which thereby links work and family, and which sends family members out to work in order to provide earnings for the family's support. In this paper we develop our earlier concept into a descriptive model of the worker-earner role by analyzing the impact of, and adaptation to, four different situations in which an individual's ability to perform the role is impaired—the life cycle squeeze; lower-class family status; disability; and old age. Our focus is upon complex national societies. Although most of the discussion deals with Western and North American families, it is to some extent carried out within the context of a comparative framework. The formalization of our model into a series of interrelated and testable propositions has not yet been carried out, although the process has been started in the sections on the life-cycle squeeze and on disability. In the meantime, through incorporating illustrations from several societies, including those in the Caribbean, Greece, and Japan, we have developed the descriptive model with some awareness of cross-national similarities and differences.

One line of evidence that indirectly confirms the importance of the worker-earner link comes from research on job satisfaction. Given our descriptive model of the worker-earner role, we would expect that extrinsic rewards, particularly income, would be important in all occupational groups and in all age groups. Voydanoff's (1978a) secondary analysis of a United States national probability sample demonstrates that extrinsic rewards, especially good pay and fringe benefits, make a significant contribution to job satisfaction in all five occupational groups included in her study. Cohn's (1979) secondary analysis of a U.S. national probability sample indicates the invariant importance of several variables, including good pay, for four age groups.

Although much of the discussion that follows may apply equally to male and female worker-earners, we will focus the discussion upon men. Despite changing sex roles and the reduced emphasis placed on success, men are still more consistently expected to play a reliable worker-earner role for the family. The 1980 data show that in the U.S., in 46 percent of white households and 52 percent of black households, both husband and wife play the worker-earner role; in 4 percent of white households and 8 percent of black households the wife only plays the worker-earner role; in approximately 15 percent of all households, neither spouse plays the worker-earner role. Consequently, the husband is the sole breadwinner in only 36 percent of white households and 27 percent of black households (U.S. Bureau of the Census, 1981:181–83).

However, despite the fact that in the majority of households both spouses work, many working wives still earn less income than their husbands. In 1979, it was found that in families in which both spouses work, wives contribute 25 percent of the family income (Johnson and Waldman, 1981) and this percentage has remained fairly stable throughout the 1970s (Johnson, 1981). Of course, these are average figures, and mask a significant percentage of cases in which the wife earns as much or more than the husband. In 1970, for example, "22 percent of wives working full-time year-round contributed over 50 percent of the total income of their respective families" (C. S. Bell, quoted in Ross and Sawhill, 1975:10).

Several aspects of wives' work and family roles help to sustain the traditional expectation of the husband as the major earner in the family; the fact that many wives still earn less than their husbands; that they work in occupations with relatively flexible points of entry and exit (which allow interruptions without serious penalties); and that they still carry a disproportionate share of housework and child care responsibilities. Thus, although wives' work and earnings are having an increasing impact upon the family's status and style of living, the economic and social rewards of the husband's job are generally still paramount (Papaneck, 1979; Johnson and Waldman, 1981). We would therefore expect that in societies in which income is the key power basis, the man's worker-earner role in many households would still be defined as the major link between work and family organization.

Considering the critical importance of the man's worker-earner role several questions follow that we shall explore below. How (and how much) does this key position of the man affect the organization of family life? What happens when the man is disabled and unable to play his key role? What happens to the lower-class family in which the man is, by definition, playing a "damaged" worker-earner role? To what extent, and in what manner, can the man's emphasis upon the worker-earner role be reduced when his wife is also playing that role and under what conditions can he escape a "damaged" definition (Safilios-Rothschild, 1976a)?

The Man's Worker-Earner Role: Circumstances Under Which It Is "Damaged"

Let us look at families in which the man has difficulty with the worker-earner role. This is a crucial role because of the strong commitments expected of the man both at work and in the family. As a result, a weak link between work and family can have a variety of important consequences. And the link is weak when the man experiences unemployment, underemployment, poorly paid employment, physical disability, mental illness, or retirement from the work force. What all these circumstances have in common is that the man's worker-earner role is damaged and that he experiences difficulty meeting the expectations of that role.

The Life Cycle Squeeze

At certain stages in the family life cycle there are "strong consumption pressures on family men whose aspirations exceed their meager resources." Wilensky (1963:119) has referred to such pressures as a life cycle squeeze. One such stage occurs when the children are adolescents, especially if they are being supported while they attend college. Another such stage occurs very early in the family life cycle, as the household and family are being established. This is a time when consumption aspirations and needs frequently outstrip income, creating pressures upon the man as breadwinner and upon the family. We shall focus upon the early family life cycle stage in this paper, and the problems that it creates for men. The extent to which men experience the life cycle squeeze depends, of course, upon a number of factors: the man's age; the man's socioeconomic status; the state of the economy and the existence of employment opportunities; and the adoption of alternative life styles.

Age

The younger the age at which men begin to establish a household and family, the more likely are they to experience the life cycle squeeze. A typical problem faced by young men is a high rate of unemployment and relatively low pay. These conditions may be temporary, but they nevertheless pinpoint a period within the life cycle in which the expectations of the worker-earner role are difficult to meet. Oppenheimer (1979) points to the relatively low pay of young men in the United States and to the decline in their relative pay over recent decades. For example, looking at the ratio of younger men's median income to men aged 45–54, she reports that for men aged 20–24, the ratio declines from .59 to .41 between 1947 and 1976; and for men aged 25–34 the ratio declines from .91 to .83. These are conditions that present a serious threat to the man's worker-earner role.

As Wilensky (1963) pointed out many years ago, the life-cycle squeeze pressures more married men than bachelors into taking second jobs. This differential persists. In 1979, 6.5 percent of married men in the United States held two jobs or more, in contrast to 4.4 percent of single men and 4.5 percent of men of other marital status. For all men, those aged 25–34years (6.4 percent) and 35–44 years (7.2 percent) had the highest percentages working at two or more jobs (U.S. Department of Labor, 1981).

Socioeconomic Status

We would expect higher socioeconomic status to be associated with a reduced level of life cycle squeeze. Since socioeconomic status, stemming from one's family of orientation, is associated with higher levels of educational, occupational, and income achievement, men of higher social status are less likely to experience difficulties with the worker-earner role during the early stages of the family life cycle (or during any stage of the cycle). The man who receives the M.B.A. degree from Stanford University and takes a position for $35,000 is not going to be squeezed to the same extent as the high school graduate working at a semiskilled job. Further details on the relationship between social class status and problems with the worker-earner role are provided in the section below on "lower-class families."

Employment Opportunities

If a society's economy is healthy, and if there are abundant opportunities for employment, then the life-cycle squeeze will be a less serious problem. This is especially the case for younger men, who have fewer skills and less experience, and who therefore experience higher rates of unemployment and depressed levels of pay. To the extent that the demand for labor increases, the employment status of younger men improves, and it becomes easier for them to meet the expectations of the worker-earner role.

Alternative Life Styles

The life cycle squeeze stems from a young couple's conventional entry into marriage and early childbearing, with the husband alone playing the role of breadwinner. As a result, young men (and women) are able to reduce or avoid life cycle squeeze problems by departing from conventional marriage and family patterns.

One way for the man to ease the strain upon his worker-earner role is to postpone marriage until he is in a better earning position. In terms of our model, marriage postponement is a solution because it reduces pressure upon the earner side of the worker-earner role (cf. Furstenberg, 1974). Another potential solution, given marriage, is to postpone or forego children. Postponed childbirth is correlated with the wife's working, another potential solution to the earning problem. Finally, given marriage and children, possible solutions are the wife's involvement in full-time or part-time work, or for the man to take a second job (Oppenheimer, 1979; Grossman, 1981). These changing trends—later marriages; later childbirth; voluntary childlessness; dramatic increases in wives' working—help to alleviate the pressure upon the man's worker-earner role.

Independent Variable

It is possible to deal with men's life cycle problem in the worker-earner role as an independent as well as a dependent variable. For example, to what extent are family stress and divorce during the early stages of the family life cycle, and perhaps other indicators of stress—such as the higher rate of suicide of young black men (Davis, 1979)—influenced by the impaired link faced by some men in their worker-earner role? Although we do not explore this issue further, we believe that it would be worth looking at men's life cycle squeeze—or more generally at the weak links men experience in their worker-earner role— as a contributing factor to other types of individual and daily stress.

Lower-Class Families

A fundamental point about lower-class families is that we are dealing with families in which the man plays a worker-earner role that is damaged. By definition, the husband/father in the lower-class family is involved in much unemployment, poorly paid employment, and unskilled and perhaps semiskilled employment. We can expect a number of consequences to stem from the damaged worker-earner role played by the lower-class man (Rodman, 1971). The consequences for the lower-class man are particularly far-reaching. He loses status, esteem, and income power, and this influences his position both in the work world and in the family world. For example, he may be held in low esteem by the members of his own family because he is not able to fulfill their expectations as to the kind of financial contribution he should be making to the family. Since he is frequently unable to fulfill these expectations, immediate problems are faced both by the members of the family as well as by the man. From the point of view of the man, since he is not held in high esteem by his own family, he would often seek gratification and relationships outside the family. This may be a factor in the explanation for the strong peer relations that develop within the lower-class community (Liebow, 1967; Wilson, 1973). The man, in association with male peers in similar circumstances, is able to develop relationships through which it is possible to gain gratification. Similarly, in extramarital relationships with other women, he may have sufficient resources available to provide for them adequately, if even only for a short period of time.

What we are suggesting is that the weakness of the worker-earner role of the male and the concomitant lack of resources for the family may lead to lower-class consequences that are generally found in those stratified societies that are ideologically open for mobility to all and in which the man is expected to be the sole or major earner (O. Lewis, 1959; Smith, 1956; Rainwater et al., 1959; Gans, 1962; Rainwater, 1966; Rodman, 1971). As stated by H. Lewis (1965:350), "In spite of the fact that many homes do not have fathers or husbands, the lower income male and father is a key figure in gaining an understanding of child rearing in the lower income or dependent family. Of particular importance is the man's ability to support and stand for the family—

to play the economic and social role wished of him, particularly by wives, mothers, and children.'' The male who cannot play this role has difficulty remaining within a given marital relationship because of lack of esteem within the relationship. As a result, there may be an adaptive tendency toward marital shifting on the part of men and women. Relationships become more contractual in order to make it easier for men and women to adapt to the shifts that may be required. Certain social patterns may also develop, for example, different kinds of marital and quasi-marital relationships that permit men and women to join and separate without becoming legally and morally bound to a relationship that becomes untenable (Rodman, 1961, 1971; Segalman and Basu, 1981:147–48).

We are making two important assumptions: (1) the husband/father is expected to be the major earner in the family; and (2) the husband/father's failure to fulfill this role adequately is defined as a personal failure. Where these assumptions do not hold, the consequences we have suggested for lower-class families would not follow. In some developing countries, such as Greece, where structural unemployment has been high over long periods of time, manhood was not defined in terms of earning capacity and, therefore, the lower-class male suffered little loss of esteem within his family, and did not become a marginal or less powerful member of the family (Safilios-Rothschild, 1967). The reason for this was that most Greek males, at one time or another, experienced difficulty in fulfilling their earner role. Due to the instability of the Greek economy, unemployment has been frequent for highly educated and skilled men as well as for unskilled workers. Unemployment was therefore not usually defined as personal failure, but rather as resulting from social and economic malfunctioning and faulty governmental policies. As a result, unemployment in Greece has tended to lead to a very different kind of outcome for the lower-class family than in the United States.

In contrast to Greek culture, both the assumptions spelled out above generally hold true in Canada and the United States. There is widespread expectation that work is important, that the male should be the major earner, and that earning incapacity is related to personal incapacity. There is even an aura of sanctity about the worker-earner role of the male, and this can be observed by the strong moral reactions that have been registered against suggestions that would sever the worker-earner link, whether through technological advance (Ad Hoc Committee on the Triple Revolution, 1965) or through increased welfare payments (Segalman and Basu, 1981).

Even within North America, however, there are differences among families in terms of the importance attached to the male's earner role, and in terms of the reactions to the loss of that role. Early research on unemployment during the Great Depression (Komarovsky, 1940; Cavan and Ranck, 1938; Bakke, 1940) indicated that the men and families who viewed the male role as dominant within the family experienced lower morale and greater stress. Recent research continues to support these findings (Voydanoff, 1982a, 1982b). Those families with a more egalitarian view of sex roles are less likely to blame the man for his unemployed status and are more likely to show better family coping and adjustment (Voydanoff, 1978b). In brief, in those societies where less stress is placed upon the male's earner role, there is higher morale and less dislocation and alteration of family structure attendant upon the male's loss of employment or his lower-status employment.

Illness, Disability, and the Sick Role

Illness and disability are socially acceptable reasons for relinquishing the occupational role as well as other normal social roles. As a result, they can become attractive possibilities for persons dissatisfied with occupational or other roles. An illness or disability might become an especially attractive alternative to working when its state is permanent and its diagnostic parameters are ambiguous. For such permanent or chronic illnesses or disabilities, however, the social legitimation of work exemption becomes fuzzy and controversial (Safilios-Rothschild, 1976b). Clearly, a major consideration in granting exemptions is the type and severity of the chronic illness or disabling condition. In addition, the following societal, structural, and normative factors affect the social legitimation of work exemption.

The State of the Economy

The objective state of the economy is an important factor, as well as the perception of the economy by policymakers who can legitimize the disabled status and its exemptions and privileges. We would expect that the greater the actual or perceived affluence of a society (and the greater the belief in a labor supply surplus), the greater the ease of granting legitimized work exemptions and disability benefits to the disabled (Larson and Spreitzer, 1970).

Symbolic Value Attached to Work

As long as the Protestant ethic infuses work with a sacred quality and views work as the key element in people's psychological and social development and adjustment, we can expect policies and programs that encourage the disabled to work "for their own good." While the vocational emphasis of rehabilitation programs in the United States often exaggerated the necessity for the disabled to become economically independent (Safilios-Rothschild, 1976b), the desirability of work has also been argued in terms of its important noneconomic benefits. During the last decade, however, the intrinsic value of work has begun to be eroded as many highly successful men questioned its sacred quality and started ranking other life sectors at least as highly as the work sector. This erosion has been facilitated by the increasingly ambiguous evaluation of occupational success in the absence of marital or personal happiness, and by the higher level of occupational instability and unemployment even among executives and scientists. Therefore, it is possible that the social milieu will eventually become less insistent upon a categorical work mandate for the disabled, and that the alternative of not working may become more acceptable, especially in middle age after the disabled person has had a long, "productive" life.

Labor Scarcity vs. Labor Abundance

We expect that the more abundant labor is within a society, and the greater the structural difficulty in reducing unemployment, the greater will be the tendency to grant disability benefits and to legitimate occupational exemptions to the disabled. This will be seen as a relatively easier and cheaper social solution than securing employment for the disabled. In the 1970s and 1980s, women's labor-force participation in virtually all age-groups, educational categories, and marital statuses has increased dramatically, has produced an abundant labor supply, and has increased competition for skilled as well as semiskilled jobs. In addition, the increasing number of older individuals, and their politically successful demand for prolonged employment, have also contributed to the present oversupply of labor.

Diversity of Life Styles

The monolithic life cycle model of individual men and women that prescribed appropriate, orderly, and age-specific marital and parental stages has been replaced by a diversity of almost equally acceptable life cycles. This diversity includes singlehood as a result of delay of marriage, rejection of marriage, or rejection of remarriage. Moreover, the monolithic model of marriage, according to which the man is the only or the main breadwinner, has diminished in importance as increasing numbers of wives and mothers have entered the labor force. In some of these families the wife's worker-earner role may be as important or more important than the husband's worker-earner role.

Because of the increasing diversity of acceptable life cycle and marital models, disabled people now have a wider range of options than in the 1950s and 1960s. In 1963 the few cases of middle-aged workers with compensable back injuries who decided to stay home and take care of the children and cook while their wives enthusiastically went back to work were considered deviants and rehabilitation failures (Safilios-Rothschild, 1963a). Today they might be considered "liberated" men. As we suggested earlier, larger numbers of successful middle-aged executives and scientists have left their jobs to "do their thing" or have radically changed their life styles and deemphasized their work role or delegated the primary earner role to their wives. This is part of a social process that is beginning to open up new options for men as they reduce the salience of work and occupational success in their lives. We could therefore hypothesize that the overall societal deexaggeration of the worker-earner role for men may in the 1980s affect the nature of findings regarding the characteristics of disabled men who return to work or to the same type of work. During the 1960s the following variables were good predictors of men's resuming the worker-earner role: a stable career pattern (Starkey, 1967); low work morale resulting from failure or serious maladjustment in the performance of the occupational role (Safilios-Rothschild, 1963b); having a job to return to (Ludwig and Adams, 1968). It is possible that a good work record, work satisfaction, occupational achievement, and the opportunity to return to work may, in the 1980s, no longer be such good predictors of a return to work. These more successful workers may, after a disability, opt out of the full-time worker-earner role into more flexible and less demanding work arrangements.

Disabled People's Social Movement

The emergence of a social movement of disabled people has advanced the rights of the disabled in several ways. On the one hand the movement has fought against discrimination and for greater job opportunities—developments that serve to strengthen the commitment of the disabled to the worker-earner role. On the other hand the movement has challenged physicians and policymakers in order to gain greater acceptance for certain disabilities and the accompanying disability benefits.

One of the strengths of the social movement stems from the willingness of those with high social status, education, and visibility to identify with the ''minority'' movement and to protest against discrimination in order to achieve a ''different but equal'' status with those defined as nondisabled (Safilios-Rothschild, 1976b). While the militant organizations of the disabled have attempted to pass and enforce a number of different ''equal rights'' laws, the main goal of media presentations, conferences, and legislation has been to increase disabled people's ''self-determination and integration into the mainstream of American life'' (DeLoach and Greer, 1981:131–46). The crux of self-determination is the greater acceptance and legitimation of self-definitions of disability rather than the definitions of others. Gaining the acceptance and legitimation of self-definitions of disability is no easy matter and raises questions that have far-reaching consequences for a needed redefinition of the relationships between physicians and disabled persons (Safilios-Rothschild, 1976b). Although this is a battle that the disabled have not won, the challenges leveled against definitions by previously omnipotent physicians and other experts have helped disabled people toward self-determinations. Thus, more of them are like the nondisabled in their choice and commitment to work roles, even while the militant movement has helped to legitimate occupational exemptions by broadening the parameters for the decisions.

Self-Definitions

Up to now we have discussed the macrosociological factors that can affect the social legitimation of work exemption for disabled people. In addition, however, to official definitions of disability arrived at by disability status definers, such as medical personnel, insurance agents, and employers, another definition weighs heavily on whether or not the disabled person returns to work. This is the disabled person's self-definition of disability, which may or may not coincide with ''expert'' definitions, especially with regard to the extent of working disability (Safilios-Rothschild, 1976b). It must be emphasized that ''expert'' definitions of disability are seldom in agreement with each other; there is disagreement not only between medical and insurance expert definitions, but also between medical definitions depending on the school of thinking the physicians represent or the medical theory to which they adhere (Safilios-Rothschild, 1970:250–85).

Within the ambiguous context of official definitions of the disability status vis-à-vis work, self-definitions become very important. Until very recently the disabled person's self-definitions were either ignored or were considered deviant and inappropriate. Self-definitions that were of lesser severity than official definitions were labeled "denial of disability"; those of greater severity than official definitions were labeled "malingering" or "hypochondriasis" (Twaddle, 1974). Increasingly, however, there has been a tendency to take self-definitions of disability into consideration for rehabilitation purposes as well as in other contexts, especially as the disabled become more aware of and militant about their rights. Self-definitions of disability may be influenced by the following factors:

1. *Background characteristics* such as age, sex, marital status, education, type of occupation, income, and work history. In the 1950s and 1960s sex was an important variable in determining whether or not a disabled person would return to work—men had much higher return rates (Safilios-Rothschild, 1970:231). This sex difference has increasingly become less important and other characteristics, such as age, education and type of occupation, are more important factors. In general, those background characteristics that may indicate a weaker attachment or link to the worker-earner role have been crucial in influencing a disabled worker's decision not to return to work. These characteristics include: middle or older age; low education; lack of occupational skills; monotonous and routine jobs; and a discontinuous work history due to structural unemployment and/or serious maladjustment in the performance of the occupational role. Within a context of low degree of attachment to work and low work satisfaction, disability may represent a more socially acceptable and less stigmatized status than inability to perform the occupational role successfully. Furthermore, disability becomes more attractive when it is compensable. Workmen's compensation payments to unskilled and semi-skilled workers (especially middle-aged ones) who become disabled may represent an attractive alternative to the irregular and unsatisfactory wages earned when employed (Safilios-Rothschild, 1970:193–204).

2. *Marital and life style*—The tendency to relinquish the worker-earner role may depend upon the type of marital and life style of the disabled man. Middle-aged men with grown-up children and working wives may, for example, have a greater tendency to partly relinquish

their worker role after disability by changing their previous occupation to one that is more flexible and less demanding.

3. *Membership in a disabled persons' militant group*—To the extent that a disabled man's consciousness has been raised by the ideology of the disabled persons' social movement and/or to the extent that he belongs to organized groups, he may perceive himself as having and he may try to obtain a wide range of occupational and life alternatives. One of these alternatives may be partial or complete withdrawal from the worker role. Members in a disabled persons' organization are also more likely to be aware of the benefits of hiring one of a growing army of lawyers who specialize in obtaining federal disability benefits for their clients (Fialka, 1982).

Old Age

The circumstances of old age also involve a weakening of the worker-earner role. This is a time in which physical strength and ability are on the decline and in which the capacity to work may be impaired. It is also a time in which the old, regardless of ability, may be subject to mandatory retirement. As a result work and income are often separated and the attenuated work role generally leads to a reduced income. Nonwork income for retired individuals is problematic. Countries vary in the adequacy of their public pension programs while individuals vary in the private retirement income provision they make (Schulz, 1976). Moreover, there are substantial national and individual variations in filial responsibility to provide support to aged parents (Treas, 1977; Gibson, 1980a).

One of the changes that has taken place in American society has been the growing emphasis placed upon financial and residential independence for the older person. As a result, the percentages of older people who maintain their own households and who maintain their financial independence have been increasing. Despite residential and economic independence, however, there is still a considerable amount of social contact and exchange of help with kinsmen.

Not merely do adult children want to maintain independence from their parents, but parents also want to maintain their independence. Because of this shared norm it is possible for close relationships to continue between adult children and their parents, and even for various kinds of help to be exchanged, without threatening independence. In this sense, as Reiss (1965) has pointed out, the development and widespread acceptance of a norm of independence may have contributed to improved relationships between older people and their married children (cf. Safilios-Rothschild, 1978; Learner et al., 1980).

During the period of old age, a person has reduced financial commitment to his family, since the children are grown by this time and are self-supporting. In addition, increasingly, more adequate Social Security and private retirement benefits are available for the older person, as well as other Social Security measures such as medical care that help to provide financial security. For these reasons, the weakening of the worker-earner role and even retirement from the work role do not necessarily lead to problems for the elderly (Streib, 1965; Barfield and Morgan, 1969). In view of a person's age, the "damaged" worker-earner role is legitimized; in view of Social Security and other measures, the financial plight consequent to a weakened worker-earner role is mitigated. In other words, certain measures have been adopted that cushion the blow that might otherwise be felt consequent to the attenuated worker-earner role. This is the case in the United States and in most industrialized societies (Schulz, 1976).

The case of Japan is particularly instructive because of the early age of formal retirement. About 50 percent of all large companies have retirement plans with mandatory retirement at age 55 (Kii, 1979). But men do not receive government pensions until age 60, and these are relatively modest old age pensions. As a result of the gap between mandatory retirement and pension eligibility, there is a potential problem with the worker-earner role. How does Japanese society deal with the problem? The government has deliberately taken a limited role in filling the gap and has instead encouraged corporations and families to do so (Vogel, 1979).

Corporations have developed some creative solutions to the problem. One system used by companies is a reemployment system—workers are retired and then rehired. Another system is an extension-of-employment system—the retirement age is not changed but workers are permitted to continue working at management's discretion. In both of these systems, described by Kii (1979), the older worker's salary and work status are typically reduced. As Vogel (1979) points out, corporations prefer these systems to greater government welfare support because it keeps governmental bureaucracy and taxation down, and because these discretionary systems increase a worker's loyalty to the company, especially to the larger companies that can provide greater assurance of support to their older workers.

As a result, Japan, which has some of the earliest mandatory retirement ages among industrialized nations, also has the highest percentage of older people who continue to work (Schulz, 1976:51). This paradoxical situation continues, despite major changes in Japanese society. In 1965, in Japan, 55 percent of Japanese men ages 65 and over were working; in 1970, the figure was 54 percent (Kii, 1979); in 1975, it was 50 percent (*Demographic Yearbook*, 1980). The comparable 1962 figures for Denmark, Britain, and the United States were 38, 28, and 32 percent, respectively (Palmore, 1975; Shanas et al., 1968). In 1970, in Denmark, it was 24 percent (*Demographic Yearbook*, 1980); in 1971, in Britain, it was 19 percent (*Demographic Yearbook*, 1974); in 1979, in the United States, it was also 19 percent (U.S. Bureau of the Census, 1980).

Family practices also cushion the potential problem faced by the elderly. As in many societies, there are attitudes of filial responsibility to elderly parents, and a variety of patterns of help and exchange take place across the generations (Safilios-Rothschild, 1978; Gibson, 1980a, 1980b). These filial attitudes have traditionally been very strong in Japan, where they include coresidence as a desirable feature. The percentage of elderly Japanese couples who live with one of their adult children is comparatively high in Japan. For example, in 1973, 79 percent of Japanese couples over age 65 were living with one of their children. The comparable figures in Denmark, Britain and the United States are 15, 28, and 17 percent, respectively (Palmore, 1975; Shanas et al., 1968). This is not simply a case in which elderly Japanese are forced to live with their children because they are unemployed and destitute. It stems rather from the stronger norms of filial responsibility in Japan and from stronger attitudes of responsibility for aged parents (Palmore, 1975; Learner et al., 1980).

The structure of corporate and government retirement support in Japan reflects the cultural attitudes of filial responsibility and helps to maintain these attitudes. Thus, employers and employees frequently make long-term commitments to each other. Despite early mandatory retirement, comparatively high percentages of older men continue to work, albeit at lower levels of pay. And comparatively high percentages of elderly Japanese live with an adult child. Significant changes, however, are currently taking place stimulated at least in part by the recession and unemployment in 1974 and by sharp increases in the percentage of Japanese elderly (Nodera, 1981). The government and labor unions have put pressure upon corporations to raise the age of mandatory retirement from 55 to 60 by 1985, and labor contracts are now providing for gradual increases in the retirement age (*Ageing International*, 1981). In addition, although filial norms and attitudes remain comparatively strong, their strength is diminishing over time and the percentage of elderly Japanese who live with their children is decreasing (Yoshiro, 1979; Chira, 1982).

The ties between adult children and their elderly parents may involve not only residence in the same household, but nearby residence, with economic ties and help and exchange of various sorts. As Safilios-Rothschild (1978:39) has pointed out in a cross-cultural overview of family structure, traditional extended families have tended to be replaced by modified extended families that involve "residential separation of the nuclear family from kin, while at the same time a close relationship is maintained between the couple and their parents through patterns of frequent visiting and communication, mutual financial assistance, baby-sitting and housework services and a variety of other exchanges and obligations." As a result, help tends to flow from parents to adult children as they are establishing their own families of procreation, thus alleviating the life cycle squeeze of the younger generation. And, reciprocally, in cases of need, help tends to flow from adult children to elderly parents, thus alleviating the poverty associated with aging and retirement in the older generation (Treas, 1977). In these ways families provide a degree of internal support and security, and a reallocation of resources, to overcome weak links in the worker-earner role at various stages of the family life cycle.

Conclusion

In this paper we have developed a descriptive model of the worker-earner role that helps us view the transactions between work and family from a different perspective. Although family variables clearly have an impact on work experience, we have focused primarily upon the impact that certain work situations have for the family. By focusing on the worker-earner role we have been able to develop a descriptive model that aids in understanding what happens when the link in that role is weak or damaged. Thus, young men face a life cycle squeeze in which their relatively low income is often insufficient to meet the high costs of establishing a household. Lower-class men frequently face the dilemma of being unable to provide the support that is expected of them within the family. Men who are disabled or who retire are also potentially in a position of not being able to provide adequately for their families. But the disabled role and the retirement role may be socially legitimized and, therefore, accompanied by social welfare or social insurance support. This tempers the impact of the damage to the worker-earner role, and it also raises interesting questions about which men are more or less likely to retain the disabled role or to take early retirement.

Although our model provides a different way of viewing the link between work and family, it clearly raises more questions than it answers. But some of the questions it raises are new, and it also suggests where to look for the answers. For example, it makes it possible to look at certain problems of young men and lower-class men, at unemployment, underemployment, and poorly paid employment, at disability and retirement, through the same analytical lenses. For each of these situations we may ask: (1) To what extent is the worker-earner role damaged? (2) How, and to what extent, are individuals or families affected by a weakening of the role? (3) How much societal tolerance or legitimation of the weakened link between work and family occurs? (What about subcultural and individual differences in tolerance or legitimation?) (4) How, and to what extent, do individuals and families vary in adapting to the weakened link? (5) To what extent do societal supports (such as social insurance or social welfare programs) compensate for damage to the worker-earner role?

Several questions that need further analysis and that stem from our perspective provide additional illustrations of the value of our approach. Are fluctuations in the average age of marriage related to the social and normative structure of the worker-earner role? Are recent rises in the average age of marriage related to rising family consumer expectations and/or to lower relative pay for younger workers, both of which make it more difficult for young men to fulfill the worker-earner role during the early stages of the family life cycle? Are young married men more likely to take a second job because of the pressure experience in the worker-earner role? A special labor force report for the United States (U.S. Department of Labor, 1981), carried out in May 1979, indicates that a higher percentage of married men with spouse present hold second jobs than men of other marital status.

Finally, while we have not addressed in great detail the issue of multiple workers in the same family, we have seen how women's involvement in the worker-earner role tends to cushion the strains resulting from weak links in the male earner role. In the past, women's entry into the work force was often a response to men's absence or to men's damaged worker-earner roles. Increasingly, however, women's involvement in the worker-earner role is an independent development that represents women's choice and reflects changing ideas about sex roles, about the compatibility of career and family orientations for women as well as men, and specifically about the breadwinning responsibility. As the financial responsibility for the family and children increasingly becomes a joint responsibility, it would be interesting to analyze the nature and effects of, and the adaptations to, weak links in women's worker-earner roles.

References

Ad Hoc Committee on the Triple Revolution
    1965   "The triple revolution: An appraisal of the major U.S. Crisis and proposals for action." Pp. 443–457 in Louis A. Ferman, Joyce L. Kornbluh, and Alan Haber (eds.), Poverty in America: A Book of Readings. Ann Arbor, Mich.: University of Michigan Press.
Ageing International
    1981   "Japan raises retirement age." 8(Winter):7
Bakke, W. Wight
    1940   The Unemployed Worker. New Haven, Conn.: Yale University Press.
Barfield, Richard E., and James N. Morgan
    1969   Early retirement. Ann Arbor, Mich.: Institute for Social Research, University of Michigan.
Cavan, Ruth S., and Katherine H. Ranck
    1938   The Family and the Depression. Chicago: University of Chicago Press.
Chira, Susan
    1982   "Japanese attitudes toward aging change." New York Times News Service, Greensboro Daily News, January 5.
Cohn, Richard M.
    1979   "Age and the satisfactions of work." Journal of Gerontology 34:264–272.
Davis, Robert
    1979   "Black suicide in the seventies: Current trends." Suicide and Life-threatening Behavior 9:131–140.
DeLoach, Charlene, and Bobby G. Greer
    1981   Adjustment to Severe Physical Disability: A Metamorphosis. New York: McGraw-Hill Book Company.
Demographic Yearbook 1973
    1974   United Nations
Demographic Yearbook 1979
    1980   United Nations
Fialka, John J.
    1982   "Growth industry: Disability-claim cases under social security are a boon to lawyers." Wall Street Journal, 14:1–22.

Furstenberg, Frank F., Jr.
    1974   "Work experiences and family life." Pp. 342–360 in James O'Toole
        (ed.), Work and the Quality of Life. Cambridge, Mass.: MIT Press.
Gans, Herbert J.
    1962   The Urban Villagers: Groups and Class in the Life of Italian-
        Americans. New York: The Free Press of Glencoe.
Gibson, Mary Jo
    1980a   "Family support for the elderly in international perspective: Part
        I." Ageing International 7(Autumn):12–17.
    1980b   "Family support for the elderly in international perspective: Part
        II, policies and programs." Ageing International 7(Winter):13–19.
Grossman, Allyson Sherman
    1981   "Working mothers and their children." Monthly Labor Review,
        May, 49–54.
Johnson, Beverly L.
    1981   Marital and Family Characteristics of the Labor Force, March, 1979.
        U.S. Department of Labor, Special Labor Force Report 237, pp.
        48–52.
Johnson, Beverly L., and Elizabeth Waldman
    1981   "Marital and family patterns of the labor force." Monthly Labor
        Review, October, 36–38.
Kii, Toshi
    1979   "Recent extension of retirement age in Japan." Monthly Labor
        Review, October, 36–38.
Komarovsky, Mirra
    1940   The Unemployed Man and His Family. New York: Dryden Press.
Larson, David L., and Elmer A. Spreitzer
    1970   "The disabled role, affluence, and the meaning of work." Journal
        of Rehabilitation, 36:29–32.
Learner, Max, James Romeis, and Marvin Sussman
    1980   "Responsibility for aging parents: Attitudes of adult children in
        Japan and the United States." Mimeographed.
Lewis, Hylan
    1965   "Child rearing among low-income families." Pp. 342–353 in Louis
        A. Ferman, Joyce L. Kornbluh, and Alan Haber (eds.), Poverty
        in America: A Book of Readings. Ann Arbor, Mich.: University
        of Michigan Press.
Lewis, Oscar
    1959   Five Families: Mexican Case Studies in the Culture of Poverty.
        New York: Basic Books.
Liebow, Eliot
    1967   Tally's Corner. Boston: Little, Brown and Company.
Ludwig, Edward D., and Shirley D. Adams
    1968   "Patient cooperation in a rehabilitation centre: Assumption of the
        client role." Journal of Health and Social Behavior 9:328–336.

Nodera, Yasuyuki
  1981   "Japanese employment policies for older workers." Aging and
            Work 4:101–108.
Oppenheimer, Valerie Kincade
  1979   "Structural sources of economic pressure for wives to work: An
            analytical framework." Journal of Family History 4:177–197.
Palmore, Erdman
  1975   The Honorable Elders. Durham, N.C.: Duke University Press.
Papanek, Hannah
  1979   "Family status production: The 'work' and 'non-work' of women."
            Signs: Journal of Women in Culture and Society 4:775–781.
Rainwater, Lee
  1966   "Crucible of identity: The Negro lower-class family." Daedalus
            95:172–216.
Rainwater, Lee, Richard P. Coleman, and Gerald Handel
  1959   Workingman's Wife. New York: Oceana.
Reiss, Paul J.
  1965   "Extended kinship relationships in American society." Pp. 204–
            210, in Hyman Rodman (ed.), Marriage, Family, and Society: A
            Reader. New York: Random House.
Rodman, Hyman
  1961   "Marital relationships in a Trinidad village." Marriage and Fam-
            ily Living 23:166–170.
  1971   Lower-class Families: The Culture of Poverty in Negro Trinidad.
            New York: Oxford University Press.
Rodman, Hyman, and Constantina Safilios-Rothschild
  1968   "Business and the American family." Pp. 313–335 in Ivar Berg
            (ed.), The Business of America. New York: Harcourt, Brace and
            World.
Ross, Heather L., and Isabel V. Sawhill
  1975   Time of Transition: The Growth of Families Headed by Women.
            Washington, D.C.: Urban Institute.
Safilios-Rothschild, Constantina
  1963a   The Reaction to Disability in Rehabilitation, Ph.D. dissertation,
            Ohio State University.
  1963b   "A typology of reactions to disability." Paper presented at the
            Michigan Sociological Association, Detroit, Mich.
  1967   "A comparison of power structure and marital satisfaction in ur-
            ban Greek and French families." Journal of Marriage and the Family
            29:345–352.
  1970   The Sociology and Social Psychology of Disability and Rehabili-
            tation. New York: Random House.
  1976a   "Dual linkages between the occupational and family systems: A
            macrosociological analysis." Signs: Journal of Women in Culture
            and Society 1:51–60.

1976b   "The self-definitions of the disabled and implications for rehabilitation." Pp. 39–56 in Gary Albrecht (ed.), The Sociology of Disability and Rehabilitation. Pittsburgh: University of Pittsburgh Press.

1978   "Trends in the family: A cross-cultural perspective." Children Today 7:38–44.

Schulz, James H.

1976   The Economics of Aging. Belmont, Calif.: Wadsworth Publishing Company.

Segalman, Ralph, and Asoke Basu

1981   Poverty in America: The Welfare Dilemma. Westport, Conn.: Greenwood Press.

Shanas, Ethel, Peter Townsend, Dorothy Wedderburn, Henning Friis, Paul Milhoj, and Jan Stehouwer

1968   Old People in Three Industrial Societies. New York: Atherton Press.

Smith, Raymond T.

1956   The Negro Family in British Guiana. London: Routledge and Kegan Paul.

Starkey, Pearl Davidoff

1967   "Sick-role retention as a factor in nonrehabilitation." Journal of Counseling Psychology 19:73–79.

Streib, Gordon F.

1965   "Intergenerational relations: Perspectives of the two generations on the older parent." Journal of Marriage and the Family 27:469–476.

Treas, Judith

1977   "Family support systems for the aged: Some social and demographic considerations." Gerontologist 17:486–491.

Twaddle, Andrew C.

1974   "The concept of health status." Social Science and Medicine 8:29–38.

U.S. Bureau of the Census

1980   Statistical Abstract of the United States: 1980. Washington, D.C.

1981   Household and Family Characteristics: March 1980. Current Population Reports, Series P–20, No. 366. Washington, D.C.

U.S. Department of Labor

1981   "Multiple job holders in May 1979." Special Labor Force Report 239. Washington, D.C.

Vogel, Ezra F.

1979   Japan as Number One. Cambridge, Mass.: Harvard University Press.

Voydanoff, Patricia

1978a   "The relationship between perceived job characteristics and job satisfaction among occupational status groups." Sociology of Work and Occupation 5:179–192.

1978b   "Unemployment and the family." Pp. 17–26 in June Sale (ed.), Readings. Pasadena: National Consortium for Children and Families.

1982a   "Unemployment and family stress." In Helena Lopata and Joseph Pleck (eds.), Research in the Interweave of Social Roles, Vol. 3. Greenwich, Conn.: JAI Press.

1982b   "Sudden unemployment and the family." In Charles R. Figlen and Hamilton I. McCubbin (eds.), Stress and the Family, Vol. 2. New York: Brunner/Mazel.

Wilensky, Harold L.

1963   "The moonlighter: A product of relative deprivation." International Relations 3:105–124.

Wilson, Peter, J.

1973   Crab Antics: The Social Anthropology of English Speaking Negro Societies of the Caribbean. New Haven, Conn.: Yale University Press.

Yoshirō, Tanaka

1979   "The plight of the elderly." Japan Quarterly 26:63–74.

Comments—Bringing Women Back In: A Critique of "Weak Links in Men's Worker-Earner Roles"

EUGEN LUPRI

I shall address three interrelated issues. First, to highlight its theoretical potential for comparative research, I would like to place Rodman and Safilios-Rothschild's insightful chapter in theoretical and historical contexts. Second, I shall show how the concept of the worker-earner role in conjunction with the notion of damaged links is most appropriate for tracing interchanges between family and work. In so doing, I shall document how these two concepts are applicable to other roles as well. Third, I shall critically assess the author's assumption that the articulation of family and work transactions is best carried out through the *male* worker-earner role. I take issue with that assumption and plead for making the proposed model more flexible and less arbitrary, so *female* worker-earners may enter it on a more permanent basis than suggested.

In any field of sociology it is essential to have an analytical framework that establishes the boundaries of empirical investigation. If two fields, like family and work, are examined simultaneously, a theoretical framework of some sort becomes even more crucial.

In family sociology, models have been developed that are mostly grounded in structural-functional theory, interaction theory, developmental theory, exchange theory, and more recently, conflict theory. Some of the models are specifically designed to investigate certain aspects of the relationship between family and economic life. In past research, economic factors in that relationship were conceptualized as independent variables, while family variables, by and large, were defined as dependent variables. The chapter under discussion falls in the latter category, stressing as it does the consequences for the family brought about by the male worker-earner's "damaged links." In recent years, more attention has been devoted to research that treats the family as an independent variable, particularly as the focus shifted from the study of internal structure and family functioning to tracing intersecting family and work roles of both spouses.

Whatever the research strategy used, it is evident that family theory, defined as a system of interrelated propositions, does not exist in family sociology today. What we have instead is a number of miniature theories. In short, family theory is noninclusive, incomplete, inconsistent, highly contradictory, and divergent in its epistemological assumptions about the nature of social phenomena. Moreover, like most theories in general sociology, family theory is highly culture-bound and its concepts are value-laden. So it follows that family sociology deals with data *as interpreted within a special type of conceptual model*. But without such a framework or model, it is not possible to identify ranges of empirical variation that are scientifically problematical.

It is within this overall theoretical context that Rodman and Safilios-Rothschild's attempt is commendable. The proposed theoretical model helps us identify crucial variables in tracing interchanges between family and work, particularly in links that are "damaged" or "weak."

The chapter is commendable in yet another way. The basic concepts of "worker-earner role" and "damaged" or "weak" links have, at least on the surface, universal applicability. For example, some of the "damaged links" observed in the worker-earner role of lower-class men may be examined in a wider cross-national setting, as the authors' in fact do. Should economic activity in different societies be described in terms of its meaning to the members of the society, or should it be measured by some objective index? The worker-earner role, as a concept, is universally defined and should prove helpful in comparative research.

The comparative approach enables us to maximize the range of variation so we can determine whether certain "damaged links" hold true independently of the varied societal settings in which they occur, or whether they occur in certain societies only. The interplay of family and work roles is empirically testable through the "worker-earner role." It is that type of conceptualization that provides the model with two essential and required properties: it can be empirically verified and it is assumed to be universally valid.

In sum, the model has the potential of becoming a theory as it contributes to our understanding of the transactions between family and work. The emphasis is on the articulation of damaged or weak links in the interchange.

On the other hand, if we are to appraise the model in terms of its theoretical inclusiveness or cross-cultural validity, a reconceptualization of what constitutes *work* along with a redefinition of the "wage-earner role" is in order. But let me first comment on the applicability of the general concept of the worker-earner role.

What I find most enlightening is that several observed "damaged links" in the male worker-earner role are strikingly paralleled in the structural barriers *women* face when they enter the world of work. For example, the authors state the case of young men in early stages of the life cycle and the difficulty they have in meeting certain expectations of the worker-earner. Solutions they suggest are to *postpone* marriage or to *postpone* having children. A much more plausible solution they suggest, but do not develop, is that the young men might be cohabiting, or even be legally married, and have children. Furthermore, their young wives might be mothers and might decide on their own to remain in the labor force. As a matter of fact, one of the most pervasive and basic changes in the contemporary family is the dramatic increase in the proportion of *married* women who work for pay. And more important is the cross-national finding that the largest increase in labor-force activity is in the groups least likely to work in the past: *mothers of preschool children*.

Perhaps the young men the authors refer to are indeed married, have children, and send their wives to work. It is much more likely that the young mothers remain in the labor force, or reenter as soon as possible. Perhaps the young wives want to work to find fulfillment. Moreover, working outside the home may have meaning and significance for them as well, contrary to what the authors assume. Recent cross-national evidence suggests that both single and married women increasingly attach greater meaning to their work roles outside the home (Lupri, 1982). Scanzoni and Scanzoni (1981:354) report interesting trend data for the United States showing that the proportion of wives who work because they *enjoy* working increased from 30 percent in 1960 to 50 percent in 1971, whereas the proportion of wives who reportedly work to supplement the family income decreased.

The thrust of my argument is that if the *male* worker-earner role is damaged, the problem may be solved by the *couple as a family unit*, which will soften the blow to the male or female as couples work out the damaged role. Cross-sectional data and aggregate figures may mislead us in identifying only the male's "damaged role" and the familial consequences. Longitudinal data are needed to trace these interrelationships for both spouses.

Another interesting example is the case of the lower-class worker-earner whose role is damaged. A lower-class family man is more likely than a middle-class man to be unemployed, underemployed, poorly paid, unskilled, and semi-skilled. The consequences for family life are far-reaching, the authors say: he loses status, esteem, and income power. Exactly the same pattern may be identified when we examine the worker-earner role of women in the labor force, although the familial consequences may differ.

A recent study of the changing roles of Canadian women in family and work showed that they remain clustered in service and clerical jobs; that their share in the overall growth in professional work is negligible; that they have less paid employment than they desire; and that Canadian women, especially those who are married, are more vulnerable than men to underemployment. Women's earnings are lower than men's, and the gap is widening (Lupri and Mills, 1981).

Like lower-class male worker-earners, women on the whole are predominantly employed in low-pay, low-skilled, low-prestige jobs. Married women, not unlike lower-class men, move in and out of the work force as their personal, and often familial, situations dictate. *Both* worker-earner roles are severely damaged, although the familial consequences may or may not differ.

It appears, then, that the proposed model sensitizes us to examine structural inequities that damage both roles, that of the male worker-earner and that of the female worker-earner. The parallel structures are most striking, even though circumstances may vary. Again, cross-national studies tend to support the notion that the plight of the employed mother is not unlike the damaged role of the lower-class man. I think the damaged role of the lower-class husband shows greater cross-national variation, while the plight of the employed wife tends to reflect an identical pattern across societies. It appears to be a universal one (Szalai et al., 1972).

Mental illness may serve as another example. Here the role of the housewife manifests parallel patterns. Not because the housewife's "links" are damaged but because there are no links at all. Technically, her job is considered not demanding, it carries little if any prestige, and it is not highly rewarded. This can be frustrating for women with considerable formal education, internalized values of equality, and the belief that they will be achieving, productive adults. Women remain essentially isolated. Their role expectations are considerably more diffuse, and less clear, than those for men. No wonder that evidence accumulating for almost four decades has consistently shown married women to have higher rates of mental illness than married men (Gove, 1972, 1978, 1979). The consequences for the family and work settings need to be explored.

Let me turn to my final point, the plea to open up the model and let *female* worker-earners enter it through the front door. Throughout their chapter, the authors allowed women to enter the model, to leave it, and to reenter it, but always, so it seems, through the back door. Working wives are introduced as highly adaptable "angels" whenever support is needed in the damaged male worker-earner role. To use another metaphor, working women are treated analytically, like night nurses always on call to heal a damaged male role. This analytical treatment strikingly parallels how women's roles have been defined traditionally, and are still defined in many industrialized countries. But theoretical concepts, to be useful, must be sensitive and receptive to capture social changes. Future family theory will need to define men's and women's role configurations in a manner that permits alternative family and work structures to emerge.

Rodman and Safilios-Rothschild's assumption that "the man (husband-father) is expected to be the major earner" is, of course, grounded in Parsonian structural-functional theory (e.g., Parsons, 1949, 1960; Rodman, 1965; Grønseth [1971] presents a critical appraisal of this notion). But why limit the model to the *male* worker-earner?

The authors underestimate the economic contribution working wives are making to the household and seriously ignore recent observations that their earnings "undoubtedly affect the general status position of the family and not just its economic position because wives' earnings will probably modify the family consumption patterns, i.e., its life style" (Oppenheimer, 1977:397). The authors are heavily influenced by Parson's assumptions of the nature and determinants of women's socioeconomic role in the family. According to Parsons, the major mechanism preventing disruptive competition between husband and wife is sex-role segregation, where the dominant male role is the occupational role and the dominant female role is that of housewife and mother (1949:13). Another proposition, and one that is of greater relevance here, is Parson's statement that "it is fundamentally by virtue of the importance of his occupational role as a component of his familial role that in our society we can unequivocally designate the husband-father as the 'instrumental leader' of the family as a system (1960:13).'' Thus, while the role of the adult male is anchored primarily in the occupational world, the female role is anchored primarily in the internal affairs of the family. It is precisely the articulation between the family and the occupational system that sharply focuses the instrumental responsibility on *one* adult *male* member.

In following Parsons, Rodman and Safilios-Rothschild seem to take "what *is* as an indication of what, almost certainly, must *be* (Morgan, 1975:46).'' The authors' image of the family and the roles husband and wife have is so tied to the functional perspective that the image masks what initially may have been an accurate observation by theoretically denying any alternative developments or any possibility of countertrends. It ignores *a priori* that it is possible, theoretically and empirically, that either husband *or* wife can perform *both* roles and that significant role changes can occur over the family life cycle (Lupri and Frideres, 1981).

My thesis is that cross-national evidence now is sufficient to redress this unintended sexual imbalance in the proposed model. No world trend is better documented than the increase in the proportion of married women who work for pay (Lupri, 1982). But more important, the largest increase in labor-force participation has been by the group generally viewed in the past as least likely to work: mothers of preschool children. Middle-aged women also show dramatic rises in work activity outside the home, indicating that young and old wives are increasingly sharing the economic burdens of contemporary family households everywhere. In almost all advanced societies, half the wives and mothers are in the labor force. In socialist countries the proportion is even higher. The dramatic increase in the proportion of married women who work for pay outside the home manifests one of the most pervasive changes in the structure of the family everywhere. The change reflects the ever-increasing intersecting of women's roles in family and work. Further, men's overall labor-force participation rates are declining in many industrialized nations (Lupri, 1982:Table 2).

Rodman and Safilios-Rothschild argue that "it is also an accurate reflection of the reality that the *man* . . . is generally the major family earner with long-term involvement in the worker-earner role." The question is, whose reality? They further argue that working mothers contribute less than one-fourth of the family income. But Oppenheimer, with recent U.S. data, has shown that the wives' contribution to family income varied considerably by occupational status: "The lower the occupational earnings group of the husband, the higher the ratio of wives' median earnings to husbands' (1977:397).''

The most important question, however, is not whether the wife's earnings equal those of her husband but the ''extent to which her earnings provide a functional substitute for upward occupational mobility on his part or a counterbalance to downward mobility (Oppenheimer, 1977:400).''

Furthermore, Rodman and Safilios-Rothschild ignore housework. International time-budget data demonstrate conclusively that when housework and paid work are summed, employed wives work between two and three hours more per day than employed husbands do. The work day is extended by another hour if she has children. In reality, then, because housework is defined as unpaid work, wives' economic contribution to family income is vastly deflated. If women, employed or nonemployed outside the home, were paid for their household labors, their economic contribution to family income would at least equal that of their husbands.

In sum, the new life-course pattern emerging for women everywhere is a pattern in which family and work roles are coordinated throughout adult life. It appears that a sexual symmetry of work roles is in the making, notwithstanding the persistence of structural barriers that impede women's full equality at home and on the job everywhere (Lupri, 1982). The unfavorable earnings position of women versus men in all societies should not deter us from recognizing the economic significance of their earnings.

In the light of changes in both female and male roles, is it still meaningful to trace the interchanges of family and work roles through the male role only? I think it is not, if we are interested in articulating the *transactions* between family and work. The model would have greater predictive power if the designation according to sex were left open for empirical investigation or, preferably, if both male and female worker-earner roles were examined simultaneously, thereby making the family the basic unit of analysis. In so doing the model would come to grips with the *unitary* character of much of family and work activity. The traditional analytical distinction of family and work as dichotomous spheres tends to reify the sexual division of labor and thereby unduly emphasizes the separation of family and work. It also perpetuates the notion of ''naturally'' different spheres for women and men as well as the double standard, so pervasive in the social structure of all industrial societies. But viewing the family as a household unit with sets of task requirements inside and outside the household would greatly enhance the explanatory potential of the proposed model. Such a perspective requires a redefinition of work for the proposed model and entails treating paid work *and* housework as *family work* (Pleck, 1977, 1978). That would begin to redress the traditional imbalance according to sex that still permeates much current theory and research in family sociology.[1]

In short, let women workers enter the model as full-fledged partners, let them enter as equal co-workers, let them enter as worker-earners who, like men, attach meaning to their work, and finally, let women enter as persons with their own identity. The model is sensitive to many significantly "damaged links" in the family-work system; it will be an even better model if we *bring women back in*.

Note

1. Because family theory is insensitive to, or even denies, domestic labor's *economic* function, it ignores the housewife as a worker-earner. Some interesting insights on how this conceptual dilemma can be remedied may be derived from Marxian perspectives. For example, Secombe (1980) presents a recent interpretation of Marx's discussion on domestic labor's relation to wage labor and how both can be conceptualized as labor power. Following Marx, Secombe (pp. 375–376) convincingly demonstrates that the commodities the wage purchases are not themselves in a finally consumable form at the point of purchase. An additional labor, housework, is necessary in order to convert commodity into family subsistence. The value the housewife creates is realized as one part of the value labor power achieves as a commodity when it is sold. In short, all labor—wage labor and domestic labor—produces value when it produces any part of a commodity that achieves equivalence in the marketplace with other commodities. Current theorizing about changes in family structure and functioning would benefit by reexamining Marx's analysis of the housewife and her labor under capitalism.

References

Gove, Walter
    1972   "Sex roles, marital status, and mental illness." Social Forces 51:34–44.
    1978   "Sex differences in mental illness among adult men and women: An examination of four questions raised regarding whether or not women actually have higher rates." Social Science and Medicine 12:187–198.

1979   "Sex, marital status, and psychiatric treatment: A research note." Social Forces 58:89–93.

Grønseth, Erik
1971   "The husband provider role: A critical appraisal." Pp. 11–31 in Andrée Michel (ed.), Family Issues of Employed Women in Europe and America. Leiden: E. J. Brill.

Lupri, Eugen
1982   "The changing positions of women and men in comparative perspective." Pp. 3–39 in Eugen Lupri (ed.), The Changing Positions of Women in Family and Society: A Cross-Cultural Comparison. Leiden: E. J. Brill.

Lupri, E., and D. L. Mills
1982   "The changing roles of Canadian women in family and work: An overview." Pp. 43–77 in Eugen Lupri (ed.), The Changing Positions of Women in Family and Society: A Cross-Cultural Comparison. Leiden: E. J. Brill.

Lupri, Eugen, and James Frideres
1981   "The quality of marriage and the passage of time: Marital satisfaction over the family life cycle." The Canadian Journal of Sociology, Special Issue on the Canadian Family 6:283–305.

Morgan, D. H. J.
1975   Social Theory and the Family. London: Routledge and Kegan Paul.

Oppenheimer, Valerie Kincade
1977   "The sociology of women's economic role in the family." American Sociological Review 42:387–406.

Parsons, Talcott
1949   "The social structure of the family." Pp. 173–201 in Ruth Anshen (ed.), The Family: Its Function and Destiny. New York: Harper and Brothers.
1960   "The American family: Its relation to personality and to the social structure." Pp. 3–33 in Talcott Parsons and Robert F. Bales, Family Socialization and Interaction Process. New York: The Free Press.

Pleck, John
1977   "The work-family role system." Social Problems 24:417–427.
1978   "Men's family work: Three perspectives and new data." The Family Coordinator 28(4):481–488.

Rodman, Hyman
1965   "Talcott Parsons' view of the changing American family." Pp. 262–292 in Hyman Rodman (ed.), Marriage, Family, and Society: A Reader. New York: Random House.

Scanzoni, Letha Dawson, and John Scanzoni
1981   Men, Women, and Change. New York: McGraw-Hill Book Company.

Secombe, H.
   1980   "The housewife and her labour under capitalism." Pp. 370–395
            in Michael Anderson (ed.), Sociology of the Family (2nd ed.).
            London: Penguin Books.
Szalai, A., et al. (eds.)
   1972   The Use of Time. The Hague: Mouton.

4

Regional Differentiation, Intra-industry Division of Labor, and Family Labor Supply in Peru

MARTA TIENDA

The purpose of this chapter is to develop and evaluate alternative measures of family labor supply and to determine how patterns of family labor supply vary according to the diverse production structures characteristic of Peru, a highly regionally differentiated country. To illustrate the implications of regional differentiation for the division of labor at the familial level, employment structures among three regions delimited by natural geography are compared. Subsequently, the extent of territorial divergence in economic development in Peru is summarized, with an index of intra-industry occupational differentiation, and the implications for the division of labor among families are discussed. The general question about how families adapt their labor-force behavior to environments characterized by limited earning opportunities and low levels of occupational differentiation is addressed through a multivariate analysis. This is accomplished by estimating the influence of heads' socioeconomic and demographic characteristics, household composition, and regional/ecological factors on two measures of

Prepared for the Fifth World Congress of Rural Sociology, Mexico, August 7–12, 1980. An earlier version was presented at the Colloquium on Family and Work Roles in Comparative Perspective held in Calgary, Alberta, Canada, on March 13–14, 1980. Research support was provided by a grant from the Graduate School of the University of Wisconsin-Madison (Project No. 190075) and the College of Agricultural and Life Sciences. Computational work was supported by a grant to the Center for Demography and Ecology from the Center of Population Research of the National Institute of Child Health and Human Development (HD-05876). The technical assistance of Gerardo Otero, Mary Miron, and Linda Clark is gratefully acknowledged.

family labor supply. Results are discussed in terms of the role of the family in maintaining the territorial division of labor by subsidizing unstable employment patterns of primary workers through increases in total family work effort.

Introduction

Sustenance activities—those involving the expenditure of human energy in the direct pursuit of food or in the production of some good or service (Browning and Gibbs, 1971)—are central for understanding how human societies adapt to their environment. Much has been said and written about how migration reflects a demographic response to changing production structures or sustenance organizations (Frisbie and Poston, 1978; Sly, 1972), but human ecologists are largely silent about the linkages among various patterns of sustenance organization and the division of labor at the familial level. Yet the most fundamental aspect of social adaptation is that which results from the pooling and exchange of resources *within* families.

There are some reasons for this serious omission in the literature. One is that for methodological reasons it is difficult to address problems that require data at more than one level of aggregation (Hannan, 1971; Dogan and Rokkan, 1969) or that involve different units of analysis in a single framework. Another concerns measurement. Quite simply, in spite of the vast literature on labor-force participation and employment, particularly that which specifies supply considerations, existing studies fail to provide clues about how to empirically grasp the notion of *family labor supply*. This is not to say that the importance of family factors has not been previously acknowledged in the study of labor-force behavior, but only to point out that economists and sociologists alike have shied away from directly measuring and empirically analyzing the work behavior of *family units*. Anthropologists share less guilt in this regard, but their qualitative approach often does not permit rigorous quantitative analysis.[1]

This chapter has two separate but related objectives. One is to develop and evaluate alternative measures of family labor supply. The second is to determine how patterns of family labor supply vary according to the diverse production structures characteristic of a highly regionally differentiated country. Selection of Peru as a case study is justified for several reasons, but two considerations are outstanding: the regional diversity manifested in terms of natural geography and socioeconomic differences between places, and the availability of survey data that lends itself to the analysis of labor supply at the individual and familial level.

To illustrate the implications of regional differentiation for the division of labor at the familial level, we begin by comparing employment structures among three regions delimited by natural geography. The extent of territorial divergence in economic development in Peru is summarized with an index of intra-industry occupational differentiation developed by Browning and Gibbs (1971). Next, the implications of occupational differentiation for the division of labor among families are discussed. Then we take up the methodology of operationalizing family labor supply and showing the extent of variation according to regional contexts and labor utilization of the household head. Finally we present a multivariate analysis that addresses the general question of how families adapt their labor-force behavior to environments characterized by limited earning opportunities and low levels of occupational differentiation. This is accomplished by estimating the influence of heads' socioeconomic and demographic characteristics, household composition, and regional/ecological factors on two measures of family labor supply. Within-region regression estimates allow for more stringent control of between-region differences in opportunity structures. Results are discussed in terms of the roles of the family in maintaining the territorial division of labor by subsidizing unstable employment patterns of primary workers through increases in total family work effort.

Peru as a Case of Unequal Regional Development

Like many Latin American nations, Peru is a country of great contrasts. These are the result of geographical factors which, coupled with an uneven development process, have resulted in extensive regional differentiation. The contrasts are illustrated by the occupational distribution in Table 4–1. Three distinct "natural" regions based on geography are commonly identified. The *costa*, a relatively narrow coastal plain that borders the Pacific Ocean, is the most developed region in terms of industrial activity, percent urban, and the concentration of governmental activity. A second distinct region, the *sierra*, splits the country from the northwest to the southwest with the towering peaks of the Andes mountains. Finally, the *selva* (the jungle region) is a largely undeveloped tropical area that forms the western end of the immense Amazon River basin (U.S. Bureau of the Census, 1971). Whereas the coastal region accounts for 11 percent of the national territory, in 1975

Table 4–1

Distribution of the Labor Force Among Major Occupations by Natural Regions of Peru, 1970
(in percent)

Occupation	Natural Region		
	Costa	Sierra	Selva
Professionals	4.5	1.8	5.2
Managers	1.8	0.4	1.7
Office employees	9.3	2.8	6.8
Sales persons	14.0	8.1	15.2
Farmers	13.5	65.2	31.2
Miners	0.2	0.8	--
Transporters	4.0	1.1	3.0
Craftsmen	22.4	7.6	12.8
Other craft	6.0	3.3	3.8
Operative workers	5.2	2.1	5.4
Service workers	19.0	6.7	14.9
Total	99.9	99.9	100.0
(N)	(17,196)	(20,106)	(1,464)

Source: 1970 National Multipurpose Survey of Peru.

it represented 46 percent of the population. Comparable figures for the *sierra* and *selva* are respectively 26 percent and 63 percent for territory and 45 percent and 9 percent for population.

Historically, social and economic development has been concentrated in the coastal region, where Lima, the capital city, is located. The largely Indian population of the *sierra* remained isolated from other areas for a long time, but recently the government has taken steps to break the isolation through improved transportation networks, educational programs, and more advanced agricultural technology. These programs are slow to develop in some areas and even slower to have an impact on the socioeconomic circumstances of the population. The current fiscal crisis has dampened these efforts to some extent and has contributed to the deterioration of the economic well-being of all sectors of the population, including the middle- and upper-income groups.

Although the natural regions are relatively homogeneous[2] with respect to physical features, they are quite heterogeneous in terms of social and economic linkages. These linkages reflect the uneven development process which has rendered contemporary Peru a nation comprised of complementary but ecologically diverse areas that crosscut the natural regions. The social division of labor is determined not only by the complexity of various forms of social organization, but also by the constraints imposed by the ecological context of the geographical regions themselves. These constraints refer to limits in the range of production possibilities within a micro-region as well as to the existing levels of technology and forms of social organization.

Occupational Differentiation: Conceptualization and Measurement

In specifying the linkages between the division of labor and sustenance organization as theoretical constructs, Browning and Gibbs (1971) argued that the extent of intra-industry occupational differentiation varies directly with the territorial division of labor and intra-national disparities in economic development.[3] Their analysis based on the Mexican case illustrates the value of using a measure of intra-industry occupational differentiation (hereafter OD) to portray divergencies in economic development at the intra-national level. Given the extent of regional differentiation in Peru, it is instructive to examine differences in the degree of occupational differentiation among natural and socioeconomic regions. This will provide a basis for subsequently interpreting the variations in patterns of family labor supply.

One measure suitable for gauging occupational differentiation is operationally defined as

$$1 - [\Sigma x^2/(\Sigma x)^2]$$

where x is the number of individuals in each occupation. Among the various advantages of this measure is its reflection of both the number of occupations and the distribution of individuals among the occupations—two aspects basic to the general notion of differentiation. Another advantage is that OD values can be compared without regard to variation in the size of the labor force of the various units under consideration, because OD is not a direct function of population size. Further strengths of the OD index include its amenability to various kinds of populations and to categories other than occupations.[4] An important disadvantage of OD is that it does not give sufficient weight to the number of occupations, which means that the index of differentiation does not change proportionately with changes in the number of occupations, given a constant distribution of individuals. This problem can be circumvented partly by using a constant number of occupations, in which case the OD values would reflect only the differences in the distribution of individuals among occupations. The maximum value of OD is defined by $1 - (1/N_c)$, where N_c is the number of categories. With 11 categories (occupations), for example, the maximum OD value is .909, but it is .750 and .800 respectively with four and five categories, assuming an even distribution of individuals.

Intra-industry Occupational Differentiation and Regional Inequality in Peru

Our analysis of regional differentiation and family labor supply is based on the 1970 National Multipurpose Survey of Peru, which was conducted in late 1970 and early 1971 by OTEMO, the Office of Technical Manpower Studies of the Ministry of Labor. The National Multipurpose Survey (NMSP) is a multilevel stratified probabilistic sample that provides a wide range of information about the Peruvian population and society. A total of 5,487 households, representing 30,360 individuals, were surveyed. (See Table 4–2.) When properly weighted, the sample is representative at the national level, for urban and rural areas and for the ten largest cities. Although not ideal, the NMSP is adequate for an inter- and intra-regional analysis based on three natural regions.[5]

In particular, the NMSP permits the computation of OD measures within industries at the inter-regional level. As shown in Table 4–3, there is appreciable variation in the industry and occupational structures characteristic of the three natural regions. For example, in the *costa*, the most industrially developed and urbanized of the three natural regions, manufacturing accounts for one-fourth of all employment. Less than 15 percent of all workers in the *selva* are so employed, and the proportion of manufacturing workers in the *sierra* is

Table 4–2

Natural Regions by Representative Primary Sampling Units from the National Multipurpose Survey of Peru, 1970

Natural Region	NMSP Primary Sampling Units	Number of Households	Individuals
Costa			
	Puira	385	2580
	Sullana	28	186
	Perliñas	25	220
	Chiclayo	427	2724
	Monsefú	16	104
	Trujillo	390	2335
	Chimbote	29	177
	Santiago De Cartavio	45	307
	Lima-Callao	903	4828
	Barranca	27	116
	San Benito	43	201
	Chincha	29	191
Sierra			
	Arequipa	479	2567
	Tacna	30	140
	Cuzco	415	1876
	San Jerónimo y Saylla	66	305
	Huancabamba	43	245
	Chocope	23	153
	Pomahuaca-San Felipe	69	414
	Oxamarca	50	245
	Chacampampa	58	228
	Ichocan	49	242
	Lamas	13	100
	Huaraz	21	129
	Marcará	46	223
	Yanama	31	167
	Huancayo	354	1868
	La Oroya	24	115
	Paucartambo	83	479
	Cayran Chaulan	58	269
	Tapo	27	131
	Abancay	23	127
	Pampachiri	33	146
	Huanta	27	151
	Paucara	30	134
	San Pedro	44	203
	Puno-Juliaca	479	2236
	Zepita	76	361
	Paratia y Cabanilla	42	195
	Huancavelica	18	94
Selva			
	Chipurana-Huimbayoc	27	194
	Iquitos	402	2654

Source: 1970 National Multipurpose Survey of Peru

Table 4–3

Distribution of the Labor Force Among Industries by Natural Regions of Peru, 1970
(in percent)

Industry	Natural Region		
	Costa	Sierra	Selva
Agriculture, Ranching	15.1	65.6	30.7
Mining	2.4	1.7	0.1
Manufacturing	25.3	9.1	13.7
Construction	4.3	1.9	4.3
Energy	0.5	0.3	0.2
Trade	17.2	9.4	18.6
Transportation	4.8	1.3	5.2
Services[a]	30.3	10.7	27.1
Total	99.9	100.0	99.9
(N)[b]	(17,196)	(20,106)	(1,464)

Source: 1970 National Multipurpose Survey of Peru.

[a]Includes domestic servants.

[b]Weighted.

lower still. In underdeveloped areas, low representation of the work force in manufacturing is usually accompanied by a relatively high share employed in agricultural activities. Using the relative size of the agricultural work force as an indicator of development, it appears that the highlands is the least developed of the natural regions. Nearly two-thirds of the labor force in the *sierra* was engaged in agricultural and ranching industries in 1970. The respective share for the *selva* is 30 percent, or approximately half that of the highlands area. By contrast, along the coastal area only one out of every five or six workers was employed in agriculture and ranching industries.

Differences among the natural regions in the relative representation of workers in mining, construction, and energy industries are negligible. However, the inter-regional differences in the relative importance of trade and service employment are noteworthy. Specifically, the *costa* and *selva* regions have more similar employment structures in that approximately 30 percent of all workers are engaged in services, whereas the respective share for the *sierra* is considerably lower, about 11 percent. Similarly, trade activities comprise about 18 percent of employment in the *costa* and *selva* regions as compared to the *sierra*, where less than 10 percent of the labor force is employed in trade. These differences are important because they have implications for the extent of occupational differentiation and the possibilities for the spread of work at the familial level.

Marked differences in economic development among the three natural regions are further illustrated in Table 4–4, which presents the in-

Table 4–4

Measures of Intra-industry Occupational Differentiation for Natural Regions of Peru, 1970

Major Industry Sectors	Natural Region			
	Costa	Sierra	Selva	Country
Agriculture, Ranching	.27	.02	.01	.06
Mining	.88	.80	--[a]	.87
Industry, Manufacturing	.48	.51	.58	.50
Construction	.57	.56	.52	.57
Energy	.00	.03	.01	.05
Trade	.44	.27	.42	.38
Transportation	.63	.59	.70	.64
Services	.61	.61	.65	.61

Source: Computed from 1970 National Multipurpose Survey of Peru.

[a]Too few cases for reliable estimate.

dex of intra-industry occupational differentiation. By itself, occupational differentiation partly reflects territorial specialization, but this is less true when expressed at the inter-industry level across regional units. The presumption is that Peru has not yet reached the point where the extent of territorial specialization is reflected in the occupational structure of particular industries, as may occur in highly industrialized areas (see Browning and Gibbs, 1971, for further discussion). Recall that with a constant number of occupations, the OD value captures only differences in the distribution of workers among the various occupations.

In general, there is little dispersion in the range of OD values among natural regions in the construction, energy, and service industries. Greatest inter-regional dispersion in the range of OD values occurs in agriculture and trade industry sectors, followed by transportation and mining. However, interpretation of the OD values in terms of differences among industries and differences among regions is complex, not only because the industrial production structure differs among regions (partly reflecting the territorial division of labor), but also because the nature of activity subsumed under the broad industry groupings differs. To illustrate the importance of differences in the nature of work, consider the OD values for agriculture. These are low for the country as a whole and for the highlands and jungle regions, but not for the coastal area. Whereas in the *sierra* and *selva* virtually all (99 and 98 percent respectively) those engaged in agriculture are farmers, this is less the case in the *costa*, where 15 percent of those engaged in agriculture and ranching hold nonfarming occupations. These include managers (3.6 percent), clerical and sales workers (3.5 percent), transportation operatives (1.7 percent), and miscellaneous craft workers and day laborers (4.5 percent).

The dispersion in OD values for mining reflects the diversity of activities entailed in extraction and transportation of ores, gravel, and sand as well as the administrative and clerical personnel associated with urban mining operations. Manufacturing has a relatively higher value in the jungle zone, compared to the coastal and highlands regions. As noted earlier, the differences in OD in manufacturing partly reflect the difference between heavy industry on the one hand and artisanal types of activities on the other. For example, in Puno and Juliaca, two highland cities, virtually all workers employed in manufacturing are craft workers, whereas in Trujillo and Lima, both coastal cities, there are substantial shares of day laborers, operatives, and various service and professional workers generally associated with larger-scale manufacturing operations.

The OD values for construction and services vary little among the natural regions, but there is considerably more intra-regional differentiation. For instance, whereas the OD values for the service sector range from .65 to .61 for the natural regions, the respective range for socioeconomic regions is between .53 and .91 for the highland area. Browning and Gibbs (1971:238) explain that relatively high values result because services include a variety of heterogeneous sub-industries that may be mutually complementary. They note that in regions where there are many professionals there are also likely to be many domestic servants. These patterns are of some consequence for the labor-force behavior of individuals and household units, as elaborated in the next section.

Implications of Intra-industry Occupational Differentiation

The significance of territorial divergence in the extent of intra-industry occupational differentiation can be appreciated in terms of employment patterns and the well-being of social units. My case is that the extent of diversity in the employment structure which reflects variation in sustenance organization shapes the ways families earn a livelihood and maintain themselves. In a certain manner, the OD values provide a general sense for the employment opportunity structures characteristic of different regions. While this information is important in its own right, its role in determining patterns of family labor supply is perhaps even more important.

Linking the extent of intra-industry occupational differentiation to economic development is essential because of the ways in which the development processes change the structure of employment so as to alter the organization of the household economy. In general, as the composition of total output shifts from predominantly extractive commodities to predominantly industrial commodities and services, the family plays a less direct role in market production (Tienda, 1979). This means that the "spread of work" among various family members (Jaffe and Stewart, 1951) will decrease in accordance with shifts in the structure of production from less to more differentiation. From a cross-sectional point of reference, the implication is that the lower the degree of intra-industry occupational differentiation, the greater the spread of work among several family members; alternatively, the higher the degree of intra-industry occupational differentiation, the lower the spread of work among several family members.

Viewed in this light, one can conceive of empirically testable propositions about the ways in which the division of labor at the household level is conditioned by structural factors—in particular, employment opportunity structures that determine individual levels of utilization as well as market conditions that are conducive to the involvement of the very young or very old. The general notion is that in areas where intra-industry occupational differentiation is low, the level of utilization of workers is also likely to be low. Hence, the need for more working members to compensate for conditions of high unemployment or underemployment will be greater. Conversely, in areas with a highly developed formal labor market, fewer members per family will be required to work to meet basic sustenance needs.

Regional differences should help explain variations in patterns of family labor supply, not only because of underlying differences in the extent of economic development which are directly correlated with employment patterns (Jaffe and Stewart, 1951), but also because geographic and environmental factors effectively constrain production possibilities and shape the resulting patterns of sustenance organizations. My basic contention is that the ability of families to adapt will be reflected by patterns of family labor supply. This idea is further developed and empirically examined in the next section.

Family Labor Supply as a Form of Economic Adaptation

Human ecologists define adaptation as the ability of social units to change or elaborate their structure as a condition of survival or viability (Micklin, 1973:5). At the microstructural level (i.e., their composition) this can be accomplished by families changing either *themselves* or their *resources* through changes in activities geared toward the acquisition of goods and services (Loomis, 1936). The intra-family division of labor reflects a family's adaptation to socioeconomic circumstances, and in the context of poverty it is a critical survival strategy (Lomnitz, 1976; Roberts, 1976; Deere, 1978b). Thus, the study of family labor supply should help clarify how households tailor market behavior in accordance with the structure of their community and the age-sex composition of the unit.

Generally speaking, it is unconventional to discuss labor supply in terms of family units. Yet social scientists have frequently acknowledged the importance of the family unit for understanding the ability of individuals to subsist in places with unstable or limited opportunities for gainful employment (Roberts, 1976; Lomnitz, 1976; Tienda and Ortega, 1982; Tienda, 1979). Deere's (1978b) notion of intra-family deployment[6] is compelling precisely because it points out that limited employment opportunities can be partly offset by involving more family members in income generation or, more generally, sustenance activities. Because many individuals earning less than the minimum for subsistence can potentially raise their level of living by remaining in a family unit, conclusions based on individual labor market outcomes which fail to consider the significance of the participation patterns of other family members may be distorted. In particular, the circumstances in which poverty arises and is resolved or alleviated depend largely on the manner in which income is derived as well as on absolute income thresholds. This means that the number of dependents to be supported should be taken into account to appreciate fully the significance of a family's capacity to adapt (Turnham, 1971).[7]

Another equally important justification for examining family labor supply rests on the historical significance of the family as a work unit. In many settings, multiple-worker households still constitute an important source of economic security for members that are too young or too old to work. The prevalence of multiple-earner (worker) households is not unique to developing areas, although its magnitude and characteristic forms differ notably from those found in industrialized areas.

For instance, in the case of subsistence agricultural economies where the family household serves as the locus of consumption and production (Rojas and Tienda, 1979; Deere, 1978a; 1978b), sustenance activities are generally shared among various family members, and the young and old are not excepted (Mueller, 1976). Alternatively, in industrialized societies where the locus of production is external to the family unit and where the distinction between economically productive and unproductive members is more clear (albeit not completely so), the notion of family labor supply may be less important, but it is by no means irrelevant. Labor economists often refer to the ''added worker''—the family member (or members) who enters the labor force—on either a temporary or a permanent basis—when the earnings of the primary workers are inadequate to meet needs or to achieve a desired standard of living.

The point is that the work behavior of individuals can be better appreciated with reference to the context in which it emerges and acquires a specific meaning. Using families as analytic units facilitates assessment of the extent to which units are able to make up the difference for one or more inadequately utilized members. However attractive the idea of analyzing labor supply at the familial level may be, operationalization continues to be problematic. There are no formulas or precedents for quantitative analyses, so two exploratory measures are proposed in the next section. These provide the basis for the descriptive and multivariate analyses that follow.

Operationalizing Family Labor Supply

Two factors are central to the measurement of family labor supply: the spread of work among various members and the level of utilization of each individual worker. The latter is particularly important because the definition of economic activity is itself affected by changes in the structure of production that result from economic development. The labor-utilization framework initially proposed by Philip Hauser and elaborated by Sullivan (1974; 1978) is generally better suited to the complexities of the labor force in developing economies than the more conventional labor-force approach, because the phenomenon of under-employment is acknowledged in the conceptual categories. Both use the working-age population as a base and distinguish between the economically active (in the labor force) and the economically inactive (not in the labor force). However, they differ in their division of the economically active. Whereas the labor-force approach divides the economically active into the employed (with a job and at work) and the unemployed (looking for work), the labor-utilization approach divides the labor force into those adequately utilized and those inadequately utilized (Sullivan, 1974:5). Inadequate utilization consists of four distinct types: unemployment, under-utilization by hours of work, under-utilization by level of income, and under-utilization by levels of skill.

The 1970 National Multipurpose Survey of Peru is particularly well suited for an analysis of family labor supply because the central objective of the study was to generate information about the employment, income, and occupational histories of individuals and because data were obtained for all individuals within households included in the sample. Persons aged 14 and over who worked during the week before the survey were considered to be in the labor force and were classified according to whether they were adequately employed, underemployed by level of income or hours of work, or unemployed.[8] For agricultural workers, a 12-month reference period was used (instead of a single week) to account for the seasonal character of much agricultural activity in Peru.[9] In addition, the labor-force status of 6- to 13-year-olds was ascertained from the household head's report that the individual had worked during the week before the survey, but unlike the adults, no information about the level of utilization is available.

Two measures of family labor supply are derived from this information. The first is simply the number of related[10] individuals within a household classified as "economically active," without regard to age differences or level of utilization, that is, the total number of family members who work outside the home. This reflects the "spread of work" among family members. A second measure is obtained by weighting the working members according to respective utilization levels, summing across all workers within a household and dividing by the number of working members. In effect, this measure is an index of average utilization. For this purpose, the following values were used:

3 = *adequately utilized*
2 = *underemployed* by hours or level of income (including independent campesinos)
1 = *economically active children* (who presumably produce between one-half to one-third of an adult equivalent)
0 = *unemployed* (who for all practical purposes are "not working")

Although it is admittedly crude, there is some justification for this measure. Ideally labor supply should be weighted on the basis of hours worked and the share of income contributed by each family member. Unfortunately, the data did not allow for this refinement because the income data are not reliable (Tienda, 1976, Appendix C) and because hours of work are not reported uniformly for all working members. Given the exploratory nature of this exercise, the crude but simple proxy is adequate for a first approximation of family labor supply.

Correlates of Family Labor Supply

Two important correlates of family labor supply stand out in the literature and merit special consideration before proceeding with the multivariate analysis. One is related to the "added worker" notion discussed by labor economists, which implies an inverse relationship between the adequacy of employment of the head (usually the primary

Table 4–5

Levels of Family Labor Supply and Labor Utilization of the Head: Peru, 1970

Head's Utilization	Number of Workers[a]	Supply Index[b]
Not in labor force	1.1	1.4
Unemployed	1.6	1.3
Campesino	2.7	1.9
Underemployed	2.0	2.0
Adequately employed	1.8	2.7
Mean	2.1[c]	2.1[c]
(N)	(4,151)	(4,151)

Source: 1970 National Multipurpose Survey of Peru.

[a]Individuals classified as in the labor force, including unemployed.

[b]Defined in text.

[c]Between group differences significant at $p < .001$.

breadwinner) and the spread of work among other family members. A second factor, regional ecological context, represents the main concern of this investigator. Table 4–5 provides insight about the former.

As expected, the average number of workers per family (indicative of the spread of work) is greater for households where the head is under-utilized, but some significant qualifications are in order. Contrary to expectation, the average number of workers is not highest among households where the head is out of the labor force or unemployed, even though these work statuses generally imply no earnings. There are several reasons this is not implausible. One is the possibility that heads who are not in the labor force are independently wealthy and do not need to work. Or, more realistically, the head may be too old to work, in which case an adequately employed adult offspring may serve as primary earner while the retired parent may still be designated the household head.[11] For the unemployed, under-utilization is often a temporary phenomenon and hence may not stimulate labor-force adjustments within the family in the short run. There is no way to monitor differences in the duration of unemployment for this group.

Notice also that the average number of workers per family is greatest for the campesino category. This is consistent with the argument that in subsistence economies, where production is organized around the household and levels of technology are generally low, several family members must participate in the work process to meet basic needs (Jaffe and Stewart, 1951; Deere, 1978b; Rojas and Tienda, 1979). Under these circumstances the amount of output is often a direct function of total labor inputs, but this depends on the manner in which peasant economies are integrated into the broader market economy, the access of individual households to capital inputs, and the availability of additional workers (Deere, 1978a). The data suggest that campesino heads require on the average one additional worker to attain a level of total labor inputs comparable to that of adequately employed heads. This is because individual workers are more likely to be under-utilized.

The pronounced influence of the head's utilization status on the average level of utilization for the family is illustrated in the second column of Table 4–5. The highest average levels of utilization correspond to households where the head is adequately utilized, whereas the lowest correspond to those where the head was not working at the time of the interview. Apparently the spread of work does serve to compensate for the low levels of utilization of one or more family members, but whether this means that individuals are better off in a material sense is open to question. This issue, which requires information on per capita income levels, cannot be addressed with these data.

Regional variation in sustenance organization is another important determinant of family labor supply. As shown in Table 4–6, the spread of work among family members is greatest in the *selva* region, where an average of three persons work per family household. In the *costa*, where there is more industrial activity and greater intra-industry occupational differentiation, the spread of work among family members is lower and the average level of worker utilization is about 20 percent higher.

Apparently the organization of production in the *sierra* and *selva* regions is more conducive to the existence of multiple-worker households, but it also places effective limits on the possibilities for adequate earnings and sustenance activities. Although the average number of workers per family is higher in the *selva* as compared to the *sierra*,

Table 4–6

Levels of Family Labor Supply According to Natural Regions: Peru, 1970

Natural Regions	Supply Measures	
	Number of Workers[a]	Supply Index[b]
Costa	1.8	2.4
Sierra	2.3	2.0
Selva	3.0	2.0
Mean (N)	2.1[c] (4,151)	2.1[c] (4,151)

Source: 1970 National Multipurpose Survey of Peru.

[a]Individuals classified as in the labor force, including unemployed.

[b]Defined in text.

[c]Between group differences significant at $p < .001$.

this is partly due to the greater under-utilization of the work force in the former region. By sending more members into the labor force, families can partly offset the inadequate incomes of individual workers. Notice that the average level of utilization for the *sierra* and *selva* is identical.

On balance, the aggregate relationships are more suggestive than conclusive, because averages conceal as much as they reveal. Also, in these descriptive bivariate tabulations, underlying differences in household composition are likely to play as much of a role in shaping patterns of family labor supply as ecological variations play in sustenance organization. The point is that family characteristics and ecological factors must be examined simultaneously, but this requires a multivariate framework. This is the thrust of the next section.

Multivariate Analysis

A number of variables are hypothesized to influence family labor supply. These fall into three categories: (1) ecological factors, notably the extent of intra-industry occupational differentiation and rural-urban residence; (2) household characteristics, including type of headship, extended or nuclear family type, and number of dependents; and (3) social and demographic characteristics of the household head, particularly educational attainment, age, sex, and labor-utilization status. The importance of the extent of occupational differentiation has been discussed sufficiently in terms of its implications for patterns of family labor supply and needs no further justification. Urban-rural residence is important because it defines the social context in which individuals obtain their motivation to behave in specified ways. Although the extent of intra-industry occupational differentiation is greater in urban areas, residence co-varies with a number of additional factors that, above and beyond sustenance organizations, are likely to influence the division of labor at the familial level.

Of the household characteristics hypothesized to influence family labor supply, the number of dependents is important because it reflects the magnitude of economic need in terms of the support demands of household members who are not in the labor force. Hence, the presence of dependents is expected to influence positively the work behavior of working age family members. Type of headship is important because of its relationship with the economic well-being of the family unit. Specifically, absence of a head is often associated with changes in the labor-force activity of other family members (Morgan et al., 1974) and with the propensity of a unit to extend through the incorporation of additional relatives (Tienda and Ortega, 1981).

In turn, extended family composition has implications for the availability of individuals to enter the labor force should the need for more income and the opportunity to enter the labor market arise (Deere, 1978a). There exists some evidence that the formation of extended-family households allows units to cope with increasing dependency burdens during life-cycle periods when support demands are great (Tienda, 1980). Therefore, extended household composition is hypothesized to affect family labor supply positively.[12] This expectation is reasonable if economic stress associated with large and/or young families can be mitigated by increasing the number of individuals who generate income. When the number of working-age adults in the family is limited, either the help of kin can be solicited or children can be sent into the labor force, and in rural areas the latter may be as viable as reliance on extended kin (Tienda, 1979). The important point is that in both cases work effort is increased.

Characteristics of the household head are important because of the well-established patterns of relationship between labor-force participation and such demographic attributes of individuals as age, sex, and race (Bowen and Finegan, 1969). There is also some empirical evidence that women and the elderly are more likely to be under-utilized than prime-age males (Sullivan, 1978), but it is unclear how this fact, which applies to workers in the United States, may influence the division of labor within families in Peru. It is conceivable that households headed by prime-aged males will, all other factors being equal, require less work input of other family members, whereas the opposite should hold for very young or very old men and most women. Some evidence for women is found in Tienda and Ortega (1982). Overall, the effects of age are likely to be weak. Male headship should be inversely related with the total labor supply of families and positively related with the average utilization of family workers.

The level of education of the head should be negatively related with the number of workers per family and positively related to the average utilization level which is dominated by the head's employment status. The income effects of education on the labor supply of the primary earner and associated substitution effects on the labor supply of other family members are documented in the labor-force participation literature. That is, at higher levels of earnings of the head, the need for other family members to work is lessened; thus other family members are apt to substitute market work for other activities, including school and leisure. Also, as illustrated in Table 4–5, the employment status of the head is itself systematically related to the labor-force behavior of other family members, and it is expected that this effect will persist even after differences due to education have been taken into account.

The basic objective of the multivariate analysis is to ascertain the unique effects of each variable identified above on the two measures of family labor supply. Accordingly, each of the dependent variables is regressed on the set of independent variables denoting the influence of ecological factors, household composition, and sociodemographic attributes of the head of the household. First, pooled regression estimates are derived using the entire sample of family households and the intra-industry occupational differentiation index corresponding to the entire country (column one of Table 4–4). Subsequently, within-region regressions are computed separately for each of the natural regions using the corresponding region-specific measures of intra-industry occupational differentiation. Special attention is devoted to the significance of inter-regional variation in sustenance organization for understanding the division of labor at the familial level.

Pooled Estimates

Table 4–7 presents the correlations among the variables included in the regression model. There is little need for extensive comment on these data except to note a few outstanding points. The most striking feature of the matrix is the generally low values of most correlations, but the few exceptions are worth comment. Notice that the supply measure which reflects the spread of work (KINWORKS) is only weakly correlated with the average utilization index for the family (SUPIND). Given our basic premise that under-utilization (manifested either as underemployment or unemployment) is a positive stimulus to increased work effort among other family members, it is satisfying to observe the inverse relationship between the total number of workers and the average utilization level. Also, the utilization level of the head is moderately associated with the supply index, which approximates the average intra-family utilization level. This association can be understood in terms of the centrality of the household head as the primary breadwinner in most units; in many units, the head is also the only earner. The fact that the zero-order correlation is not higher speaks to the importance of the economic activity of other family members and justifies the need to study the intra-family division of labor.

The associations between the OD measures and the urban dummy variable also deserve comment. These moderately strong associations are to be expected, because a highly differentiated occupational and industrial structure is intrinsic to the increased organizational complexity implied by urbanity. Because the latter taps much broader dimensions of social organization than the OD measures, it is appropriate to include both variables in the analytical model. Finally, the unusually strong negative correlation that occurs between the type of headship and the sex of the head is noteworthy. Spouse-absent households comprise approximately one-fourth of all families in Peru. The strong negative association between sex and headship reflects the fact that most households are headed by males whose spouse is present and that single-parent family households are more likely to be headed by women.

The results of the pooled regressions of family labor supply are shown

Table 4-7

Zero-order Correlations, Means, and Standard Deviations of Variables Used in Regression Analysis of Family Labor Supply

Variable Names[a]	(1)	(2)	(3)	(4)	(5)	(6)	(7)	(8)	(9)	(10)	(11)	(12)	X̄	S.D
1. KINWORKS	1.000												2.14	1.33
2. SUPIND	-.173	1.000											2.13	.66
3. EDATAIN	-.253	.347	1.000										4.07	4.10
4. AGE	.147	-.126	-.189	1.000									43.81	13.59
5. MALE	.128	.213	.133	-.085	1.000								.86	.35
6. UTIZ	.071	.624	.263	-.247	.339	1.000							2.14	.81
7. ONEHEAD	-.119	-.189	-.133	.175	-.825	-.306	1.000						.18	.38
8. EXT	.163	.014	-.035	.209	-.105	-.060	.128	1.000					.33	.47
9. KINDEPNC	.198	-.056	-.106	-.085	.074	.034	-.106	.146	1.000				2.74	1.91
10. URBAN	-.315	.381	.522	-.087	-.028	.214	-.000	.088	-.019	1.000			.51	.50
11. IOD	-.276	.351	.441	-.121	-.009	.266	-.011	.021	-.020	.676	1.000		.30	.26
12. ODN	-.284	.368	.461	-.115	-.002	.273	-.013	.031	-.004	.704	.970	1.000	.29	.27

Source: 1970 National Multipurpose Survey of Peru.

[a] 1-Number of kin workers
2-Index of family labor supply
3-Educational attainment of the head
4-Age of the head
5-Dummy variable, coded 1 if head is a male
6-Level of utilization of the head

7-Dummy variable, coded 1 if family has only one head (parent absent)
8-Dummy variable, coded 1 if household contains 1 or more extended family members
9-Number of family members under 14 years of age
10-Dummy variable, coded 1 if family resides in urban areas
11-Intraindustry occupational differentiation index, total country scores
12-Intraindustry occupational differentiation index, natural region scores

in Table 4–8. As expected, head's education lowers the spread of work among family members, because higher levels of schooling imply better prospects for adequate employment and earning capacity. This, in turn, reduces the need for supplementary income from other family members. The positive effect of the head's utilization status on both supply measures reflects the head's position as primary worker within

Table 4–8

Pooled Regressions of Family Labor Supply: Effects[a] of Head's Characteristics, Household Composition, and Ecological/Organizational Aspects of the Territorial Division of Labor
(Standard Errors in Parentheses)

Independent Variables	Dependent Variables	
	Number of Kin Workers	Labor Supply Index
Head's Characteristics[b]		
Education	-.033 (.005)	.013 (.002)
Age	.013 (.001)	.002 (.000)
Utilization	.298 (.026)	.443 (.010)
Family Composition		
Headship	-.353 (.086)	.026* (.035)
Extended Type	.442 (.041)	.052 (.017)
Number of Dependents	.107 (.010)	.023 (.004)
Ecological/Organizational		
Urban	-.594 (.053)	.254 (.022)
IOD[c]	-.585 (.010)	.107 (.040)
Constant	1.124	.847
R^2	.228	.468
F	136.5	404.9
d.f.	9/4141	9/4141

Source: Computed from 1970 National Multipurpose Survey of Peru.

[a]Unstandardized regression coefficients.

[b]Net of sex of head of household.

[c]Intra-industry occupational differentiation index.

*Not significant at $p \leq .05$.

most households, a circumstance evident especially in the utilization weighted index. Sex of the head is related only weakly with the labor supply index, which measures the average utilization level of all workers, indicating that male heads have a slight advantage over female heads in terms of being adequately employed (that is, not under-utilized).

Compared to households where both spouses (heads) are present, those with a missing spouse generally have one less eligible adult to send into the labor force should the need to increase labor supply arise. This demographic circumstance constrains possibilities for a greater spread of work among family members. Type of leadership apparently has little to do with the average utilization status of all working members, once other pertinent variables are adequately controlled. However, the formation of extended-family households can partly offset the negative effects of single-parent headship, because the presence of an adult relative often serves as a replacement for the missing spouse (Tienda and Ortega, 1979). This is because the incorporation of non-nuclear relatives potentially allows for a reallocation of domestic and market work roles within the family. Consistent with this agreement, our results show that extended households have, on average, about one-half worker more than nuclear units. To the extent that non-nuclear family members also offset under-utilization of one or more family members, the effect of extended-family composition would be lessened in the supply measure which is adjusted by the utilization levels of all family workers (column 2). Overall, these results provide some support for the argument that extended-family formation may be an important mechanism enabling families to adjust their economic behavior (Deere, 1978a; Tienda, 1980). This is particularly important for single-headed households, which are (all factors considered) more apt to feature extended structures (Tienda and Ortega, 1982).

As hypothesized, the number of dependents in a family serves as a positive stimulus for the total family work effort. Specifically, for each additional dependent there is an increase of one-tenth of a worker per family. A lessened but statistically significant influence of dependents emerges for the utilization weighted supply index. The fact that the latter influence is not stronger may partly reflect differences in the economic activity of dependents. That is, in some contexts, children under 14 enter the labor force to supplement family earnings, but their overall contribution may be small if not negligible. In this sample as many as five children ages 6 to 13 were reported to be in the labor force per family, in addition to the adult workers. This circumstance would result in an increased spread of work but relatively little influence on the utilization weighted supply measure.

The influence of ecological and organizational factors on family labor supply conforms to expectations. In urban areas the average number of workers per family is considerably lower compared to rural areas. The reason for this is the better employment conditions in cities and towns, which permit better utilization of individual workers. Our earlier point that urbanization is not a perfect substitute for the employment structure is confirmed by the equally strong and statistically significant effect of the intra-industry occupational differentiation index on the family labor supply measures. Specifically, places with highly differentiated industry employment structures permit families to concentrate the work load on one or two members, who are, in turn, more likely to be adequately utilized in terms of hours of work and level of earnings. Presumably this permits a more efficient division of labor within the family and reduces the share of family effort devoted to sustenance activities, both within and outside the labor market.

In terms of the overall fit of the model, the results are encouraging, because in spite of the low range of variation in the dependent variables, the total variance explained ranges from 23 percent for the number of workers per family to a high of nearly 50 percent for the labor supply index.

Within-Region Regressions

Within-region regressions permit a decomposition of the pooled estimates as well as a fine-tuning of the importance of occupational differentiation as measured by the more precise region-specific intra-industry indexes. Table 4–9 shows that the explanatory power of the model is highest for the *selva* where approximately 50 percent of the variation in the two labor supply measures is accounted for by the selected characteristics of the head, family structure, and sustenance organization. In the *sierra*, between 22 percent and 48 percent of the variance in labor supply is explained, whereas the lowest r^2 statistics correspond to the *costa*, the most socially and economically differentiated of the three regions.

Within-region education effects on labor supply are in the expected direction for the coastal and highland regions and are basically similar in magnitude to those obtained in the pooled model. In the jungle region, however, the influence of the educational attainment of the head

Table 4-9

Within Natural Region Regressions of Family Labor Supply: Effects[a] of Head's Characteristics, Household Composition, and Ecological/Organizational Aspects of the Territorial Division of Labor (Standard Errors in Parentheses)

Natural Region and Dependent Variable	Independent Variables								Constant	R^2 [b]	F	D.F.
	Education	Age	Utilization	Headship	Extended	Dependents	Urban	ODN				
1. Costa												
Number of workers	-.041 (.006)	.017 (.002)	.272 (.031)	-.081* (.122)	.573 (.055)	.028 (.013)	-.420 (.089)	-.209* (.170)	.750	.190	44.6	9/1161
Supply Index	.011 (.004)	.002* (.001)	.444 (.017)	-.043* (.069)	-.021* (.031)	-.004* (.008)	.205 (.051)	-.009* (.097)	1.043	.373	111.2	9/1161
2. Sierra												
Number of workers	-.036 (.009)	.011 (.002)	.388 (.043)	-.470 (.117)	.319 (.058)	.156 (.014)	-.584 (.076)	-.782 (.134)	1.042	.220	73.9	9/2356
Supply Index	.014 (.003)	.002* (.001)	.461 (.013)	.58* (.036)	.104 (.018)	-.041 (.004)	.209 (.024)	.147 (.042)	.800	.483	246.3	9/2356
3. Selva												
Number of workers	-.017* (.051)	.042 (.013)	.197* (.209)	.062* (.810)	.785 (.293)	.242 (.066)	-.938 (.392)	-1.828 (.694)	.140	.504	13.8	9/104
Supply Index	-.016* (.017)	-.001* (.004)	.394 (.069)	.142* (.266)	.090* (.096)	.003* (.022)	.268 (.129)	.406* (.228)	.555	.460	11.7	9/104

Source: Computed from 1970 National Multipurpose Survey of Peru.

[a] Unstandardized regression coefficient.

[b] Adjusted for degrees of freedom.

*Not significant.

is not statistically reliable. This suggests that the ascriptive bases of social stratification may be more pronounced in the *selva*, where agriculture accounts for approximately one-third of all employment. The more pronounced age effects in the *selva* further support this claim, as the spread of work among several family members is greater among households headed by older individuals. In other words, systems of land tenure and inheritance are likely to be more important in determining patterns of family labor supply than the acquisition of education per se or other achieved statuses.

Among the family composition variables, headship has the least significant influence on the patterns of family labor supply except for the *sierra* region, where, like the pooled model, male-headed households have about one-half worker less than the female-headed units. Extended-family composition influences the spread of work (number of workers) positively in all the regions, but the magnitude of the effects differs notably. Extended families have more workers than pure nuclear types, as expected, but in the *costa* this means about .6 of an additional worker per household, whereas in the *sierra* and *selva* increased labor supply effects are respectively .3 and .8 of additional worker per family unit. Of course, increases in the number of workers per household unit do not automatically insure that basic needs will be met, but presumably increased labor inputs will partly compensate for the low average levels of utilization of individual workers.

As was observed for the pooled estimates, the number of dependents in a family positively influences the number of working members in all regions, but the magnitude of the effect differs notably. For example, in the *costa* the number of dependents exerts mild effects on the spread of work, but in the *sierra* and *selva* regions the presence of each additional dependent requires between one-tenth to one-fifth of an additional family worker. Only in the *sierra* does the presence of dependents alter the average utilization level of households (supply index). The reason for this is mostly that in the highlands, where two-thirds of the labor force is engaged in agricultural activities, the young and very old are usually "economically active," but these groups are more likely to be underemployed than prime-age males. Consequently, the average utilization level drops.

The most important message in Table 4–9 emerges from a comparison of the effects of the OD measures and the head's labor utilization status on the labor-supply measures among the three regions. Along the more developed coastal area, the extent of intra-industry occupational differentiation has little to do with the patterns of family labor supply, whereas the effects of the head's utilization level are quite pronounced. A different picture emerges in the *selva*, where the head's employment status is important in determining the average utilization level among all household workers (supply index) but where the OD measure exerts a strong negative effect on the spread of work among family members. Still a third pattern emerges for the *sierra*, where both the OD index and head's utilization status are significant predictors of family work patterns. The basic message is that in places where the employment structure is more diversified, as in the *costa*, the mode of insertion of the head determines the intra-family division of labor. This situation contrasts with areas characterized by less differentiated structures where, because of poor and unstable employment conditions, both the opportunity structure as well as the ability of the heads to secure adequate employment determine the spread of work and the likelihood that any family member will be fully utilized. Clearly the forms of economic adaptation reflected in the inter-region patterns of family labor supply involve more than increasing the spread of work. The strategies families use to earn a livelihood must be tailored to the available opportunities within a given locality.

In many ways these results echo those presented in Tables 4–5 and 4–6 and underscore the need to consider both individual and structural or ecological factors to explain the intra-family division of labor. A second important inference has to do with the advantage of directly operationalizing sustenance organization rather than relying on a crude proxy-reflecting level of urbanization to capture differences in the structure of production. This advantage is because, as shown, the urbanization reflects ecological dimensions different from those reflected by the OD indexes. The effect of urbanization is basically constant across regions, and thus it does not contribute to the specification of the between-region differences as the OD index does.

Conclusions and Implications

In setting forth objectives, I proposed to develop and empirically evaluate alternative measures of family labor supply and to determine how the extent of regional differentiation in Peru shapes the intra-family division of labor in terms of the spread of work and the adequacy of labor utilization. The results, while suggestive, leave room for a good deal of improvement and further analysis. My success in operationalizing family labor supply was modest, given the constraints imposed by the survey data. Further refinements are needed to adequately differentiate labor inputs in terms of hours of work and the relative share of income generated by each family member. The labor-utilization framework permitted a crude approximation of variable labor inputs at the familial level, because differences in the degree and kind of under-utilization are poorly represented. Perhaps the greatest weakness stems from failure to acknowledge the importance of non-market work in the family division of labor. Unfortunately, it is too easy to argue that this sin of omission reflects the state of the art, although this is certainly true.

The importance of establishing differences in forms of economic adaptation resides in the salient intra-national diversity in Peru. Analysis of the relationship between the levels of utilization and the extent of intra-industry occupational differentiation among diverse ecological contexts has provided insights about the structural dimensions of Peru's regional differentiation in terms of how the family system operates to accommodate the development of new economic activities. These, in turn, have implications for the range of job alternatives and the mechanisms of reallocation of market and non-market activity within families. My basic point is that the particular socioeconomic and cultural setting in which a family finds itself ultimately determines the nature of adjustments made to meet sustenance needs. The division of labor is an intrinsic part of this adjustment and is manifested both in micro-structural and macro-structural terms. At the micro level, the interplay of the availability and need for resources shapes the division of labor between market and non-market activity, but this also depends on whether all income of all members goes into a common fund from which distribution is made, how and by whom distribution is controlled, and for what purposes and to whom it is allocated for consumption (Levy, 1949:27).

A question arises as to whether the results generated from a single case study can be generalized. While the main advantage of this approach is that it permits greater penetration into the sociocultural complex in which family sustenance strategies acquire specific meanings, the basic disadvantage is that the findings cannot automatically be generalized to other settings. There are, conceivably, elements of the Peruvian case study that would apply to other societies, but the commonalities and rich lines of variance must be spelled out. I have tried to highlight the importance of such diversity only by specifying intra-national differences in family work patterns in terms of contrasts between natural regions. This exercise has been instructive, given that Peru's internal social and economic differentiation has been exacerbated by the uneven process of economic development. However, this cross-sectional approach is only suggestive about the patterns likely to emerge from a cross-national comparison among nations at various stages of development. And, in the Peruvian case, a regional typology of ten socioeconomic regions based on functional integration of economic activities proved to be no more enlightening than that based on natural regions.[13]

In spite of the many shortcomings of this analysis, future research along similar lines should be encouraged, because the intra-family division of labor is not well understood in terms of diverse patterns of sustenance organization. Yet this is central to the study of the role of the family in the process of economic development. My attempt to examine how the intra-industry division of labor influences family labor supply produced results that are generally consistent with academic writings about the relationship between economic development and patterns of labor-force participation, but this effort is only a beginning.

In setting forth a research agenda, it is worthwhile to encourage further specification of the mix of activities used to maintain families in diverse economic settings. The work of Torres (1976) and Deere (1978a; 1978b) is suggestive along these lines, because it shows how the household income-generation processes among peasant groups in the Peruvian *sierra* are conditioned by the local and regional context. Specifically, Torres shows that migration for work and commercialization of goods are basic ingredients of subsistence strategies devised by the *comuneros*. Among older cohorts the propensity to combine commercialization activities with agricultural occupations is more prevalent than among the younger groups, but this strategy also requires a greater reliance on family labor for exploiting communal landholdings. Deere's study illustrates how the intra-familial division of labor by sex is shaped by the degree of integration of the peasant household into the product market and by the social valuation of men's and women's work.

An additional consideration that should be ranked high on research agendas is the detailing of the *content* of household sustenance strategies by explicitly showing how new opportunities are pursued over the family life career. It is important to specify not only *who* (i.e., dependents, relatives, parents) shares the family support burden, but also *when* (i.e., at what periods of the family life cycle). What I am proposing, essentially, is an empirical specification of the complementarity of domestic and market work activities within the household unit, along with a description of how the changing expression of the allocation of work reflects a rational and collective effort. Of course, none of these goals is worth pursuing until greater precision in the measurement of family labor inputs is attained.

Notes

1. Anthropological studies provide a good deal of descriptive information about the labor-force participation of women and children, but until recently (Cain, 1978; Tienda, 1979), little quantitative analysis of the labor-force activity of children was available. Analysts of women's labor-force participation in developing countries usually lament the inappropriateness of census data for studying the employment status of women, particularly those employed in agricultural activities (Singelmann and Tienda, 1979).

2. Below is a depiction of a transversal (although exaggerated) cut of Peruvian territory, viewed from south to north.

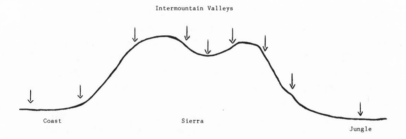

The areas within each two arrows represent different "micro-regions." The differences among them reflect the combined effects of altitude, rainfall, and latitude and are manifested in terms of characteristic flora and climate. On the west side of the mountains, there is very little rainfall; thus artificial irrigation systems have been used in agriculture since the time of the Incas. The highlands cover a broad range of elevations, including snow-capped peaks of over 6,000 meters. Between the two ridges of mountains there are agricultural and cattle-raising valleys. In the southern part of Peru, near Cuzco, human settlements are found at altitudes from 3,800 to 4,800 meters. This makes the Cuzco area, along with the *altiplano* of Puno and Bolivia to the south, the part of the world where humans have adapted to the highest altitudes. High-altitude agriculture has been possible because of the proximity of the equator, which offsets the cold temperatures associated with high altitude. However, cultivation in the highlands is restricted to narrow valley floors. Rainfall in the Amazonian forest area is much higher than in the Andes, averaging 2,000 millimeters or more. The corresponding amount for the Andean area is about 650 millimeters a year. On the other hand, the coastal strip is almost entirely devoid of precipitation. Along the coast, rivers and wells are the only sources of water. Coastal agriculture is based on the intensive cultivation of carefully irrigated narrow strips. In the humid lowlands of the jungle, east from the Andes, bananas, pineapples, citrus fruits, cocoa, coffee, rubber, and other tropical crops are grown. Much of this is commercial production for exchange with the highlands and the coast, and even to export overseas (especially coffee and rubber).

3. Browning and Gibbs (1971) implied not that economic development is reflected only by intra-industry occupational differentiation, but that the latter is one of several alternatives for analyzing the relation between differentiation and development.

4. For example, the OD index can be used to measure occupational differentiation within industries, in which case industries would represent a population of sorts.

5. A few limitations in the representation of natural regions are exposed by a cross-classification of observations by natural and socioeconomic regions. The most obvious is the absence of primary sampling units from the central and lower *selva* region. However, this limitation is not serious, because the jungle region is very sparsely settled and thus the bias is not likely to be great. Basically, this means that results for the *selva* region will be representative only of the northern *selva*. Overall, the NMSP does permit a first approximation of the patterns of variation of family labor supply at the level of natural regions, although more in-depth analyses based on socioeconomic criteria would require a sampling framework tailored to a specified regional scheme.

6. In her work, Deere (1978b) defines intra-familial deployment as the process by which familial labor is allocated to a range of activities required to reproduce the peasant household's level of subsistence consumption and possibly to generate a surplus.

7. Deere's studies (1978a, 1978b) also call attention to the distinction between market and non-market work, appropriately emphasizing that both must be considered in any assessment of the division of labor at the familial level. However, most census-type surveys, including ours reported in this volume, do not consider unrenumerated domestic activities as work. Thus, our analysis is delimited to market work, as represented by the conventional labor-force concept.

8. Women who did not work outside the home were not considered to be in the labor force.

9. Basically this means that the estimate of unemployment will be lower than if only a one-week reference period were used, whereas the prevalence of underemployment will be somewhat higher. Otherwise the size of the labor force will be quite similar to that of the 1972 census (see Tienda, 1976, for further discussion).

10. The decision to exclude unrelated members such as domestics, pensioners, and guests from the measurement of family labor supply is based on the notion that "inmates" (the term Hammel and Laslett, 1974, use to identify semi-permanent household residents) are not fully integrated into the household economy, as blood-related individuals are. The transient nature of guest

relationships is reason enough to substantiate this claim for visitors. Pensioners, on the other hand, provide a source of income for the family, but usually they do not interact with the family members in the same way or to the same extent that blood relatives do.

11. This would be the use among extended households, where an elderly parent is designated head for reasons of deference or respect but where an adult offspring is for all practical purposes primary earner and head.

12. Deere's (1978a) evidence based on a single case study in the Peruvian *sierra* shows that extended households comprised of a parent and one or more adult offspring were better able to capitalize their productive process and to enter into commodity production. This economic possibility depended on utilization of labor power of grown sons and daughters.

13. These results are not reported because of space limitations, but they may be obtained from the author.

References

Bowen, William G., and T. Aldrich Finegan
    1969   The Economics of Labor Force Participation. Princeton, N.J.: Princeton University Press.

Browning, Harley L., and Jack P. Gibbs
    1971   "Intraindustry division of labor: The states of Mexico." Demography 8:233–245.

Cain, Mead T.
    1978   "The household life cycle and economic mobility in rural Bangladesh." Population and Development Review 4:421–438.

Deere, Carmen Diana
    1978a   "The differentiation of the peasantry and family structure: A Peruvian case study." Journal of Family History 5:422–438.
    1978b   "Intra-familial labor deployment and the formation of peasant household income: A case study of the Peruvian Sierra." Paper prepared for the Conference on Women in Poverty: What Do We Know? International Center for Research on Women.

Dogan, Mattei, and Stein Rokkan
    1969   Quantitative Ecological Analysis in the Social Sciences. Cambridge, Mass.: M.I.T. Press.

Frisbie, W. Parker, and Dudley L. Poston Jr.
    1978   Sustenance Organization and Migration in Nonmetropolitan America. Iowa City: University of Iowa Press.

Hammel, E. A., and Peter Laslett
    1974   "Comparing household structure over time and between cultures." Comparative Studies in Society and History 16:73–109.

Hannan, Michael T.
    1971   Aggregation and Disaggregation in Sociology. Lexington, Mass.: Lexington Books.

Jaffe, A. J., and Charles D. Stewart
    1951   Manpower Resources and Utilization. New York: John Wiley and Sons.
Levy, Marion J., Jr.
    1949   The Family Revolution in Modern China. Cambridge, Mass.: Harvard University Press.
Lomnitz, Larissa
    1976   "Migration and network in Latin America." Pp. 133–150 in Alejandro Portes and Harley L. Browning (eds.), Current Perspectives in Latin American Urban Research. Austin: University of Texas Press.
Loomis, Charles P.
    1936   "Study of the life cycle of families." Rural Sociology 1:180–199.
Micklin, Michael
    1973   "Introduction: A framework for the study of human ecology." Pp. 3–19 in Michael Micklin (ed.), Population, Environment, and Social Organization. Hinsdale, Ill.: Dryden Press.
Morgan, James N., Katherine Dickenson, Jonathan Dickenson, Jacob Benus, and Greg Duncan
    1974   Five Thousand Families—Patterns of Economic Progress. Vol. 1. An Analysis of the First Five Years of the Panel Study of Income Dynamics. Ann Arbor, Mich.: Survey Research Center, Institute for Social Research, University of Michigan.
Mueller, Eva
    1976   "The economic value of children in peasant agriculture." Pp. 98–153 in Ronald G. Ridaker (ed.), Population and Development. Baltimore: Johns Hopkins University Press.
Roberts, Bryan
    1976   "The provincial urban system and the process of dependency." Pp. 99–132 in Alejandro Portes and Harley L. Browning (eds.), Current Perspectives in Latin American Urban Research. Austin: University of Texas Press.
Rojas, Alicia, and Marta Tienda
    1979   "Dependency rates in peasant economies: Theoretical considerations and alternative measures." CDE Working Paper 79–33. Madison, Wisc.: University of Wisconsin.
Singelmann, Joachim, and Marta Tienda
    1979   "Changes in industry structure and female employment in Latin America: 1950–1970." Sociology and Social Research 63:370–391.
Sly, David F.
    1972   "Migration and ecological complex." American Sociological Review 37.
Sullivan, Teresa A.
    1974   "New approaches to labor force measurement: Uses for census

data.'' Asian and Pacific Census Newsletter, East-West Population Institute 1:5–8.

1978   Marginal Workers, Marginal Jobs: The Underutilization of American Workers. Austin: University of Texas Press.

Tienda, Marta

1976   ''Macro and micro contexts of age and economic dependency: An assessment with Peruvian data.'' Ph.D. dissertation, University of Texas.

1979   ''The economic activity of children in Peru: Labor force behavior in rural and urban contexts.'' Rural Sociology 44:370–391.

1980   ''Age and economic dependency in Peru: A family life cycle analysis.'' Journal of Marriage and the Family 42:153–166.

Tienda, Marta, and Sylvia Ortega Salazar

1982   ''Female-headed households and extended family formation in urban and rural Peru.'' Demografia y Economia 16:64–89.

Torres, Mario J.

1976   ''Forms of economic adaptation of peasants in Peruvian highland communities.'' Ph.D. dissertation, University of Texas.

Turnham, David

1971   The Employment Problem in Less Developed Countries: A Review of the Evidence. Paris: Organization for Economic Cooperation and Development.

U.S. Bureau of the Census

1971   Population of Peru, Estimates and Projections: 1962–2002. Demographic Reports for Foreign Countries, Series P–96, No. 4. Washington, D.C.: U.S. Government Printing Office.

Comments—Tienda's "Regional Differentiation, Intra-industry Division of Labor, and Family Labor Supply in Peru"

JOSEPH E. DiSANTO

Most of us in sociology have been repeatedly reminded of the importance of concept formation and measurement (e.g., Blalock and Blalock, 1968; McGinnis, 1969; Campbell, 1969; Hempel, 1952; Sjoberg, 1959; Zeller and Carmines, 1980). Yet with some exceptions we tend to pay insufficient attention to these issues in doing research. The excuses proffered are varied. One of the most common is of the following type: "Although it is admittedly crude, there is some justification for this measure. Ideally . . . Unfortunately, the data did not allow for this refinement because the . . . data are not reliable . . . and because. . . . Given the exploratory nature of this exercise, the crude but simple proxy is adequate for a first approximation of family labor supply" (Tienda).

Part of Tienda's dilemma is the result of reliance on a secondary data base. If we rely on such data, however, simple caveats will not suffice to escape responsibility for data limitations. In such circumstances, we have an even greater responsibility to indicate how these limitations might affect our results. This is particularly germane when our findings are only weakly supported by our analysis.

We cannot excuse our insufficiently supported findings under the rubric "exploratory research." Exploratory research requires proportionately more attention to concept formation, variable construction, and measurement, rather than less. Moreover, it is questionable research strategy to argue that "rigorous quantitative analysis" is the *sine qua non* for good research, as Tienda implies, and then to create a variable that is supposed to reflect the concept "family labor supply" and to measure this variable with "unreliable" data simply because the data are "quantifiable."

Tienda states that one of her objectives is "to develop and evaluate alternative measures of family labor supply." First, the concept "family labor supply" is obfuscated by use of the concept "division of labor" at the familial/household level in at least nine different places. It is unclear whether these two concepts are considered equivalent. Second, there is an insufficient attempt to evaluate alternative measures of family labor supply. Although two measures are used, these appear to be measuring two different dimensions of the concept. These dimensions are "spread of work" and "level of utilization" of family workers.

Spread of work is measured by the number of economically active, related individuals working outside the home. Unfortunately, as Tienda notes, women working in the home are excluded. This limitation is apparently the result of the way the original data set was collected and/or classified. However, this limitation is serious with respect to rural families, especially in less developed regions. This limitation would also affect the validity of the measure of utilization. Tienda's chapter would have been improved had the implications of these data limitations been explored.

"Inadequate utilization," Tienda states, "consists of four distinct types: unemployment, under-utilization by hours of work, and under-utilization by level of income, and under-utilization by levels of skill." Her data were classified as (a) unemployed; (b) underemployed by level of income or hours of work, which relates to her second and third types; and (c) adequately employed. It is not clear, but I assume that "adequately employed" relates to her fourth type, "under-utilization by levels of skill." Tienda goes on to construct a weighted index from that data as classified with the addition of giving economically active children a lesser weight. The reason offered by Tienda for giving children a lesser weight is the presumption that they produce between one-half to one-third of an adult equivalent. Although this is a minor point (no pun intended), I have difficulty in accepting this reason; I feel it is insufficiently supported.

Perhaps of more importance is the weight given to the indicator "underemployed by level of income or hours of work." It is given a weight of 2 on a scale of 0 to 3. This is done regardless of the assertion made by Tienda that "income data are not reliable . . . and . . . hours of work are not reported uniformly for all working members." From Tienda's chapter, it is not possible to ascertain the degree of unreliability of income data, nor is it possible to determine the lack of uniformity in reporting hours of work, although there is a reference to another chapter where this is discussed. Therefore it is impossible to determine the validity of the indicator "underemployed by level of income or hours of work."

Tienda's second objective is "to determine how patterns of family labor supply vary according to the diverse production structures characteristic of a highly regionally differentiated country." Having discussed her dependent variable, family labor supply, I will briefly discuss her main independent variable, "diverse production structure."

The dimension of diverse production structures that is developed most in the chapter is intra-industry occupational differentiation (OD). An OD was calculated for each of several broad industry groupings, e.g., agriculture/ranching, mining, industry/manufacturing (see Table 4–4). Two questions arise. First, are these groupings too broad to be useful in explanation when shifting from the macro–level region and country to the micro-level of family? I am not questioning the usefulness of these broad groupings for prediction so much as their usefulness for explanation.

The second question is how are these ODs weighted and combined into overall indexes of diverse population structures at both the regional level and the country level? Perhaps they are not, but then I fail to understand how they are used in the regression equations.

Several other independent variables were used as well. Tienda groups all the independent variables into three categories: (1) ecological factors; (2) household characteristics; and (3) "social and demographic characteristics of the household head, particularly educational attainment, age, sex, and labor-utilization status." It is the third category that is of some concern. The dependent variable, family labor supply, presumably includes the head as part of the family. In part this variable is operationalized using "skill" (I expect education is related very directly to skill) and utilization of the head. Now we encounter these listed as independent variables as well as components of the dependent variable, SUPIND. Any relationships between the dependent variable (SUPIND) and the independent variables education of head (EDATAIN) and level of utilization of head (UTIZ) would be somewhat tautological, that is, a part-whole correlation (see Table 4–7). Although the data are not given, I would also suspect that the inter-item correlations in SUPIND would be low.

Given Tienda's measurement problems, I find it difficult to take seriously the multiple regression and multiple correlation analyses. These analyses are presented in Tables 4–8 and 4–9. One additional comment might be added with regard to these analyses. Although the means and standard deviations are given for all variables in Table 4–6, a measure of skewness would have been useful.

The reliance on the particular data base used by Tienda places a severe limitation on the theoretical exposition of the problem she has chosen to study. It is safe to say that she is attempting to address the problem of how families as units (one level of analysis) use their resources to adapt their sustenance activities to the larger regional opportunity structure, as indicated by occupational differentiation of the region (a higher-order level of analysis).

Tienda recognizes the aggregation problem from a methodological perspective when she states, ''For methodological reasons, it is difficult to address problems that require data at more than one level of aggregation . . . or that involve different units of analysis in a single framework.'' There are, however, theoretical issues involved in shifts of units and levels of analysis as well. One of the more important issues as it relates to Tienda's theoretical problem is the part values play; specifically, work values and other values associated with different roles within the family must assume importance at the family level of analysis. This issue is not given sufficient theoretical exposition in Tienda's chapter. It is precisely this kind of issue that prompted Schnore's (1965) classic paper, ''The Myth of Human Ecology.'' In his ''Conclusions'' to that paper, Schnore quotes Ernest Burgess. I can do no better than indicate that Burgess' remarks apply to both theoretical and methodological issues:

It is possible to inquire how ecological processes work, without the necessity of doing research on the social-psychological processes. It is also possible to inquire about the social-psychological processes without doing research on the ecological aspects. These are two different ways of looking at human behavior. . . . While it is true that both approaches can be brought together to produce significant findings on particular problems, their joint use should be conscious and deliberate. Many researchers unwittingly mix the two; as a consequence they make a mess of their studies.

References

Blalock, H. M., and A. Blalock (eds.)
    1968   Methodology in Social Research. New York: McGraw-Hill Book Company.

Burgess, E.W.
 1953   "The ecology and social psychology of the city." Pp. 80 in Don-
         ald J. Bogue (ed.), Needed Urban and Metropolitan Research.
         Oxford, Ohio, and Chicago: Scripps Foundation for Research in
         Population Problems, and Population Research and Training Cen-
         ter, University of Chicago.
Campbell, D. T., et al.
 1969   "Definitional versus multiple operationalism." *et al.* 2(Summer):14–
         17.
Hempel, C. G.
 1952   "Fundamentals of concept formation in empirical science." Inter-
         national Encyclopedia of Unified Science, Volume I–II, Chicago:
         University of Chicago Press.
McGinnis, Robert
 1969   "Measurement and sociological theory." *et al.* 2(Summer):7–9.
Schnore, Leo
 1965   "The myth of human ecology. Pp. 29–43 in L. Schnore, The Ur-
         ban Scene. New York: The Free Press.
Sjoberg, Gideon
 1959   "Operationalism and social research." Pp. 603–627 in Llewellyn
         Gross (ed.), Symposium on Sociological Theory. Evanston, Ill.:
         Row Peterson and Company.
Zeller, R. A., and E. G. Carmines
 1980   Measurement in the Social Sciences. New York: Cambridge Uni-
         versity Press, 1980.

5

Linking Work and Family: Notes from Trinidad

HYMAN RODMAN

In many ways my chapter is radically different from Marta Tienda's, but in one way it is really quite similar, because I am also addressing the question of responses to economic need. She is dealing with a demographic response to economic need, and I am dealing with social and cultural responses. She is using demographic data, I am using ethnographic data. She is focusing on the United States, I am focusing on Trinidad. She uses status as a variable, while I am dealing with a relatively homogeneous poverty-level group. She has data on several different racial and ethnic groups, while my data are based on one group. In my chapter "Weak Links in Men's Worker-Earner Roles: A Comparative Perspective," I pointed out that there were several ways in which the man's worker-earner role might be jeopardized. I left the elaboration of the "weak links" in lower-class men's roles for this chapter.

In this chapter I present specific details and a general analysis of the lower-class family in Trinidad with the underlying question of whether this might be a step toward a general theory of lower-class families. The ethnographic present is from 1956 to 1968. I was in Trinidad on four occasions during that period, and I will be basing this chapter primarily on ethnographic data, although survey data were also collected.[1]

The chapter will illustrate the utility of thinking in terms of the worker-earner role.[2] It demonstrates how the weakness of that role on the part of the lower-class man in Trinidad has many consequences for individual family members and for the family system as a whole.

Friending, Living, and Married

There are three different kinds of marital relationships in Trinidad: *friending, living,* and *married.* In a *friending* relationship, the man visits the woman at irregular intervals for sexual purposes, and he has some financial responsibilities to that woman and to any children she may bear for him. If she does have children, he will ordinarily support them. He might also set up house with the woman whether she bears children or not (at that point they would be entering into a *living* relationship). The *friending* relationship in Trinidad is usually a temporary arrangement. Since a man has an economic responsibility to the children, and since his resources are limited, he is concerned about whether a particular child is actually his child. Men therefore often visit women they are *friending* with at irregular intervals to see whether they are available. They do this, as they might say, to see whether they can "bounce up" somebody else—that is, to discover whether the woman is faithful. Fidelity is expected within all three of the marital relationships in Trinidad (Rodman, 1969). Other patterns also reflect men's concerns about whether the woman is being faithful. It is a biological fact that a woman is sure that a child is hers, but a man cannot be sure. In Trinidad people wonder, "Does this child resemble the man?" Does the child have a splotch on the right leg that somehow confirms it is really the man's child? Does it have his eyes or his nose or his sheepish look so that he will be persuaded that that particular child is his child?

Black calypsonians in Trinidad make use of infidelity as a theme, often relating it to the multiracial nature of Trinidad society. As a result, we hear calypsos about black women who bear children that appear to be Chinese or Portuguese or who have blue eyes.[3] Other calypsos illustrate infidelity between members of different classes; for example, the calypsos "Buxom, Buxom" tells of the boy who "knows" his schoolmaster's wife.[4]

One of the phrases heard in Trinidad has to do with a woman "horning" a man. Standard dictionaries tell us that it was used in England from the fifteenth to the nineteenth century and means infidelity. It is a common term in current use in Trinidad.

In the *living* relationship, the man and woman live together but are not married. A common saying in the West Indies is "Better a good *livin'* than a bad marriage." The same expression is used in the Spanish-speaking, French-speaking, Dutch-speaking, and English-speaking islands. In the *living* relationship, the man and the woman often refer to each other as husband and wife. As a result, when somebody was talking about "my wife" (or "my husband") and I did not know the nature of the relationship, I asked a standard question: "Do you mean your married wife?" I would then be told, "Yes, she's my married wife" or "No, she's not my married wife, we're living together."

Another term that a man and a woman in a *living* relationship use in referring to each other is "keeper." Each will refer to the other as "keeper." Trinidad is a highly sex-segregated society. It is the woman's job to *keep* house. She cooks, washes, cleans, and takes care of the children. It's the man's job to *keep* money flowing into the house. If either party does not fulfill the expected role, you get a fairly quick reciprocal response from the other party. A strong *quid pro quo* element comes into play far more quickly than would be the case in middle-class American society. In other words, you're not your spouse's keeper unless your spouse is your keeper.

The *living* relationship is more stable than the *friending* relationship but it does not occur as frequently as *friending*. There is a somewhat casual attitude between the sexes which makes it easier for separations to occur. Although such an attitude is by no means universal, the following examples illustrate the attitude. I was interviewing a man who had been through five *living* relationships, asking a series of questions about each of these relationships. By the time I was asking him about the fourth relationship (how long did it last? why did it break up? etc.), his gestures were clearly showing impatience with my inability to understand him. He stopped my questions and said, "Look, for you to understan', a woman like a bus, man. This one gone? Don' get vex, you catch the nex' one!" Or, as a woman said about the *living* relationship, more briefly and philosophically, "You *live* today and you part tomorrow."

In a *married* relationship, a marriage has been performed and the union is legal. Marriage is more stable than *living*, but it occurs less frequently. Most women say they want to get married, and most men say they do not. People give a variety of reasons for this difference. For example, women say the reason they want to marry is to be entitled to wear a ring and to be referred to as Mistress instead of Miss. Even though these are the most frequent reasons given, I found myself in situations where these reasons were simply not operating. For example, someone is continually referring to *Miss* Rose and I know that she is married. Why do they not refer to her by the more prestigious form of address? "Well, she's been Miss Rose for so long, there's no reason for us to change it. We're just accustomed to calling her Miss Rose so we continue to call her Miss Rose."

According to my interpretation, women have two major reasons for desiring a legal marriage. The first is the legal right this gives them for financial support from their husband (which has limited value because these are lower-class men with very few resources). The second is that with marriage they are legally entitled to inherit their husband's estate. Otherwise there is the danger that somebody else will file a legal claim to the estate. Since the estate may include a small house or a piece of land, it is of some importance. In normative terms, nobody else should file a claim—the woman in the *living* relationship ought to inherit. But legally somebody else may claim the inheritance. As a result, women usually prefer marriage.

Men, however, say they are afraid of the legal ties of marriage. They point out that these ties are hard to break and that they are not sure they can trust a woman after marriage. There are a variety of apocryphal stories told by men about women's laziness and infidelity after marriage.

One of the terms I use in describing *friending, living,* and *married* relationships is "marital-shifting." I use it to refer to two different kinds of transitions. A man and woman may enter into a *friending* relationship and subsequently shift from *friending* to *living* and from *living* to *married.* When relationship shifts occur, they are almost always in the *friending* to *living* to *married* direction. But a large majority of relationships terminate rather than shift (Voydanoff and Rodman, 1978).

Another kind of shift I refer to is the shift from a relationship with one person to a relationship with another. A man and woman may be *friending* for a short period of time; the relationship may break; subsequently the man may set up a new *friending* relationship with another woman, and the woman may set up a new *friending* relationship with another man.

The Parent-Child Relationship

In the parent-child relationship it is the father's job to *mind* the child and the mother's job to *care* for the child. *Minding* the child refers to financial support, and that is the father's responsibility. *Caring* for the child refers to social support and nurturance, and that is the mother's responsibility.

If the father does not *mind* the child—for example, he may not recognize the child as his own and he may leave the woman—what happens? The "child-shifting" pattern typically comes into play at that point. The woman turns the care of her child over to another woman and goes to work to earn some income that can help to *mind* the child. Ordinarily her child would be turned over to the care of her own mother or her sister or some other female relative.

In child-shifting, the woman typically leaves the child with someone permanently. She does not reclaim the child at a later time even if she subsequently becomes part of a stable relationship. In discussing children's and parent's feelings of affection in these dual relationships, one hears a fairly consistent response. Children talk of their affection for biological parents and social parents in a rather sophisticated, rational manner: "It depends on how they treated me." They talk about whether their biological parents maintained contact with them, the kind of contact, the extent to which their biological parents made contributions to the household, gave them gifts, and showed them affection. They also talk about the kind of treatment they received from their social parents. Nobody attempts (as middle-class North American social workers might) to hide the dual relationship, and there is no concern about any possible trauma to the child. Moreover, there is no evidence of disabilities that stem from these dualities.

In many cases, parents have favourite children. They do not try to hide their favouritism. North American parents might have feelings of favouritism, but they try hard not to let it show. In Trinidad there is not the same kind of normative concern about treating all children equally. Parents explain their favouritism in a straightforward way. "It depends on how the child treats me"—one child treats me better than another, or one child obeys me better than another. Again, we have a rational form of calculation to account for favouritism.

Weakness in the Worker-Earner Role

Given certain weaknesses in the man's worker-earner role, there can be a series of consequences for the family. In this case, I am referring to possible consequences for the lower-class family in Trinidad and perhaps for other lower-class settings as well.

I did my field work in a rural village in Trinidad. Somebody owns some land in about half the households in the village, but not one household is able to earn a living off the land. Villagers rely on wage labour, for the most part day work on one of the nearby coconut estates. This employment is irregular. When it rains there is no work and no pay. In checking the records on one estate, I found that workers averaged about three working days a week over a four-week period. There is a good deal of poverty in the village. The key problem is the weak worker-earner role of the man. The man finds it difficult or impossible to fulfill the worker-earner role he is expected to fulfill. In contrast, the woman is able to fulfill the role that is expected of her. She is able to take care of the household and the children.

As a result of the man's difficulty, he experiences a loss of esteem, even within his own family. He may have a marginal status within his family. This tends to lead to marital separations—either because the man decides to remove himself from an untenable situation or because the woman pushes him out. The casual attitude between partners contributes to separations and cushions the separations that occur. The alternative marital relationships, and the marital shifting pattern, make it possible for the man to end the relationship. He may continue to make occasional financial contributions, depending on the nature of the relationship he has established with the woman and his children, and depending on his economic resources. But he is subsequently able to enter into another relationship, and in this other relationship, at least temporarily, he may be able to provide reasonably adequate financial support. I am suggesting that the existence of alternative relationships and of the marital-shifting pattern make it possible for the man to cope with the problems that stem from his worker-earner role.

This leaves the woman in a potentially difficult situation. She is left with the children and without financial resources. The child-shifting pattern, however, makes it possible for her to turn the care of the children over to someone else while she goes to work. In Alvin Toffler's (1970) discussion of post-industrial society and the future of the family, he predicts that in the early stages of the life cycle people will concentrate on working and in later stages they will concentrate on childrearing. There are many women in Trinidad who currently follow that sequence.

Conclusion

When people talk about lower-class families, they occasionally refer to promiscuity, immorality, and pathology. For example, the Moynihan Report (1965) referred to the pathology of the Negro family and generated a great deal of controversy.[5] More frequently, social commentators refer to illegitimacy, unmarried mothers, common-law unions, and deserting fathers as the problems of the lower-class family. My own interpretation turns these conventional ideas upside down. I avoid terms like illegitimacy and desertion and instead use native terms like *friending* and *living* or coin value-neutral terms like marital-shifting and child-shifting. In effect, I suggest that the marital and parental patterns often referred to as the problems of the lower class are instead the attempted solutions of lower-class families to some of the more basic economic and political problems that they face.

Notes

1. For more details, including the survey data, see Rodman (1971) and Voydanoff and Rodman (1978).

2. See in this volume my chapter "Weak Links in Men's Worker-Earner Roles: A Comparative Perspective" for further details.

3. The specific calypso referred to is "Man Smart but Women Smarter" by King Radio.

4. "Buxom, Buxom" by Mighty Panther tells of a boy and his schoolmaster arguing about who "knows" the most girls by saying "Buxom" for girls they have had as they walk by. The schoolmaster feels blue as the boy calls out "Buxom" when the teacher's wife passes by.

5. For additional details on this controversy, see Moynihan (1967) and Rainwater and Yancey (1967).

References

Moynihan Report
    1965   The Negro Family: The Case for National Action. Washington, D.C.: Department of Labor.

Moynihan, Daniel P.
    1967   "The President and the Negro: The moment lost." Commentary 43:31–45.

Rainwater, Lee, and William L. Yancey
    1967   The Moynihan Report and the Politics of Controversy. Cambridge, Mass.: MIT Press.

Rodman, Hyman
    1969   "Fidelity and forms of marriage: The consensual union in the Caribbean." Pp. 94–107 in Gerhard Neubeck (ed.), Extramarital Relations. Englewood Cliffs, N.J.: Prentice-Hall.
    1971   Lower-class Families: The Culture of Poverty in Negro Trinidad. New York: Oxford University Press.

Toffler, Alvin
  1970   Future Shock. New York: Random House.
Voydanoff, Patricia, and Hyman Rodman
  1978   ''Marital careers in Trinidad.'' Journal of Marriage and the Family 40:157–163.

Comments—Rodman's "Linking Work and Family: Notes from Trinidad"

JAMES S. FRIDERES

This chapter by Hyman Rodman, "Linking Work and Family," attempts to link the male economic position with that of family structure. He also tries to make a logical connection between marital and sexual behaviour, which culminates in his implicit "lower class normative system."

The paper may be considered heuristic in that it may lead to some reassessment of the conventional theoretical perspectives regarding marriage, family patterns, and divorce. However, one must ask what differences have been delineated by Rodman in his typology of "marital relationships" beyond those discussed by Clarke (1957) in her study of Jamaica—permanent concubinage, temporary concubinage, and the fatherless family.

American family sociologists have focused on economic and social marginality as determinants of matrifocality. Unfortunately, cultural factors have rarely been examined, and the present work is no exception. However, the work of Tanner (1974) suggests that positive cultural conceptions of women's kin roles, an absence of extreme cultural dichotomization of role expectations for women and men, and relatively equal participation of men and women in general societal role systems form a constellation of features critical to the effective functioning of matrifocality. It is unfortunate that cultural factors are summarily dismissed as irrelevant (or at least not important enough to be discussed).

On the other hand, Rodman may argue that Trinidad is not a true matrifocal society. In either case, we need to weigh the evidence for such a claim. For example, within the kinship system of Trinidad the mother's role is central, but the contributions of men are highly valued. Does this provide evidence of something less than matrifocality? Or, to what extent does the mother have some degree of control over the kin unit's economic resources? How critically involved is she in kin-related decision-making processes? In other words, to what extent does the structural component of matrifocality relate to both economic and political power with the kin group? These questions must be answered before a more complete explanatory sketch can be developed and more specific hypotheses tested.

Rodman, coming from a society that deals oddly with women, chooses the traditional procedure in his treatment of them. Women are seen as something of an anachronism. As some family researchers have pointed out, men are classified in terms of ranked, institutional positions; women are simply women, and their activities, interests, and differences receive only idiosyncratic note. To a certain extent, women are seen as deviant or, at best, manipulators. Hence, it does not surprise us to find that the focus of the chapter is on men and, in the end, their role in determining the family structure.

Rodman also takes a very traditional approach in that illegitimacy is explained (and assumed solely explained) from the perspective of ''maternity without consideration of paternity'' or its social and ethnic milieu. To be sure, marital patterns eventually culminate in a dyadic relationship, but this does not mean that one can ignore the overall social value system within which such behaviour occurs. Rodman does acknowledge the context, but unfortunately it is quickly forgotten; for example, we find no mention of the different pattern in urban versus rural areas, between various classes or between ethnic groups. The work of Frelich (1970) would be germane to cite in this regard. He points out that a variety of cultures exist in Trinidad and that one must be cautious in generalizing beyond one. In his work he found substantially different marital patterns among the East Indian, Creole, mixed Indian-Creole and the local black.

Rodman also chooses not to provide the reader with an appropriate historical perspective of Trinidad, more specifically, the family in Trinidad. For example, what has been the consequence of the historical forces deriving from a pervasive plantation system lasting nearly 300 years? The reader should be made aware that the patterns of sexual behaviour and mating were (and still remain) structurally regulated by legal prescriptions and mores. In addition, these patterns are inextricably tied to the value system emerging from a slave system but nevertheless shared by the whole society at one level or another (Manyoni, 1980). For example, during the period 1808 to 1821, fewer than 450 marriages were conducted involving slaves or free coloured individuals.

The chapter demonstrates the need for a more detailed historical and macro-approach to facile explanations of extramarital mating patterns among the so-called lower-class segment of Trinidad. If Rodman's objective was to depict another culture's way of life, he succeeded, but if his goal was to fill in some theoretical or methodological gap in the area of family studies, he did not succeed.

References

Clarke, E.
  1957   My Mother Who Fathered Me. New York: George Allen and Unwin.
Frelich, M.
  1970   "Mohawk heroes and Trinidadian peasants." Pp. 185–250 in M. Frelich (ed.), Marginal Natives. New York: Harper and Row.
Manyoni, J.
  1980   "Extra-marital mating patterns in Caribbean family studies: A methodological excursus." Anthropoligica 22:85–119.
Tanner, N.
  1974   "Matrifocality in Indonesia and Africa and among black Americans." Pp. 129–156 in M. Z. Rosaldo and L. Lamphere (eds.), Women, Culture, and Society. Stanford, California: Stanford University Press.

6

Household Composition and Income-Generation Strategies Among Non-Hispanic Whites, Blacks, and Hispanic-Origin Groups in the United States

RONALD ANGEL AND MARTA TIENDA

A great deal has been written concerning the racial and ethnic dimensions of social and economic inequality in the United States, especially with respect to occupational status and earnings differentials. While numerous studies reveal the socioeconomic cost of race (Farley, 1977; Featherman and Hauser, 1976; Parcel, 1979; Beck et al., 1978), few have examined the socioeconomic significance of Hispanic origin in as comprehensive a fashion. Yet during the 1970s, the Spanish-origin population in the United States grew at a faster rate than that of the total population. Research investigating how the labor-force experiences of various Hispanic groups differ from those of the native Anglo and black populations is not only limited but also of generally poor quality (see Tienda, 1981, 1979 for review).

The relative lack of study of Hispanic-origin groups in the United States does not mean that Spanish origin is unimportant. For example,

Prepared for the Colloquium on Family and Work Roles in Comparative Perspective held in Calgary, Alberta, Canada, on March 13–14, 1980. Research support was provided by a grant from the U.S. Department of Labor (No. 21–55–79–27) and the College of Agricultural and Life Sciences. Computational work was supported by a grant to the Center for Demography and Ecology from the Center of Population Research of the National Institute of Child Health and Human Development (HD-05876). The authors benefited from useful comments from Hallinan Winsborough.

Duncan and his associates (1972) reported that among the non-black population, individuals of Latin American origin suffered the greatest income, educational, and occupational disadvantages. Because of different immigration and assimilation experiences, there exist noteworthy differences among the Hispanic national-origin groups, in terms of both occupational and earnings attainments (Portes and Bach, 1980; Newman, 1978; U.S. Bureau of the Census, 1976).

The attempts of racial and ethnic minorities to deal with poverty are likely to be influenced by cultural norms that determine how individuals pool both monetary and non-monetary resources. Living arrangements that facilitate the pooling of resources can have profound effects on the ability of households to cope with poverty. The extent to which cultural beliefs about the sharing of resources facilitate the inclusion of non-nuclear members into a household may greatly influence the earnings potential and the amount of domestic help available to the unit. Residential enclaves and co-residence patterns can facilitate greater interaction among relatives and community members and can foster higher levels of non-pecuniary exchanges of goods and services. In light of the higher incidence of poverty and disadvantages experienced by blacks and Hispanics, it seems likely that the earnings of individuals other than the head are a potentially important supplement to household income for these groups. Thus, the practice of including non-nuclear members can help raise a household's aggregate economic well-being, not only because of the possibility of contributing to total income, but also by increasing the flexibility of the household in allocating market and domestic work roles among members.

Persisting economic disadvantages among minority households lead us to the question that has motivated the present research: To what extent does inclusion of individuals other than the head, the wife of the head, or the children of the head in family households reflect an economic response for compensating for the disadvantages faced by ethnic and racial minority family heads, and to what extent do differences in the prevalence of extended households reflect variations due to ethnic (cultural) preference? We shall refer to the inclusion of individuals other than nuclear family members as the formation of an extended household. Non-nuclear individuals may be other relatives or non-relatives, including both children and adults. To address this question, we examine the relationship between household composition and the sources of household income, paying special attention to the relative importance of poverty status and minority status (race or Hispanic origin) in determining the propensity of a household to extend.

Our strategy entails first outlining demographic differences in the size and structure of non-Hispanic, white, black, Mexican, Puerto Rican, Central/South American, and other Spanish origin households. Subsequently, differences in the propensity to form extended-family households are examined in relation to two types of headship arrangements: female-headed and husband-wife. The economic significance of doubling up is examined by partitioning household income into the relative contributions of nuclear and non-nuclear family members and comparing the relative shares among poor and non-poor households. Finally, a logit analysis is performed to determine the major factors related to the propensity to form extended households among the various racial and ethnic groups.

Data

Our empirical analysis is based on special tabulations from the 1976 Survey of Income and Education (SIE), a public-use microdata file consisting of 151,000 households. Because of its unusually large sample size, the SIE has become an important intercensal survey for the study of the socioeconomic and demographic characteristics of the non-institutionalized population of the United States. For the present analysis, Spanish-origin households were deliberately oversampled. When properly weighted, the sample is representative of the general population of the United States. Only family households, that is, those including a minimal dyad consisting of a head and other relative, are included in the analysis.

Household Composition and Income Sources: Relative Shares of Nuclear and Non-nuclear Members

As shown in Table 6-1, there is a great diversity in the demographic characteristics of non-Hispanic white, black, and Spanish-origin households. Most family households are headed by a husband and wife, but a substantial share of the total are headed by women, especially for blacks and Puerto Ricans. Among blacks, female-headed households comprise 38 percent of the total, whereas about one-third of all Puerto Rican families are female-headed. For the remaining Hispanic-origin groups, the population of households headed by single women is lower, ranging between 10 percent for non-Hispanic whites to around 18 percent for Mexican, Central/South American, and other Spanish origin households.

Table 6–1

Selected Demographic Characteristics of Family Households by Race or Hispanic National Origin: United States, 1976
(Means or Percents)[a]

| Demographic Characteristics | Race or National Origin | | | | | |
	Non-Hispanics	Black	Mexican	Puerto Rican	Central/ South American[b]	Other Spanish
Type of Headship						
Husband-wife	89.5	62.0	82.5	65.7	83.1	81.5
Female head	10.5	38.0	17.5	34.3	16.9	18.5
	(19,177)	(8,000)	(2,030)	(507)	(376)	(681)
Median Household Income	$14,986	$9,017	$9,785	$7,962	$11,325	$11,749
Education						
Husband-wife	12.1	10.0	9.0	9.7	11.2	10.7
Female head	11.3	10.2	7.8	8.2	10.4	10.2
Mean Household Size						
All persons	*3.3*	*3.9*	*4.2*	*3.8*	*3.6*	*3.5*
Persons under 18	*1.1*	*1.8*	*2.0*	*1.9*	*1.3*	*1.3*
Persons 18+	*2.2*	*2.1*	*2.2*	*1.9*	*2.3*	*2.2*
Non-nuclear members Percent of total	3.6	10.5	5.5	4.5	8.3	6.0
Extended Families[c] as Percent of Total	8.1	22.8	12.0	11.4	20.3	13.2
Number of Persons Presently Employed						
Total	*1.43*	*1.23*	*1.34*	*.90*	*1.46*	*1.28*
Nuclear	*1.40*	*1.17*	*1.30*	*.88*	*1.36*	*1.25*
Non-nuclear	*.03*	*.06*	*.05*	*.02*	*.10*	*.03*
Proportion Below Poverty						
Husband-wife	.04	.14	.16	.17	.12	.10
Female head	.20	.47	.48	.58	.43	.34

[a]Means are in italics.

[b]Includes Cubans.

[c]Defined as a family containing one or more non-nuclear relatives.

Non-Hispanic whites have the smallest family households, with an average size of 3.3 persons, whereas Mexicans have the largest families, averaging 4.2 persons per unit. Families with income below poverty are larger still, with an average of 4.6 persons per household. Among Mexicans, the larger family size is due to the persistence of high fertility (Bradshaw and Bean, 1972) and to norms that favor large families (Edington and Hays, 1978). The slightly smaller average family size for Puerto Ricans and blacks is to be expected in light of the greater prevalence of single-parent households among these groups and their lower fertility relative to Mexicans. Central/South American and other Spanish households are more similar to non-Hispanic whites than to other Hispanic groups in terms of average size.

Among non-Hispanic whites, the presence of non-nuclear members accounts for less than 4 percent of household membership, on average, whereas among blacks, non-nuclear members comprise about 10 percent of the total. The Hispanic groups fall between these two extremes and exhibit considerable diversity among themselves. Notice, for example, that while non-nuclear members comprise between 5.5 and 4.5 percent of the membership of Puerto Rican and Mexican family households, they account for 8 percent of Central/South American households. Given that the latter group is economically better off than either Mexicans or Puerto Ricans, one might infer that the greater tendency to form extended households reflects cultural preferences. However, it is important to consider that virtually all the Central/South American heads are foreign-born. Thus, it is conceivable that many of these first-generation heads of household have had to shoulder the responsibility of helping new waves of immigrants adjust to the host society. For Cubans, who comprise roughly half this group, the pattern of breaking up and reconstituting families in the United States is common. It is possible that many families have never been fully reunited; thus the greater prevalence of extended-family households among Cubans may reflect this outcome.

Clearly, the propensity to incorporate non-nuclear members is greatest among black households, of which approximately 23 percent are extended. If this were due primarily to the higher prevalence of female-headed households among blacks, one might expect that Puerto Ricans would exhibit a similarly high proportion of extended households. This is not the case, and in fact, the proportion of extended households among Puerto Ricans is only slightly higher than that of non-Hispanic whites, but it is notably lower than that characteristic of all other Hispanic-origin groups. The reasons for this outcome are not immediately apparent from the tabular data but are addressed further in the multivariate analysis. With approximately 15 percent of all households containing one or more non-nuclear members, Mexican or other Spanish origin households are intermediate between Puerto Ricans and Central/South Americans in the prevalence of extended-household structure.

Evidence in Table 6–1 concerning the economic motivations to form extended households is weak, and indirect at best. For example, contrary to expectation, non-Hispanic whites have, on average, more workers per family. Thus the higher total family income of this group is partially attributable to the greater labor inputs of family members. While the average number of workers per family among Mexican and Central/South American households is relatively similar to that of non-Hispanic whites, the corresponding median family incomes are considerably lower. This serves to illustrate the well-documented labor market disadvantages faced by minority groups. Along the same lines, blacks and other Spanish family households are similar in that they both have an average of about 1.2 workers per unit but differ in that the latter enjoy much higher household incomes. For Puerto Ricans, the average number of persons in the labor force is slightly less than one, reflecting the exceedingly high unemployment rates characteristic of this group, as well as the prevalence of discouraged workers (Cooney, 1979a; Tienda, 1980).

It is important first to examine differentials in extended-household composition according to type of headship, since female-headed households are more likely to experience economic hardships (Ross and Sawhill, 1975; Cutright, 1974; Sweet, 1972) and thus should be more inclined to seek alternative living arrangements to compensate for the loss of an earner. The special significance of headship for the formation of extended-family households stems from the fact that units lacking one parent are frequently handicapped in their ability to provide adequately for domestic needs. This results because single parents are unable to devote full time to labor-market and domestic activities unless someone can be recruited on a paying or non-paying basis to share these functions. Presumably the formation of extended households affords single-parent households a practical way of ensuring the social and economic viability of the family unit. The basic hypothesis is that female-headed households are more likely to contain one or more non-nuclear members, compared to units where both spouses are present. If there are economic dimensions to this demographic response, the work earnings of non-nuclear members should comprise a greater share of total household income.

Table 6–2 addresses the first question concerning the higher propensity of female-headed households to extend. Not only do the data support our expectation, but a clear pattern emerges between the type of headship, race or national origin, and extended-family composition. First, among all groups, female-headed households are smaller, on average, than their two-headed counterparts. This is manifested in terms of both smaller nuclear cores and total unit size. Among all groups, spouse-absent households have uniformly larger non-nuclear components, a phenomenon which partly reflects the fact that these units have more space for an additional person as well as, perhaps, a greater desire to replace the missing spouse (Tienda, 1980). The fact that parent-absent households remain smaller than those with two spouses, even after adding non-nuclear individuals to their membership, shows that the spouse-replacement mechanism only partly compensates for the loss of a spouse.

Differentials in the propensity for female-headed and husband-wife to extend are best appreciated by considering the size of the non-nuclear component as a share of total household membership. These data show that among units with two spouses, non-nuclear members comprise a trivial share of non-Hispanic white households and those headed by persons of other Spanish origin. This is not the case for minority households, especially those headed by women, in which non-nuclear members comprise between 12 and 17 percent of household membership. Puerto Ricans are the exception to this pattern. According to the economic argument, Puerto Rican households headed by single women should be more inclined to extend because of the unfavorable economic circumstances in which most find themselves (Cooney, 1979b). However, because the incomes of Puerto Ricans generally are lower than those of other Hispanic-origin groups, this alternative may not be particularly attractive. Under some circumstances the incorporation of an additional member may decrease the economic well-being of the unit. Given the chronically high unemployment rates experienced by Puerto Ricans (Cooney, 1979a), the possibility of increasing rather than decreasing economic dependency burdens is very real. Thus, the alternative of receiving income transfers in the form of direct public assistance payments and other non-cash benefits may be more practical, not only because it affords the female head the opportunity to devote more time to domestic functions, but also because other members are apt to be less crowded than if an additional person were added to the unit. Further insight into this matter is provided below.

From an economic perspective, the most pertinent question is whether the observed differences in extended family structure (Table 6–1) among minority and non-minority households actually result in increases in household income either through the direct contributions of the non-nuclear members or through the increased market activity of other nuclear family members, which is presumably facilitated by the presence

Table 6–2

Mean Size of Family Households by Type of Headship and Race or Hispanic National Origin: United States, 1976

Type of Headship and Nuclear/Extended Components

Race or National Origin	Husband-Wife Families					Female-Headed Families				
	Total Members	Nuclear Members	Non-Nuclear Members	Non-Nuclear as Percent of Total	(N)	Total Members	Nuclear Members	Non-Nuclear Members	Non-Nuclear as Percent of Total	(N)
Non-Hispanc White	3.39	3.32	.07	2.1	(17,220)	2.86	2.47	.39	13.6	(1,957)
Black	4.02	3.75	.27	6.7	(4,990)	3.74	3.16	.58	15.5	(3,010)
Mexican	4.36	4.22	.14	3.2	(1,683)	3.85	3.40	.45	11.5	(347)
Puerto Rican	3.99	3.84	.15	3.8	(339)	3.47	3.29	.18	5.2	(168)
Central/South American[a]	3.78	3.55	.23	6.1	(316)	2.92	2.48	.44	15.1	(60)
Other Spanish	3.57	3.47	.10	2.8	(567)	3.38	2.81	.57	16.9	(114)

Source: 1976 Survey of Income and Education, U.S. Bureau of Census.

[a] Includes Cubans.

of non-nuclear members. Because female-headed households are considerably more likely to be poor compared to their husband-wife counterparts, the income contribution of non-nuclear members is expected to be more substantial in these units. The information in Table 6–3 addresses this issue in part.

Relatively few husband-wife households contain non-nuclear members with earnings; thus the earnings of non-nuclear members as a share of all work income are trivial, in both poor and non-poor households.[1] The general conclusion from these data is that within the context of normative family structure (i.e., those with two heads), non-nuclear members probably benefit more from extended living arrangements than do nuclear members. This statement must be qualified by acknowledging that the presence of non-nuclear members increases the flexibility of households in coping with economic hardship by facilitating alternative work arrangements among nuclear members. In other words, to the extent that the non-nuclear members assume a greater share of the domestic work roles, it is possible for nuclear members to reallocate time between market and non-market work. This internal reallocation of household and market work roles cannot be assessed with these data, but it is an important dimension of the interface between work and familial roles that deserves more careful attention.

In contrast to households in which both spouses are present, the income contributions on non-nuclear members in female-headed households are quite substantial, especially for those with incomes above poverty level. The relative earnings contribution of non-nuclear members ranges from a low of 14 percent for blacks to 24 percent for Central/South Americans. This share is greater for all four Hispanic groups than either non-Hispanic whites or blacks. The relative income contributions of non-nuclear members is especially high among Puerto Rican and Central/South American non-poor, female-headed households, two groups that have atypical immigration experiences. For Central/South Americans, a group which includes Cubans, the relative importance of non-nuclear members may reflect the dislocation associated with emigration from Cuba and the subsequent need to pool resources in the United States, both for financial and psychological reasons. For Puerto Ricans, the back-and-forth movement from Puerto Rico typical of this group, as well as their concentration in the Northeast, may again increase the need to pool resources or share living quarters. Overall, these results suggest that the inclusion of non-nuclear members may help alleviate poverty but that not all groups are equally able to draw the resources of non-nuclear members.

Table 6-3

Share of Household Earnings Contributed by Nuclear and Non-nuclear Members by Type of Headship and Race or Hispanic National Origin: United States, 1975 (In Percent)

Type of Headship, Poverty Status, and Nuclear/Non-nuclear Components

Race or National Origin	Husband-Wife Families				Female-Headed Families			
	Poor		Non-Poor		Poor		Non-Poor	
	Nuclear	Non-Nuclear	Nuclear	Non-Nuclear	Nuclear	Non-Nuclear	Nuclear	Non-Nuclear
Non-Hispanic	100.0	0.0	99.0	1.0	92.0	8.0	85.0	15.0
Black	99.0	1.0	99.0	1.0	96.0	4.0	86.0	14.0
Mexican	99.0	1.0	99.0	1.0	99.0	1.0	79.0	21.0
Puerto Rican	99.0	1.0	99.0	1.0	100.0	0.0	77.0	23.0
Central/South American[a]	86.0	14.0	98.0	2.0	90.0	10.0	76.0	24.0
Other Spanish	100.0	—[b]	100.0	—[b]	94.0	6.0	80.0	20.0
(N)[c]	(1,284)	(27)	(21,593)	(601)	(958)	(90)	(3,043)	(608)

Source: 1976 Survey of Income and Education.

[a] Includes Cubans.

[b] Cell sizes too small for reliable estimates.

[c] N's refer to subset of households with earnings.

In light of the higher relative contributions by non-nuclear members among Hispanic households, another possible explanation is that Spanish-origin groups have different culturally determined tastes for living arrangements and the provision of mutual aid among relatives. Perhaps the most general conclusion to be derived from the information in Table 6–3 is that the formation of extended households is at least partially an attempt to deal with poverty, even though group-specific factors play an important determining role. Unfortunately, our data do not allow us to determine to what extent non-poor female-headed households in which non-nuclear relatives contribute significantly to family income were poor prior to the inclusion of the non-nuclear members. Neither is it possible to ascertain whether the income contributions of non-nuclear members in poor households actually serve to attenuate the economic hardship that would exist in their absence, but our data for female-headed units is suggestive in this regard. These questions cannot be addressed directly with readily available data, but the information in Table 6–4 illuminates some of the significant dimensions.

This information puts into clearer perspective the importance of the earnings contributions of non-nuclear members because it permits us to assess the economic argument in terms of the adequacy of the earnings of the primary worker and the supplementary earnings of other non-nuclear workers. Earnings comprise the bulk of total household income for most family households; but non-work income, including various sorts of transfer payments, interest and dividend income, and other non-work income, is quite substantial, even in husband-wife families. Among households headed by single women, non-work income accounts for between 22 and 66 percent of total household income. There clearly exists greater flexibility for placing additional family members in the labor force among husband-wife families where the wife is usually the preferred secondary earner. From this standpoint, non-nuclear members are third in the queue of additional workers, and possibly fourth if adult children of the head are also present.

In general, the earnings of non-nuclear members comprise a smaller share of household income than the earnings of secondary nuclear earners, with the notable exception of Central/South American female-headed units in which the earnings of non-nuclear workers are approximately twice as great as for secondary nuclear (wife and own children) workers. Puerto Ricans also evidence a slight tendency in this direction, but the magnitude of the differential is considerably smaller. However, the economic significance of the presence of non-nuclear members must be appreciated in light of the fact that female-headed

Table 6-4

Components of Family Household Income by Type of Headship, Source of Income, and Race or Hispanic National Origin: United States, 1975
(Mean Income in 1975 Dollars)

Type of Headship and Source of Income

Race or National Origin	Husband-Wife Families Head's Work Earnings	Other Nuclear Earnings	Non-Nuclear Earnings	Other Nonwork Income	Total	Female-Headed Families Head's Work Earnings	Other Nuclear Earnings	Non-Nuclear Earnings	Other Nonwork Income	Total
Non-Hispanic White Mean (%)	$11,582 (66.0)	$ 3,407 (19.4)	$ 90 (.5)	$ 2,464 (14.0)	$17,549 (99.9)	$ 3,858 (37.7)	$ 1,902 (18.6)	$ 997 (9.7)	$ 3,479 (34.0)	$10,236 (100.0)
Black Mean (%)	7,709 (56.6)	4,122 (30.2)	170 (1.2)	1,631 (12.0)	13,632 (100.0)	2,939 (42.9)	885 (12.9)	589 (8.6)	2,437 (35.6)	6,850 (100.0)
Mexican Mean (%)	7,925 (65.8)	2,651 (22.0)	123 (1.0)	1,344 (11.2)	12,042 (100.0)	2,283 (35.6)	966 (15.0)	758 (11.8)	2,409 (37.5)	5,417 (99.9)
Puerto Rican Mean (%)	8,018 (66.7)	2,397 (20.0)	115 (1.0)	1,483 (12.3)	12,012 (100.0)	1,150 (20.6)	322 (5.8)	426 (7.6)	3,672 (65.9)	5,569 (99.9)
Central/South American[a] Mean (%)	10,047 (66.1)	3,689 (24.3)	326 (2.1)	1,134 (7.5)	15,205 (100.0)	3,546 (50.8)	630 (9.0)	1,238 (17.7)	1,568 (22.5)	6,982 (100.0)
Other Spanish Mean (%)	9,795 (66.3)	2,895 (19.6)	26 (.2)	2,053 (13.9)	14,773 (100.0)	3,033 (34.3)	1,092 (12.4)	1,022 (11.6)	3,683 (41.7)	8,830 (100.0)

Source: 1976 Survey of Income and Education.

[a] Includes Cubans.

households are more likely to qualify for various forms of public assistance. In fact, the welfare system is designed to discourage further
income contributions from other family members. Thus, differences in
living arrangements which are rooted in economic need are also shaped
by institutional factors that place ceilings on the acceptable contributions of secondary workers. Violation of these norms, even in the interest of improving economic welfare, often results in the loss of benefits. Unfortunately, the question of whether the welfare system actually
encourages the formation of female-headed households is largely in-
determinate (Ross and Sawhill, 1975).

Basically, these tabular results are consistent with evidence concerning the relatively greater income share contributed by secondary workers among black households (Sweet, 1973). A recent finding is the importance of secondary nuclear earners among Spanish-origin families.
Although Hispanic wives and other nuclear members contribute a lower
share of total household income than their black counterparts, they account for a higher share of total household income than non-Hispanic
white secondary earners.

Race, Ethnicity, and Extended-Household Structure:
Further Considerations

The previous discussion focused on the relationship between race and
ethnicity, economic need, and the likelihood that family households
will extend, that is, incorporate individuals other than the wife or children of the head. Our view of the underlying relationships is summarized in Figure 6-1. We maintain that the various sociodemographic
variables for which we have measures are related to the three unmeasured constructs shown in the boxes. These unmeasured constructs
represent (1) economic need, which is a function of the adequacy of
family income for households of differing age and size composition;
(2) tastes for particular living arrangements, which reflect both social
class and cultural preferences for doubling up or maintaining an isolated nuclear family structure; and (3) the propensity to extend as governed by spatial as well as other social dimensions, most notably non-
normative headship structure.

In the present analysis, economic need is measured by the ratio of
household income to poverty.[2] Tastes for different living arrangements
are influenced by education of the head, which we use as a proxy for

Figure 6–1

Summary of Conceptual Relationships: Measured and Unmeasured Constructs

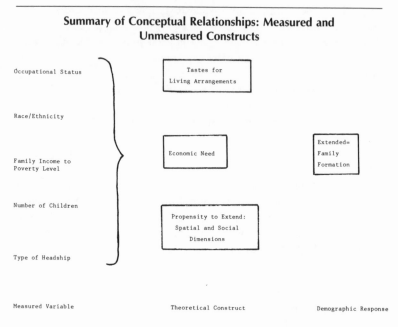

Measured Variable	Theoretical Construct	Demographic Response

social class. Racial and ethnic group membership may be related to cultural norms in living arrangements which differ from those of the larger society. The concept of the propensity to extend is tapped in the present analysis by the type of headship, which reflects the underlying need to compensate for the incompleteness of the unit. A husband-wife-children household comprised of parents and children may be normatively more closed than a female-headed unit, which is already somewhat deviant compared to the societal ideal of a two-spouse family.

From this more general perspective, it would seem unlikely that a simple economic argument would suffice to explain choices in family living arrangements. What follows is an attempt to investigate the interactions of race and ethnicity with selected sociodemographic variables that the existing literature shows to be related to economic well-being and alternative living arrangements. The major focus of the multivariate analysis is to ascertain the importance of headship and race or ethnicity to the propensity to form extended households in light of the adequacy or inadequacy of family income.

Logit Analysis

We employ a logit analysis[3] to investigate the impact of ethnicity and economic need on the propensity to form an extended-family household. Using this technique, we predict the likelihood that a household will contain non-nuclear members conditional on (1) race or Hispanic origin; (2) type of headship—husband-wife or female-headed; (3) income adequacy measured as the ratio of household income to poverty; and (4) the education of the head of the household. To perform the logit analysis, all dependent and independent variables are cross-tabulated. The table that results contains 144 cells and is based on a total sample of 30,757 households. Table 6–5 presents a detailed description of the variable categories used for the cross tabulation. The logit analysis permits us to examine the impact of the four independent variables on the natural logarithm of the odds of a household falling

Table 6–5

Symbols and Description of Variables Used in Logit Analysis

Symbol	Variable Name and Category Description
(EX)	Family Type
	(1) Not Extended
	(2) Extended
(ET)	Ethnicity or Race
	(1) Non-Hispanic White
	(2) Mexican American
	(3) Puerto Rican
	(4) Central/South American, Including Cuban
	(5) Other Spanish
	(6) Black
(PV)	Poverty Status-Ratio of Household Income to Poverty
	(1) Below or equal to 150% of poverty ratio
	(2) Above 150% of poverty ratio
(HD)	Type of Headship
	(1) Male head, husband-wife household
	(2) Female-headed household
(ED)	Education of Head
	(1) 0 through 8 years
	(2) 9 through 12 years
	(3) 13 or more years

into the category "extended" as opposed to the category "not extended."

The equations we estimate are presented in Table 6–6, which presents a nested hierarchy of logit models in which each equation contains all the terms in prior models plus additional interactions between independent variables and the likelihood of extension. The grand mean represents the log odds of extension of a household which falls into the omitted category on all the independent variables. The second set of terms adds to the grand mean the net effects of the independent variables, while the third and fourth set of terms add higher-order interactions between selected independent variables and the probability of a household extending. The fifth term represents the saturated model, which describes the table perfectly since it exactly reproduces the observed cell frequencies.

Although the logit model is linear in its logarithmic specification, it reflects non-linearity in the actual probabilities of forming extended households. This means that, whereas the influence of the independent variables is additive in a logarithmic form, this influence actually represents a multiplicative effect on the odds of extension. A particular logit coefficient is important, therefore, insofar as it interacts with the

Table 6–6

A Nested Hierarchy of Possible Logit Models for Analyzing the Effect of Race or Ethnicity (ET), Poverty Status (PV), Educational Level (ED) and Type of Headship (HD) on the Likelihood of Extension (EX)

$$\text{Logit (Extension)} = \text{Ln}\left(\frac{\text{Extended}}{\text{Non-Extended}}\right) =$$

1. W (Grand Mean)

2. $+ W_{ET} + W_{PV} + W_{HD}$ Indenpendent effects of ET, PV, ED, HD

3. $+ W_{ET,PV} + W_{ET,ED} + W_{ET,HD} + W_{PV,HD} + W_{ED,HD}$

         Two-Way interactions of ET, PV, ED, HD

4. $+ W_{ET,PV,ED} + W_{ET,PV,HD} + W_{ET,ED,HD} + W_{PV,ED,HD}$

         Three-way interactions of ET, PV, ED, HD

5. $+ W_{ET,PC,ED,HD}$ Four-way effect of ET, PV, ED, HD
                        (Saturated Model)

other variables in the equation, enhancing or diminishing their effects. We present both the additive logit coefficients and their anti-logs, the multiplicative parameters.

The first step in the analysis is to determine what subset of possible independent and interaction terms is necessary to describe the influence of the independent variable on the likelihood of forming extended-family households. For this purpose, interaction terms are added to the basic model in a logical sequence which reflects our hypotheses concerning the propensity to form extended-family households. This is done until the log-likelihood chi square (G^2) is low relative to its associated degrees of freedom (Bishop, Fienberg, and Holland, 1975). At this point, there is sufficient information to describe the interactions in the table and to reduce the entire set of potentially complex interactions to a smaller subset of more dominant and substantively interpretable interactions. Ultimately, the most parsimonious model consistent with our substantive interests is used.

Our primary substantive concern with the relationship between ethnicity and extended-household formation requires us first to ascertain the existence of significant two-way interactions between ethnicity (ET) and extension (EX). The model-selection process begins with establishing the amount of log-likelihood chi square (G^2) that is *not* attributable to the joint interaction of the independent variables and extended-household structure. This is a measure of the total amount of association between extended-household structure and the independent variable, which remains to be explained. Subsequently this G^2 is partitioned into components accounted for by the various independent variables and interactions among the independent variables and extension. What we are asking is, how do the four independent variables affect the likelihood of forming an extended-family household?

Model 1 in Table 6–7 is a baseline to establish the amount of G^2 not attributable to the interaction of the independent variables and the dependent variable—extended versus non-extended household structure. At step one, $G^2 = 3,002$ with 71 degrees of freedom. Models 2 through 5 successively add two-way interactions between the independent variables and extended-household structure. All two-way interactions significantly reduce G^2 relative to their associated degrees of freedom. Models 6 through 11 introduce three-way interactions between the independent variables and extension. Again, all the three-way interactions shown prove to contribute significantly to the explanation of the log odds of forming an extended household.

The bottom half of Table 6–7 presents tests for the various interac-

Table 6–7

A Comparison of Models of the Interaction of Race and Ethnicity (ET), Type of Household (HD), Head's Education (ED), Ratio of Family Income to Poverty (PV), and Extended Household (EX)

		Likelihood Ratio		
Marginals Fit[a]		df^b	G^2	P
1.	(EX)	71	3002	.0000
2.	(ET, EX)	66	1889	.0000
3.	(ET, EX) (EX, PV)	65	1868	.0000
4.	(ET, EX) (EX, PV) (EX, HD)	64	788	.0000
5.	(ET, EX) (EX, PV) (EX, HD) (EX, ED)	62	389	.0000
6.	(EX, HD) (EX, ED) (ET, EX, PV)	57	363	.0000
7.	(EX, ED) (ET, EX, PV) (ET, EX, HD)	52	231	.0000
8.	(ET, EX, PV) (ET, EX, HD) (ET, EX, ED)	42	145	.0000
9.	(ET, EX, PV) (ET, EX, HD) (ET, EX, ED) (EX, PV, HD)	41	66	.0086
10.	(ET, EX, PV) (ET, EX, HD) (ET, EX, ED) (ET, PV, HD) (EX, PV, ED)	39	55	.0420
11.	(ET, EX, PV) (ET, EX, HD) (ET, EX, ED) (ET, PV, HD) (EX, PV, ED) (EX, HD, ED)	37	46	.1582
	Model 5 - Model 6	5	26	<.001
	(Test for ET, EX, PV interaction)			
	Model 6 - Model 7	5	132	<.001
	(Test for ET, EX, HD interaction)			
	Model 7 - Model 8	10	86	<.001
	(Test for ET, EX, ED interaction)			

Table 6–7 (Continued)

Marginals Fit[a]	Likelihood Ratio		
	df[b]	G^2	P
Model 8 – Model 9 (Test for EX, PV, HD interaction)	1	79	<.001
Model 9 – Model 10 (Test for EX, PV, ED interaction	2	11	<.005
Model 10 – Model 11 (Test for EX, HD, ED interaction	2	9	<.025

[a]All models contain the interaction between ET, PV, HD, ED.

[b]Degrees of freedom.

tions introduced in models 2 through 11. Since these models form a nested hierarchy, the relative contribution of any one independent variable or interaction is ascertained by subtracting the likelihood ratio chi-square and associated degrees of freedom of the model in which the term appears from the immediately preceding model in which it is not included. The change in chi-square relative to the associated loss in degrees of freedom provides a measure of the influence of a particular variable or interaction term.

Subtracting model 2 from model 1 indicates that ethnicity has a pronounced impact on the propensity to extend since it reduces chi-squared by 1,113 while using up only five degrees of freedom. Subtracting model 3 from model 2 indicates that while poverty has a significant influence on the log odds of extension, its impact is far smaller than the effect of ethnicity. The difference between models 3 and 4 shows that female headship has a dramatic impact on the likelihood of extension, reducing chi-squared by 1,080 while using only one degree of freedom. Finally, the strong influence of education on the likelihood of extension is illustrated by the difference in G^2 and degrees of freedom between model 6 and model 5.

The three-way interactions presented in models 6 through 11 in Table 6–7 have less of an impact than some of the two-way interactions, but they do add significantly to the analysis. In particular, the three-way interactions between ethnicity, extension, and female headship (models 6–7); ethnicity, extension, and education (models 7–8); and extension, poverty, and female headship (models 8–9) have important impacts on the likelihood of extension. Model 11 is our final choice for describing the data because it best addresses all interactions of substantive interest and fits the data better than any of the previous models.

Results

Table 6–8 presents the logit and multiplicative coefficients for the non-interactive influence of the independent variables on the propensity to form an extended household. The logit coefficients represent the increment or decrement in the log odds of forming an extended household associated with membership in a particular category of the relevant independent variable. The multiplicative parameters are the antilogs of the logit coefficients and represent the multiplicative impact of the independent variable on the actual odds of extension. Table 6–9 presents the coefficients for the effects of interactions among independent variables on the log odds of extension. For dichotomous independent variables, these coefficients refer to membership in the second category: above 150 percent of poverty, and female-headed household. For education, the reference category is 0–8 years of school. Non-Hispanic whites are the omitted category for ethnicity and race; thus the impact of race and ethnicity is expressed relative to the majority group. In order to compute the likelihood that a household with a particular set of characteristics will be extended, the relevant logit coefficients are added to the grand mean (or the relevant multiplicative parameters are multiplied together).

Model 2 in Table 6–8 illustrates the independent effect of race and ethnicity on the propensity to extend. This equation reveals the gross effects of race and ethnicity, taking non-Hispanic whites as the reference. The grand mean indicates that non-Hispanic white households are only .083 times as likely to extend as to remain nuclear. The coefficients for the various minority groups reflect the increment to that propensity associated with minority-group membership. All these coefficients are large and significant. Being Central/South American or black has an extremely large impact on the likelihood of extension. For Central/South Americans, ethnicity has a multiplicative impact of 2.989, while for blacks this impact is 3.525. For Mexicans, Puerto Ricans, and other Spanish, the multiplicative factor is approximately 1.5.

In model 11 (Table 6–8) the grand mean (− 2.494) reflects the log odds of extension for a household with the following characteristics:

Table 6–8

Logit and Tau Parameters Describing the Direct Effects of Race or Ethnicity (ET), Poverty Status (PV), Female Headship (HD), and Education (ED) on the Likelihood of Forming an Extended Household (EX)
(Standard Errors in Parentheses)

Independent Variables	Model 2 Logit[a]	Model 2 Tau	Model 11 Logit[a]	Model 11 Tau
Grand Mean	-2.485** (.027)	0.083	-2.494** (.103)	0.083
Mexican	0.405** (.076)	1.499	.417** (.169)	1.517
Puerto Rican	0.443** (.142)	1.557	.134 (.339)	1.143
Central/South American	1.095** (.1319)	2.989	.209 (.387)	1.232
Other Spanish	0.414** (.125)	1.513	.329 (.296)	1.390
Black	1.260** (.038)	3.525	1.593** (.108)	4.918
Poverty Status			-.046 (.104)	0.955
Female Head			1.518** (.109)	4.563
Education 9–12			-.512** (.116)	0.600
Education 13+			-.855** (.174)	0.425

**Significant at .01

[1] For ethnicity the reference category is non-Hispanic white.
For education the reference category is 0–8 years of school.
For poverty status the reference category is below 150% of poverty.

non-Hispanic white ET (1); husband-wife headship HD (1); below 150 percent of the poverty threshold PV (1); and a household head with 0–8 years of education ED (1). The multiplicative parameter indicates that such a household is only .083 times as likely to contain one or more non-nuclear members as to be nuclear. Overall, the coefficients in Tables 6–8 and 6–9 give some idea of the relative impact of various factors on the probability of forming extended households. In general, results indicate that, although extended-family structure is typically rare

Table 6–9

Logit and Tau Parameters Describing the Effects of Interactions Between Race or Ethnicity (ET), Poverty Status (PV), Female Headship (HD), and Education (ED) on the Likelihood of Forming an Extended Household—Model 11 (Standard Errors in Parentheses)

Interaction	Logit[a]	Tau
Mexican x Poverty	.269 (.181)	1.309
Puerto Rican x Poverty	.593* (.343)	1.813
Central/S. American x Poverty	.377 (.360)	3.458
Other Spanish x Poverty	-.251 (.303)	0.778
Black x Poverty	-.151 (.101)	0.860
Mexican x Female Head	-.697** (.183)	0.498
Puerto Rican x Female Head	-1.142** (.337)	0.319
Central/S. American x Female Head	-.806** (.343)	0.447
Other Spanish x Female Head	-.089 (.283)	0.915
Black x Female Head	-.663** (.091)	0.515
Mexican x Education 9-12	-.395* (.083)	0.674
Mexican x Education 13+	-.079 (.246)	0.924
Puerto Rican x Education 9-12	.187 (.318)	1.206
Puerto Rican x Education 13+	-.073 (.343)	0.930
Central/S. American x Education 8-12	.951** (.362)	2.588
Central/S. American x Education 13+	1.143** (.391)	3.136
Other Spanish x Education 8-12	-.035 (.305)	0.966
Other Spanish x Education 13+	.617 (.377)	1.853

Table 6–9 (Continued)

Interaction	Logit[a]	Tau
Black x Education 8-12	-.538** (.100)	0.584
Black x Education 13+	-.758** (.131)	0.469
Poverty x Education 8-12	.227* (.099)	1.255
Poverty x Education 13+	.311* (.163)	1.365
Female Head x Education 8-12	-.213* (.097)	0.803
Female Head x Education 13+	.102 (.127)	1.107
Female Head x Poverty	.741** (.094)	2.098

*Significant at .05   **Significant at .01

[a]For ethnicity the reference category in Non-Hispanic white.
For education the reference category is 0-8 years of school.
For poverty status the reference category is below 150% of poverty.

among U.S. households, several factors have a substantial impact on the propensity of households to include one or more non-nuclear members. Apparently, poverty status is not one of them.

In model 11, which adds a number of control variables and interaction terms to model 2, only Mexican ethnicity and race retain significant independent impacts on the likelihood of extension. Mexican ethnicity exerts a multiplicative impact of about 1.5, whereas race has an even larger impact in this equation (4.918) than in model 2. The differences in the independent impact of ethnicity between models 2 and 11 reflects the fact that group differences in the propensity to extend are largely associated with the control variables. The effects of the controls in Table 6–8 show that whereas poverty status has an insignificant independent impact on the odds, female headship and educational level have large and highly significant effects. Female headship is associated with a multiplicative parameter of 4.563, reflecting a much greater propensity for female-headed households to include nonnuclear members, compared to husband-wife households. Education, on the other hand, exerts a large negative impact on the propensity to extend. Specifically, 9 to 12 years of education is associated with a multiplicative parameter of .600, whereas 13 or more years of education is associated with a multiplicative parameter of .425. These parameters indicate that the higher the educational level of the head of household, the lower the likelihood that the household will contain non-nuclear individuals.

The interaction effects presented in Table 6–9 add some insight into the phenomenon of extended-household formation. The interaction between poverty status and ethnicity is insignificant for all groups except Puerto Ricans, for whom being 150 percent of poverty is associated with an increase in likelihood of extension. It is plausible that, for this group, including non-nuclear members has an impact on the poverty level of the aggregate unit.

The interaction of female headship and ethnicity has a consistently significant negative impact on the likelihood of extension for "Other Spanish." Above and beyond the independent impacts of female headship and ethnicity, being a female-headed minority household has a dampening effect on the likelihood of extension. It must be remembered, however, that the effects of female headship and low education are such that, despite the negative coefficients associated with the interaction of female headship and ethnicity, a female-headed household in which the head has little education is considerably more likely to extend than a husband-wife household. This is especially true for Mexicans and blacks, for whom the independent effect of race and ethnicity is statistically significant. The interaction of poverty status and female headship indicates that being a female-headed household with income above 150 percent of poverty increases the likelihood of extension (multiplicative parameter = 2.098). One interpretation is that female-headed households rely on the extension mechanism in order to increase household income, but our data do not permit us to disentangle the casual direction of the effect.

The interaction of education and ethnicity has an inconsistent impact on the propensity to extend for the various groups. For Mexicans, 9 to 12 years of education for the head is associated with a significantly decreased likelihood of extension relative to lower educational levels. This is also true for blacks. For Central/South Americans, on the other hand, higher levels of education are associated with substantial and significant increases in the propensity to extend. As noted in our prior discussion, education is likely to be associated with tastes for different living arrangements as well as with differing earning potentials. It is conceivable that higher educational levels are associated with middle-class norms and tastes for more private living arrangements. This interpretation holds for blacks and somewhat for Mexicans for whom higher educational levels appear to be associated with the ability to realize more private living arrangements. It is possible that the living arrangements of Central/South Americans are influenced by their immigration experience. That is, the higher prevalence of extended-household structure probably reflects the necessity of incorporating individuals who have not yet become totally independent in a new society. For this group the achievement of higher educational levels, especially if this was attained abroad, might not operate to reduce tastes for extended-living arrangements. The interactions of poverty status and education have small but significant positive impacts on the likelihood of extension. The interaction of female headship and 9 to 12 years of education has a small but significant negative impact on the likelihood of extension. These interactions, though significant, are small and do not warrant an extensive substantive interpretation.

Conclusion

Our analysis leads us to the general conclusion that while economic hardship may slightly increase the probability that a household will include non-nuclear members, the likelihood of extension is greatly influenced by other factors, such as group-specific preferences for alternative living arrangements and the sex and education of the head of household. To be sure, the phenomenon of extension is typically rare in the United States, but the propensity to extend appears to be associated with race and ethnicity. Insofar as racial and ethnic minorities suffer from lower levels of education and contain higher proportions of female-headed households, our results indicate that they will be more likely to extend, since education and female headship prove to be strong correlates of extended-household structure. Our analysis indicates that non-Hispanic whites are the least likely to form extended households, whereas blacks are most likely to do so. For the latter, the propensity to extend is not altered when we control for income adequacy, headship, and education, indicating that race has a pronounced independent effect on the propensity to extend. Considering the pervasive economic deprivation suffered by the black population, extension probably represents a long-term adaptation to poverty.

For the Hispanic-origin groups, a single generalization about cultural or economic motivations governing the propensity to form extended households is not possible. In general, it appears that the level of income adequacy has little independent association with the propensity to extend for any group, with the exceptions of Puerto Ricans, who are more likely to be extended at level of income above 150 percent of poverty, and of female-headed households above 150 percent of poverty, who are also more likely to be extended. In light of the economic disadvantages suffered by Puerto Ricans and by female-headed households of any race or ethnicity, these groups may be particularly motivated to raise aggregate household income by incorporating non-nuclear members.

Female headship and education seem to be major determinants of household structure. Indeed, next to race, female headship exerts the largest independent impact, greatly increasing the probability of extension. Education, on the other hand, has a significant dampening impact on extension. We argued that higher levels of education may be associated with tastes for more private family living arrangements, but we also observed that various racial and ethnic groups differ in the impact education has on their propensity to extend. Insofar as education is associated with higher income, the economic argument would predict that higher levels of education would be associated with the possibility of maintaining more private family living arrangements. This phenomenon may be at work for blacks and to some extent for Mexicans. Central/South Americans, on the other hand, appear to be more likely to include non-nuclear members at the higher educational levels. We suggested that this outcome may reflect the distinctive immigration experience of this group.

It is conceivable that we failed to include pertinent variables that differentiate our group in the analysis. This is particularly salient for the Hispanic-origin groups, who are known to differ in two important respects, immigrant composition and regional residence. While it might seem appropriate to infer that cultural norms favoring extended-family living arrangements are more prevalent among the Hispanic-origin groups, our sense is that this conclusion would be premature, except on a tentative basis, because there exist important compositional differences among these groups which must be systematically monitored to adequately isolate cultural effects from economic effects. The potential importance of immigrant composition has been acknowledged, but the pattern of geographic concentration requires that we qualify our findings. Puerto Ricans are concentrated in the Northeast, Mexicans in the Southwest, and Cubans in the Southeast. Each of these areas has associated advantages and disadvantages in terms of employment and wage opportunities. For example, the economic enclaves in Miami afford Cubans economic shelters unlike those of any other group in the United States, except, perhaps, Jews (Wilson and Portes, 1980). Puerto Ricans generally cannot avail themselves of comparable economic networks that are conducive to the improvement of their socioeconomic circumstances.

To appreciate fully the significance of our analysis, we must acknowledge its limitations. Any analysis of the monetary exchanges based on co-residence patterns will reveal only a partial view of the economic argument. A more complete picture requires investigation of the patterns of interaction which transcend the narrow focus on living arrangements. In this regard, among all groups, it is not only the patterns of co-residence that are of interest, but also the patterns of residential propinquity which in turn facilitate economic assistance, either in goods or in kind. From this perspective, the residential concentration of the Hispanic-origin groups acquires a special relevance for this line of investigation.

Notes

1. This ratio is based on the non-farm poverty cutoffs in 1976, as reported in Table A–2 of Current Population Reports, Series P–60, No. 106, "Characteristics of the Population Below the Poverty Level: 1975." Washington, D.C.: U.S. Government Printing Office. Although poverty cutoffs were coded in the Survey of Income and Education, these were based on family income and thus do not take into account the earnings or unearned income of nonnuclear members. As such, these measures were inappropriate for our analyses, which are based on households.

2. Although 150 percent of the official poverty threshold may appear to be an arbitrarily high cutoff point for distinguishing between poor and non-poor households, we wish to emphasize that the official poverty threshold, as currently constructed, represents an unrealistically low subsistence minimum basket of goods. When originally developed, this standard was intended as a short-term or emergency minimum subsistence level. Yet the official poverty levels have become rigidified as absolute and acceptable minimums for families of designated characteristics. For our purposes, 150 percent of the poverty threshold represents a more realistic standard for designating poverty.

3. The logit analyses are based on a software package entitled "The GLIM System, Release 3: Generalised Linear Interactive Modelling," by R. J. Baker and J. A. Nelder, Oxford, Engl.: Numerical Algorithms Group, 1978.

References

Beck, E. M., Patrick M. Horan, and Charles M. Tolbert II
    1978   "Stratification in a dual economy." American Sociological Review 43:704–720.

Bishop, Y. M. M., S. E. Fienberg, and P. W. Holland
1975   Discrete Multivariate Analysis: Theory and Practice. Cambridge, Mass.: MIT Press.

Bradshaw, Benjamin S., and Frank Bean
1972   "Some aspects of fertility of Mexican Americans." Pp. 141–164 in Charles F. Westoff and Robert Parke, Jr. (eds.), Commission on Population Growth and the American Future, Research Reports, Vol. 1, Demographic and Social Aspects.

Cooney, Rosemary Santana
1979a   "Intercity variations in Puerto Rican female participation." Journal of Human Resources 14:222–235.
1979b   "Demographic components of growth in white, black and Puerto Rican female headed families: A comparison of the Cutright and Ross/Sawhill methodologies." Social Science Research 8:144–158.

Cutright, Phillips
1974   "Components of change in the number of female family heads aged 15–44: United States, 1940–70." Journal of Marriage and the Family 36:714–721.

Duncan, Otis D., David L. Featherman, and Beverly Duncan
1972   Socioeconomic Background and Achievement. New York: Seminar Press.

Edington, E., and L. Hays
1978   "Difference in family size and marriage age expectation and aspirations of Anglo, Mexican Americans, and native American rural youth." Adolescence 13:393–400.

Farley, Reynolds
1977   "Trends in racial inequalities: Have the gains of the 1960's disappeared in the 1970's?" American Sociological Review 42:189–208.

Featherman, David L., and Robert M. Hauser
1976   "Changes in the socioeconomic stratification of the races, 1962–1973." American Journal of Sociology 82:621–651.

Newman, Morris J.
1978   "A profile of Hispanics in the U.S. work force." Monthly Labor Review 101:3–14.

Parcel, Toby L.
1979   "Regional labor markets and earnings." American Sociological Review 44:262–279.

Portes, Alejandro, and Robert Bach
1980   "Immigrant earnings: Cuban and Mexican immigrants in the United States." International Migration Review 14:315–341.

Ross, Heather L., and Isabel V. Sawhill
1975   Time of Transition: The Growth of Families Headed by Women. Washington, D.C.: The Urban Institute.

Sweet, J. A.
  1972   "The living arrangements of separated, widowed, and divorced
          mothers." Demography 9:143–157.
  1973   Women in the Labor Force. New York: Seminar Press.
Tienda, Marta
  1979   "Socioeconomic attainment and ethnicity: Labor market experi-
          ence of native and immigrant Hispanics in the U.S." Research
          Proposal to the Office of Research and Development Employment
          and Training Administration. U.S. Department of Labor.
  1980   "Child and spouse replacement mechanisms: A life cycle perspec-
          tive on family composition in Peru." International Journal of So-
          ciology of the Family 10:67–80.
  1981   "The Mexican American minority."In Amos Hawley (ed.), The
          Future of Nonmetropolitan America. Chapel Hill: University of
          North Carolina Press.
U.S. Bureau of the Census
  1975   Current Population Reports, Series P–20, No. 291. "Household
          and family characteristics: March 1975." Washington: U.S. Gov-
          ernment Printing Office.
  1976   Current Population Reports, Series P–20, No. 302. "Persons of
          Spanish origin in the United States: March 1976." Washington:
          U.S. Government Printing Office.
Wilson, Kenneth, and Alejandro Portes
  1980   "Immigrant enclaves: An analysis of the labor market experiences
          of Cubans in Miami." American Journal of Sociology 86:295–319.

Comments—Angel and Tienda's "Household Composition and Income-Generation Strategies Among Non-Hispanic Whites, Blacks, and Hispanic-Origin Groups in the United States"

RICHARD A. WANNER

The conventional wisdom in sociology regarding trends in family structure has been that in all industrialized societies the isolated nuclear family has become the norm, while even in developing nations the extended family, incorporating more than two generations of consanguineal or affinal kin, is rapidly facing extinction as industrialization advances. Theorists like Goode (1963) have pointed out that features of industrial society, including the need for geographic mobility, a high degree of intergenerational social mobility, the assumption of family functions by other institutions, and greater emphasis on personal achievement, make the nuclear family a more functional form. More recent scholarship, however, has argued that the extended family has never existed on a wide scale in the United States or in other industrial societies. For example, Laslett (1972) has shown that only about 6 percent of households in the 100 English communities he studied for the 250-year period between 1574 and 1821 contained three or more generations, while Bane (1976) indicated that the nuclear family was never the predominant form in the United States, even during the agrarian colonial period. By 1970, approximately 7.5 percent of U.S. households contained relatives other than parents or children, a figure in line with those of earlier periods (U.S. Bureau of the Census, 1973).

Angel and Tienda's data, however, seem to suggest something else. Though not the dominant form, the "extended family" constitutes a sizeable proportion of households in the United States, particularly among Hispanic and non-Hispanic minority groups. But are these extended families in the accepted sense? In their usage, an extended household is any that contains individuals other than nuclear family members. In addition, Angel and Tienda argue that "non-nuclear individuals may be other relatives or non-relatives, including both children and adults." These households are in no sense limited to "extended families." They may contain boarders, live-in lovers, children of friends or relatives, or elderly relatives, or they may simply be families doubling up to save on rent. If a revolution in household composition is taking place in Western industrial societies, it is a revolution in the degree to which unrelated individuals are forming households. Indeed, the Swedish census has for several years had a separate category for households comprised of an adult male and adult female who are unmarried. A major difficulty with Angel and Tienda's analysis is that each of these forms of "extension" may be a response to very different forces. Taking in a boarder is clearly a response to financial exigency in most cases, but acquiring a spouse without benefit of clergy is not likely to be. In view of this, it is interesting that in Angel and Tienda's data the female-headed families, regardless of racial or ethnic background, are most likely to incorporate a non-nuclear member. Thus, an adequate test of the thesis that the addition of non-nuclear members to a household is a response to poverty demands that the nature of the relationship of the non-nuclear members to the head of household be established.

A second, related issue, mentioned only briefly by Angel and Tienda in their conclusion but crucial to a test of their hypothesis, is the degree to which economic cooperation among the poor can be established without the formation of joint or extended households. In her study of the black community in a small midwestern city she called "the Flats," Stack (1974) found that extended networks of economically cooperative kin and friends were formed to provide economic stability and a reasonable degree of economic security in a community where large numbers of persons depend on welfare for their livelihood. In the context of Angel and Tienda's problem, Stack points out that "these networks extend well beyond household boundaries and represent relatively stable social relationships which are maintained in the face of uncertain economic conditions and fluctuations in daily economic status" (1979:56). This suggests that Angel and Tienda's finding of only a minor effect of poverty status on houshold extension does not mean that economic cooperation in the form of "extended" relationships is not an important means of coping with financial difficulty among the poor. It may be that the addition of non-nuclear members to a household is just a minor form such cooperation takes.

Another issue raised by Angel and Tienda's analysis is the causal ordering of the basic variables: extended household formation, family income level, and cultural preference for extended households. As the authors themselves point out, longitudinal data are required to convincingly separate economic effects from cultural effects; that is, it must be shown that the addition of non-nuclear members typically occurs *after* a life event that reduces a family's economic standing. In addition, it must be shown that these additional members add to a family's viability either by contributing earnings or by releasing another family member to enter the labour force. One could argue that the causal ordering should run in the opposite direction from that proposed by Angel and Tienda: the formation of extended households, resulting perhaps from cultural preferences, may have the secondary effect of mitigating economic hardship. In this alternative model, the direct effect of extension on economic need would not be estimated in the presence of a control for cultural preferences, and might well be substantial, particularly if some control is introduced for type of non-nuclear membership in the household.

In light of Angel and Tienda's inference that the living arrangements of Central/South Americans are influenced by their immigration experience, it would appear to be important in such an analysis to pay attention to the immigration composition of not only the emigrants from other countries but also internal migrants as well. I refer particularly to blacks, whose migration experience consists largely of movement from a predominantly rural, agrarian South to the industrial North and West. Careful attention to migration would allow one to address several issues raised in the chapter. Of particular importance is the authors' suggestion that in view of the far higher probability of extension among blacks, irrespective of income adequacy, headship, or education, extension of the household probably represents a long-term adaptation to poverty. While this is certainly plausible, it is also possible that extension is more prevalent among blacks born in the rural South where, presumably, there is greater normative support for the formation of extended households. After again controlling for the character of the non-nuclear members, one could compare these explanations of contrasting extension among migrants from the South and non-migrants. A higher propensity to add non-nuclear members among the migrants would offer support for the cultural explanation.

Despite these difficulties in measurement and model specification, Angel and Tienda's research resurrects a venerable issue that is likely to gain in importance: What are the social and cultural factors that influence the structure of the family? Even more fundamental, What direction is family structure likely to take in the future, in a post-industrial society in which jobs for the unskilled are rapidly disappearing? The formation of extended households may be a temporary phenomenon brought about by a coincidence of immigration experience and temporary economic need, or it may become a more permanent adaptation to an era of increasing job insecurity, scarcity, and hyper-inflation. While future research must use a more realistic classification of household structures and examine the problem longitudinally, Angel and Tienda have at least delineated the issues and established guidelines for the development of a model that can be used to address those issues.

References

Bane, Mary Jo
    1976   Here to Stay: American Families in the Twentieth Century. New York: Basic Books.
Goode, William J.
    1963   World Revolution and Family Patterns. New York: The Free Press.
Laslett, Peter
    1972   "Mean household size since the sixteenth century." Pp. 125–158 in Peter Laslett and Richard Wall (eds.), Household and Family in Past Time. Cambridge: Cambridge University Press.
Stack, Carol B.
    1974   All Our Kin: Strategies for Survival in the Black Community. New York: Harper and Row.
    1979   "Extended familial networks: An emerging model for the 21st century family." Pp. 49–62 in David Pearce Snyder (ed.), The Family in Post-industrial America. Boulder, Colo.: Westview Press.
U.S. Bureau of the Census
    1973   Census of Population, 1970: Family Composition. Final Report PC(2)–4A. Washington, D.C.: U.S. Government Printing Office.

7

Family-Work Interdependence: A Concluding Paradigm

Pierre L. van den Berghe

Any contribution to this symposium at this stage is a test of stamina if nothing else. I face the same level of frustration as I had in my other talk in that again I would need at least four or five hours of time to present the case for sociobiology. Since I cannot state the case extensively, I can only hope to do two things—amuse you or irritate you. I cannot hope to convince you, except for those who are already convinced and already know the literature.

The chapters of the other participants, luckily, fit in neat progression, and I am going to address them in the order of best fit to my model. I will start with Hyman Rodman, graduating to Marta Tienda. Let me begin by trying to state the case for sociobiology.

The basic paradigm is one that says that individual organisms, human or nonhuman, behave for the maximization of their inclusive fitness. Inclusive fitness is the sum of the individual's own reproductive success, and it is the reproductive success of all related organisms discounted by the degree of relationship with ego, which is called the coefficient of relationship. The coefficient of relationship, or r, is very easily quantifiable in a species such as our own. We share exactly one-half of our genes with each of our parents, and with our children. Full siblings share, on the average, half of their genes. On the average, 25 percent of our genes are shared with grandparents or grandchildren or

This is an edited transcript of impromptu verbal remarks. Selected deletions have been made which refer directly to the papers in the companion volume, *Work, Organizations, and Society: Comparative Convergences*.

nephews, nieces, uncles, aunts, and half-siblings. We share .125 of our genes with first cousins and so on. The basic equation that gives the formula for predicting "altruism" in a model of maximization of inclusive fitness was first formulated not by Edward Wilson, who is by no means the founding father of sociobiology, but by W. B. Hamilton of the University of Michigan. "Altruism" will occur if $K > 1/r$, where K is the ratio of benefits to costs in the interaction and r is the coefficient of relationship between the altruist and the beneficiary.

Very simply put, this means that if I do my brother a good turn, he has to get more than twice as much benefit out of it as it costs me to do him a good turn, because he only shares half the genes with me. If my genetic makeup is to be ahead of the game by sacrificing something of my fitness to my brother's fitness, my brother has to get more than twice as much out of it as it costs me to be an altruist. That, in a nutshell, is what makes for what biologists unfortunately call "altruism." I say "unfortunately" because when biologists talk about altruism they mean selfishness. I don't like "selfishness" either, because selfishness implies volition or cognition and the model does not imply any consciousness of motivation at all. So, I prefer to use a nonvolitional term, such as nepotism. The tendency to favor kin over nonkin and close kin over distant kin is·what I call "nepotism," without any attribution of value judgment to the term.

There is a massive amount of data on humans and nonhumans that show that a good deal of animal sociality is explainable in terms of organisms doing each other good turns to the extent that they are related to each other and to the extent that they can maximize their inclusive fitness by doing so. Humans are obviously nepotistic in all human societies. There is no human society in which nepotism is not an obvious cement of human sociality. But so are all other social species from invertebrates to lower vertebrates, to higher vertebrates, to primates, to *Homo sapiens*. Again, you have to take me on faith, but there are several books that summarize clearly the abundant evidence. The models of inclusive fitness have been tested mostly with the "eusocial" insects, primarily the *Hymenoptera* (ants, wasps, bees). Insects are very nice to work with because in an average-size room you could keep about 250 ant societies. You can literally create huge samples and make very accurate testing of mathematical models on ant societies in a way which we would never be able to do with human societies. That's why the overwhelming mass of the evidence in support of the model comes from the social insects. The fragmentary evidence we have about more complex and bigger organisms points in the same direction, however. Kin selection, or nepotism as I prefer it called, is one of the cements of animal sociality.

Another cement of animal sociality is what Robert Trivers has called "reciprocal altruism." Again, the "altruism" is only apparent. You're not altruistic unless you get something out of it, which means you are not an altruist at all. I call it simply "reciprocity," an established term in social science. It is clear that reciprocity in humans is quite important too as a cement of sociality.

The third mechanism of sociality, which becomes increasingly important in more and more complex societies, is coercion, which consists of using the means of violence to extract surplus production in order to increase the fitness of the ruling class at the expense of everybody else. That's parasitism, indeed, intraspecific and intrasocietal parasitism, in biological terms. That becomes increasingly important with the rise of the state, and the more centrally organized a society becomes, the more coercion grows relative to nepotism and reciprocity. Coercion looms larger and larger as human societies become more complex and more stratified.

Let us get back to the family setting. What we call the human family is basically our species' way of being reproductively successful. There are basically two sets of relationships within the family: blood and marriage or, in biological terms, mating. The mating relationship is a pair bond between reproductive adults, whether officially married or not. All three mechanisms of sociality operate within the family: nepotism, reciprocity, and coercion. Nepotism operates in terms of relatives by blood; reciprocity works both with consanguine relatives and affines but is especially important between mates. Coercion, too, is important. The family is a micro-tyranny in which some people exercise more power than others. So all three of those factors operate together and, I would suggest, define the structure of a human family. The particular form that the human family takes is primarily determined by the particular form that the human pair bond takes. We are a particular kind of animal that developed a particular kind of mating arrangement. Mating arrangements in nature vary enormously, all the way from something close to promiscuity to rigid, lifelong monogamy, via polygyny. All human anatomical and physiological characteristics, in terms of sexual dimorphism and bimaturism, point to the fact that we have a tendency to be slightly polygynous. We are much less polygynous that some species, but we are clearly not the kind of species that mate once for life. We are something in between, but further away from the promiscuous end of the spectrum than from the monogamous end of the spectrum. We tend to form relatively stable, relatively long-lasting relationships in the human pair bond. All of those statements are totally meaningless except when the comparative method is used across species. Again, you have to take all that on faith, because I can't even begin to bring the animal evidence to bear on these arguments. The point is that it is absolutely impossible to understand the nature of the human pair bond except by comparison with other species.

The theory of parental investment, presented by Trivers, is highly relevant here. The theory of parental investment really asks the question: Why sexual reproduction? Now, this is a technical question, and it would take me at least 45 minutes to go into the biological arguments why sexual reproduction is so successful. Basically reproduction is explainable in terms of producing genetic diversity by reshuffling the genetic material. Sexual reproduction produces a much wider range of phenotypes on which environmental forces can select. Organisms that reproduce sexually are capable of much faster evolution than organisms that reproduce asexually, because asexual organisms have to rely on mutation for evolutionary change. Sexual organisms can adapt much more quickly to unstable environments. Sexual reproduction is one of the several mechanisms that allow organisms to track environmental change faster than what was possible before. Another mechanism, especially important in our species, is culture. Human culture is a bag of tricks of our species to accelerate our pace of adaptation to environmental change. So culture is to be seen as one in a series of quantum jumps, in speed of evolution and adaptability of species, as we go from simple to complex organisms.

Parental investment theory says simply that sexual reproduction is a device whereby the two morphs of the species (male and female) specialize in producing, respectively, a lot of very small and energetically cheap gametes (sperms) and a few relatively big and therefore expensive gametes (eggs). In a nutshell, eggs are expensive, sperms are cheap. That being the case, the reproductive ceiling on the female is invariably much lower than the reproductive ceiling on the male. The *mean* reproduction of males and females is always exactly the same, but the *range* of reproductive success is much greater for males than it is for females. Very simply, in human terms, it means that the woman is biologically incapable of having more than something like 15 or 20 children; 5 or 6 live births was about the practical ceiling that was feasible in most hunting-and-gathering societies. For a man the sky is virtually the limit. Some highly successful males in stratified, polygynous societies can look forward to having hundreds of children. Two consequences flow from that asymmetry in reproductive potential. One is that the female invests more in individual offspring than the male does. With a few exceptions (like seahorses, where the male does a great deal of nurturance), females furnish the bulk of parental investment. Another way of putting that is that males parasitize females. Why? Because each gets an equal genetic benefit from producing offspring, but the investment of the male is almost invariably considerably smaller than it is for the females.

The parasitism is relatively acute in the case of the human species because we are primates, which means that we have very slowly maturing young requiring a long gestation and lactation period, followed by a long infant dependency. We produce very few offspring, but therefore very costly offspring, who suffer relatively low mortality rates. We do so by having females who are producing the bulk of a very heavy parental investment. However, we are not the kind of species in which the male makes little or no parental contribution. We are a species where the male contribution is variable, but considerable on the average. There is no human society where it is expected that the male would make no parental investment. There are some species where the male contributes strictly nothing but his sperm. We are not such a species. Males are expected to contribute; but if you add up the energetic investment of a woman into an offspring and compare it to that of a man, you find that the bulk of the cost is borne by women in all human societies. However, you also find that the contribution of the male is seldom if ever completely superfluous. If there is a male pair-bonded to a woman, the two together can, on balance, be more successful in raising offspring than the mother alone could be. The human male makes an appreciable, valuable contribution, albeit a lower one than the female. Since there is an asymmetry in that parental contribution, the male has both an incentive and an opportunity to desert his mate, if, by doing so, he does not appreciably endanger his offspring's chance of survival; and, if he does, he increases his chances of producing more offspring with other mates. Desertion can, under some circumstances, become an attractive proposition to him. That pair bond is a successful formula to raise human offspring, but the arrangement is flexible, as in most features of human social organization. One can make some precise determinations of ecological conditions under which it becomes more or less advantageous for the male to desert or not desert the female, or to invest more or less into his offspring with one female, or to adopt mixed strategies of sticking with one female but having affairs on the side. Females, of course, evolve counter-strategies, such as cuckolding, whereby the husband can be fooled into investing in children of hers that are unrelated to the husband. So the model simply assumes that each sex is out to exploit the other; each party tries, consciously or not, to maximize its own fitness, and couples only stick together to the extent that the benefits are greater than the costs for both parties. If there is an asymmetry in that balance of cost-benefit for one of the two partners, that pair bond can be expected to break. Indeed, under many conditions, that's exactly what it does.

We're coming to this marvelous ethnographic description of Trinidad which Rodman gave us, all of which fits beautifully the kind of model that I am presenting here. Not only does his ethnographic description fit what I am talking about, but if you read just about any ethnography, you find that kinship systems across the world fit uncannily well this kind of very simple model of parental investment, nepotism, and kin selection. Throughout the world, despite considerable variety of cultural forms, cultural systems of norms surrounding marriage and kinship provide an extremely close fit to the predictions generated by that model. Let us take the case of the matrifocal family. Traditionally, the so-called matrifocal family has been associated with the lower class, especially with the proletariat of certain societies that are supposedly highly disorganized as a consequence of slavery, for example, the Caribbean pattern or the Afro-American pattern. In fact, you find this matrifocal pattern appearing at all class levels, in ecological settings that all fit the paradigm. You find that the less mandatory or the less beneficial paternal investment becomes, the more fragile the pair bond. If the male contributes very little or indeed is parasitic on the woman, then why shouldn't she kick the bum out? There are basically two types of situations that will lead to matrifocal families. Either the male has attractive mating opportunities with other females, or his contribution to the offspring is highly dispensable. In the first case, the matrifocality is primarily male-induced; in the second case, it is female-induced. The two factors may, of course, be simultaneously present, and reinforce each other. So why keep a pair bond? This is precisely the kind of situation that Rodman was describing to us.

Let us look at the proletariat of highly urbanized societies. You have a situation where the Social Security system and modern hygiene practically insure the survival of nearly all children. The mortality rate is somewhat higher for blacks than whites in the United States, but it is a difference of the order of 20 per 1,000, versus 50 per 1,000, which by human historical terms is a mere fraction of what it was in preindustrial societies. The black ghetto, proletarian male knows that, even if he deserts his woman, his children have a very high probability of physical survival. He also knows that, being in the status of a despised pariah, the probability of his children improving their life situation is infinitesimal. Under such circumstances it makes eminently good sense for the male to produce as many children as possible and to leave women holding the babies and go on welfare payments. It increases his fitness. It is a very rational choice, compared to the alternative of curtailing his reproduction and investing more heavily in fewer offspring. Their upward mobility is blocked in any case, but if they are assured physical survival, then his paternal investment is essentially wasted.

This is not the only scenario which will produce matrifocal families. Take a woman with higher education, let's say a divorced woman with a couple of kids getting a law degree, and setting herself up in a law practice. All of a sudden, she earns quite enough to raise her own children by herself, so why should she have a resident male, or why shouldn't she enter a lesbian relationship with another woman and set up a two-woman household? In other words, if the female has access to resources, which makes the presence of a male superfluous or relatively superfluous, then why have a male around except perhaps for sexual recreation?

The kind of framework derived from a strictly sociobiological model is highly reductionist. In the social sciences, reduction is a dirty word; in the natural sciences, it's the name of the game. When I say that you ought to be a reductionist, I am not saying that you ought to stop at reductionism but that you are to start out by going to the lowest level of analysis which seems to make sense, and see how much of the variance you explain. Having done that, you go on to the next higher level, trying to explain as much of the residual as you can at the next level. I am not foreclosing the possibility or value of doing higher levels of analysis. I am merely suggesting that some of us would find it profitable to start at the biological level and see how much it explains. I don't expect it to explain everything, but I do expect it to explain more parsimoniously a great many phenomena that we currently try to account for in needlessly complex, inconsistent, conflicting, and *ad hoc* ways.

Rodman gave us a body of observational data at the individual level. Now of course the model of reductionism that I am presenting is a model of individual actors behaving selfishly to maximize their inclusive fitness. So the test of this kind of model is best if you have individual data. Going into the field and doing painstaking observational, anthropological studies is very time-consuming and, in the nature of the case, it is best done at the micro-level. If you are going to observe people closely over a long period of time, you can only observe a limited number.

This is true also of animal behavior. Virtually no animal behaviorist publishes anything about any species of animal that hasn't been subjected to at least a couple of thousand hours of observation. So this is a problem which is not unique to human behavior. It is very painstaking to gather individual-level data. That's why the overwhelming majority of social scientists find it much cheaper, more convenient, and faster to use aggregate data, often collected by others, and to subject them to secondary analysis. I am not blaming them for doing that. It's not a wrong strategy. It's a cheap strategy of publication which therefore increases their fitness, so it makes good sense that they should follow that course.

Let me turn to Marta Tienda's work, which I think is very valuable in that she does accept the basic insight that the family unit is indeed the one that matters, if no longer as a unit of production, then certainly as a unit of consumption. She does have a good intuitive understanding of why relatives stick together, why they help each other, why parents support their children and vice versa. She understands at the gut level the mechanics of what I call nepotism and reciprocity. We all do, at the gut level. We have only become professionally deformed not to want to recognize it, but deep down, we know what it is all about. Obviously, the family, including the extended family, is the important unit of analysis to study occupational patterns. It's asinine to try to study an economy, particularly at the micro-level, without incorporating the individual in the context of his or her kin, that is, without treating the family group as a basic unit of economic analysis. Practically everybody who uses aggregate data apologizes for using aggregate data and for doing secondary analysis, and realizes that individual-level data and primary data collected by the researcher to test hypotheses of his own creation would be by far preferable. I do not think we even disagree as to methodology. We simply do the best we can with the available data and try to piece out of it as much as we can.

No doubt I have done considerable violence to the thoughts of the contributors of this volume in my ruthless attempt to reduce their thinking to mine. For this, I apologize, with the hope that they will take it in the good spirit in which is was meant. I strongly feel that, as social scientists, our main *raison d'être* is to be provocative. I think I have succeeded and I therefore close on a note of satisfaction.

8

A Selected Annotated Bibliography on Family and Work in Comparative Perspective

Merlin B. Brinkerhoff and Margaret I. Price

Constructing an annotated bibliography is not an easy task. It is impossible to be both exhaustive and selective, yet, readers desire some modicum of both characteristics. Choosing a fairly specific topic that combines three areas, comparative treatments of the interdependence of family and work, delimits the efforts somewhat; that is, references must treat both *family* and *work* and be *comparative*. Judgment enters into selection procedures when considering the degree to which both family and work must be evident (i.e., implications broadly hinted at versus actual data analyses linking the two systems) and when deciding how "comparative" is to be defined.

The work and family spheres are usually treated separately, in part because of specialization practices within and between disciplines. Psychologists Gutek, Nakamura, and Nieva (1981) argue in a survey of the area that the interdependence of family and work has received little research interest because family and work are "viewed as complementary spheres each belonging to one sex only. Work is for men; family responsibility and home maintenance is for women." We concur with this observation. Furthermore, we suggest that one of the consequences of the recent women's movement has been to point out this gap. Much of the recent research tying family and work together focuses on women's dual roles at home and in the economy (see, e.g., Fogarty, Rapoport, and Rapoport, 1971; Hoffman and Nye, 1974; Blake, 1974; Oppenheimer, 1979; Pleck, 1976; Safilios-Rothschild, 1976; Sawhill, 1977; UNESCO, 1978). (Most of these works fail to be comparative, even in the broadest sense.) Very little research investigates the implications of men's work roles for the family. (For some exceptions, see Mortimer, Hall, and Hill, 1978.) Similarly, familial implications of the work roles of children are ignored. (For an exception, see Rodgers and Standing, 1981.) Likewise, the impact of family roles on the work system remains largely unexplored. One of the major difficulties is the sheer breadth of the topic(s).

In a review essay, Osmond (1981) notes that comparative research on the family has grown exponentially in the past decade. She attributes this to rapid change in the family and the modification of women's roles. Her essay focuses on macro-level research because she contends it "appears to be more theoretically oriented and methodologically sophisticated than are studies of micro-social-psychological family processes" (Osmond 1981:169). Our bibliographic efforts do not lead to such a clear-cut conclusion. Much of the macro-level comparative work appears broad and illustrative. Much of it is almost armchair comparative analysis, which is only suggestive of hypotheses, at best, that is, it does not attempt to test empirical propositions. Of course, many of these macro-level sources merit attention (see, e.g., Boulding, 1976; Cancian, Goodman, and Smith, 1978).

Cogswell and Sussman (1972:1) define "comparative" as inclusive of five approaches: (1) "collection of data in two or more societies . . . ; (2) replication in one or more societies of studies previously completed in other societies; (3) secondary analysis . . . ; (4) comparison and synthesis of findings in published studies for two or more societies or cultures . . . ; and (5) placing the findings of one-society investigations in the context of other studies." Where we would like to be somewhat more restrictive in our usage of the term, we have included some of each of these types of studies in our bibliographic entries. We have, however, attempted to minimize including those that are merely illustrative, such as textbooks (see, e.g., Nimkoff, 1965), or Cogswell and Sussman's fifth type. While we would ideally like to restrict ourselves to their first type, there would be very few studies to include.

How did we arrive at these bibliographic sources? Three different computer searches were undertaken, using such key words as family, marital, sex role, gender, dual career, two career, work, employment, labor-force participation, industrialization, cross-cultural, cross-national, and comparative. Many of the sources that turned up following this procedure were not applicable, that is, they incorporated one or two, but not all three, of the major topics. Many computer retrieval systems include only key words found in the titles of articles or books, which are often misleading. The bulk of the bibliographic sources that were included were ferreted out only through diligent digging in the library. From those sources finally discovered, the compilers were forced to be selective. For example, studies that cursorily treated work as participation in a subsistence economy and its effect on the family are omitted. A large number of these studies are based on Murdoch's ethnographic data in the HARF (Human Area Relations Files). We were also somewhat limited by library resources; for example, it was nearly impossible to acquire papers read at conferences for inspection to see if they were appropriate. In short, no pretensions of exhaustiveness are suggested; it is hoped that those works selected for annotation will prove useful and will lead to additional valuable sources.

We were somewhat torn between presenting the annotated bibliography alphabetically or thematically, settling on the latter, being fully cognizant that there is considerable ambiguity. Of course, some sources could and should be included under more than one of the following six categories in which they have been placed: (1) Demographic Factors and Women's Work and Family Roles; (2) Sexual Stratification: Power, Division of Labor, and Life Satisfactions; (3) Societal Development and Women's Roles; (4) Dual Careers: Role Compatibility; (5) Policies and Services: Their Relationships to Women's Roles in Family and Work; and (6) Family Influences on Work Aspirations and Involvement. It is hoped that the classification will help more than hinder your use of the annotated bibliography.

Selective Annotated Bibliography

Demographic Factors and Women's Work and Family Roles

de Boer, Connie
    1977   "The polls: Women at work." The Public Opinion Quarterly 41(2):268–277.
        This article presents compilations of data gathered by Gallup International in 70 countries to determine whether the feminist movement had changed public attitudes toward women in society and at work. Public opinion data concerning changes in the opportunity structure, attitudes toward working mothers, and the suitability of women for certain occupations are presented.

Fogarty, Michael Patrick, Rhonda Rapoport, and Robert Rapoport
  1971   Sex, Career, and Family: Including an International Re-
          view of Women's Roles. London: George Allen and Un-
          win.
          This study deals with many complex problems surrounding
          family and work. Information on the experiences of Eastern
          Europe and Western countries is included. Topics covered
          in this book are: the special problem of women's promotion
          to top jobs; an international review of experience; studies
          of family and work careers and occupational prospects.

Michel, Andrée (ed.)
  1971   Family Issues of Employed Women in Europe and Amer-
          ica. Atlantic Highlands, N.J.: Humanities Press.
          This volume contains articles that focus on the problem of
          working women in Europe and America in relation to their
          family involvement. Because each contributor examines only
          one society, it is necessary for readers to analyze the ma-
          terial and to prepare their own cross-national comparisons.

Myrdal, Alva, and Viola Klein
  1956   Women's Two Roles: Home and Work. London: Rou-
          tledge and Kegan Paul.
          This book examines the social changes and needs accom-
          panying the increasing employment of women outside the
          home in advanced Western societies. One conclusion de-
          rived from the study is that even though the increased em-
          ployment of women is not a temporary phenomenon, there
          has been no fundamental reorganization of society in order
          to make this development beneficial to all concerned. The
          economic and psychological implications of women's in-
          creased employment are discussed, as well as suggestions
          for the reorganization of family life.

Papanek, Hanna
  1973   "Men, women, and work: Reflections on the two-person
          career." American Journal of Sociology 78:852–872.
          This article is concerned with aspects of American wom-
          en's "vicarious achievement" through their husbands' jobs
          in a special combination of roles called the "two-person
          single career." The two-person single career is prevalent
          where an explicit ideology of educational equality between
          the sexes conflicts with an implicit inequality of occupa-

tional access, as in American society. A social control mechanism that channels the occupational aspirations of educated women into the noncompetitive "two-person career" results from this conflict. The American situation is contrasted with information on the kinds of education and training women in Pakistan, Bangladesh, and India receive for work.

Ross, Aileen D.
1977   "Some comments on the home roles of businesswomen in India, Australia, and Canada." Journal of Comparative Family Studies 8(3):327–340.
Using interview data from Australia, India, and Canada, this study focuses on the conflict entailed in having to deal with the demanding work of a career and still carry on the roles of wife, household manager, and possibly mother. The article describes some of the role conflicts and problems that working couples encounter. For example, because of pressures and frustration, the wife may find it difficult to attain satisfaction from either home or work. This article provides suggestions from three areas in which husbands and their working wives must adjust, the realms of authority, responsibility, and their personal relations.

Sexual Stratification: Power, Division of Labor, and Life Satisfactions

Ankarloo, Bengt
1979   "Argriculture and women's work: Directions of change in the West, 1700–1900." Journal of Family History 4(2):111–120.
This article focuses on the specific issues involved in women's work and family organization during the transition from a feudal to a capitalist mode of production within agriculture and from rural to urban-industrial patterns of life. Information from Scandinavia, Europe, and the United States is presented and discussed.

Boserup, Ester
1970   Women's Role in Economic Development. London: George Allen and Unwin.
This volume focuses on the new sexual division of labor patterns that emerge along with economic and social devel-

opment. The author identifies and explains the significance of these patterns from the point of view of development policies. Data from national censuses, from official statistics, and from special surveys provide the basis for the overview and comparison of female employment patterns in various world regions. The book is divided into three sections: the village, the town, and transition from village to town. The author concludes that while development and urbanization increase the employment rate of women, it is important to provide new educational programs to reduce the productivity gap between male and female labor and to allow women to fit into their new way of life. Another effect of increasing female education and productivity may be the lowering of the birth rate.

Branca, Patricia

1975   "A new perspective on women's work: A comparative typology." Journal of Social History 9(2):129–153.

In this article the author suggests a more complex approach to the study of women's work. She proposes the use of a multigeographical analysis from which three conclusions emerge: (1) multigeographical analysis illuminates the differences between the work experiences of single women compared to those of married women; (2) it illustrates women's ability to initiate change in work roles even in traditional settings; (3) it emphasizes the need to refocus the stages of women's work history, placing greater stress on the late nineteenth and twentieth centuries, rather than on the classic period of industrialization. Examples from different societies, time periods, and types of work organization are used to illustrate the value of the dual geographical approach.

Brinkerhoff, Merlin B., and Victor Castillo-Vales

1983   "Family happiness and life satisfactions: Some comparative explorations from two Mexican and Canadian samples." Revista Mexicana de Sociologia.

Survey data comparing 464 couples from a western Canadian city and 264 couples from a southeastern Mexican community illustrated both differences and similarities in life satisfactions, marital happiness, etc. Mexican wives reported lower marital/familial satisfaction; both Canadian spouses were happier when the wife worked, while Mexican working wives were more dissatisfied; socioeconomic status is more strongly related to life and marital satisfaction in Mexico than in Canada. Overall, many of the results remain somewhat inconclusive.

Brinkerhoff, Merlin B., and Eugen Lupri
1983   "Conjugal power and family relationship: Some theoretical and methodological issues." Pp. 202–219 in K. Ishwaran (ed.), The Canadian Family. Revised Edition. Toronto: Gage Publishing.

Interviews of both husbands and wives in a western Canadian city are employed to critically evaluate familial power studies based on decision-making in various societies. Intra-couple analyses shows spouses are incongruent on questions of who makes the decisions. Decision-making items must be examined in terms of the frequency with which a specific decision is made as well as the importance of the decision. Their data show that wives may appear powerful because they make more decisions but that the decisions are of relatively low importance to the dyad.

Cooney, Rosemary Santana
1975   "Female professional work opportunities: A cross-national study." Demography 12:107–120.

Utilizing census data from European countries, the United States, Canada, Australia, and New Zealand, this study examines the interrelationship of economic and demographic variables affecting female participation and sexual equality within the professional sector of the labor force. Findings indicate that females' being employed in the professions is positively related to economic development. However, the rate of professional participation is not significantly associated with greater sexual equality within the professional sector. Economic factors that affect the female participation rate were found to be distinct from structural factors, such as economic growth rate and working-age male deficiency, influencing sexual equality within the professional sector. It implies for the family that as economic development and extrafamilial paid employment increases, there is an increase in economic independence and egalitarianism between spouses.

Gandhi, Madhu M.
   1980   ''Comparative occupational patterns among women in the
            United States and India.'' The Journal of Family Welfare
            27(1):46–58.
            Utilizing data from the Demographic Yearbooks and other
            published sources, this article examines and compares the
            occupational patterns among women in a developing nation
            and an industrialized nation, India and the United States.
            Comparisons are made of the economically active popula-
            tions by sex and age, by urban and rural residence, by in-
            dustry, and by marital status. The author predicts that par-
            ticipation of women in the labor force will increase in both
            countries in the future. The following suggestions are put
            forward in order to aid this development: greater opportu-
            nity for education and jobs; better wages and promotional
            avenues, and better child-care centers for working mothers.

Haavio-Mannila, Elina
   1971   ''Convergences between East and West: Tradition and
            modernity in sex roles in Sweden, Finland, and the Soviet
            Union.'' Acta Sociologica 14(1–2):114–125.
            This article focuses on the influence of economic, ideolog-
            ical, and historical factors on sex roles in Sweden, Finland,
            and the Soviet Union. It concludes that cross-cultural vari-
            ation in sex roles is connected with the time and rate of
            technological development. It deduces that because the pro-
            portion of employed women in Sweden has increased since
            1960, whereas an opposite trend may emerge in the Soviet
            Union, a convergence of communist and capitalist patterns
            of women's labor-force participation may result. The study
            also describes how little change has occurred within the
            familial division of labor, compared to the changes in the
            economic role of women generally in these countries. Fin-
            land is described as having a favorable base for women's
            emancipation. However, a shortage of child-care facilities
            requires a change in the state's or the employer's attitude
            toward this problem.

Hutter, Mark
   1981   The Changing Family: Comparative Perspectives. New
            York: John Wiley and Sons.
            This exceptional text brings together cross-cultural and his-

torical evidence of the effects of patriarchy on the male-female relationships and ultimately on the family. Basically, the author argues that over time a dichotomization of the private and public spheres (privatization of the family) has resulted in differential involvement of men and women in the worlds of work and household with concomitant variations in power, prestige, and authority. The book provides an excellent literature review, because it presents secondary data as well as many case analyses with exemplars. Special attention should be paid to chapters 9, ("Sex Roles in Changing Societies") and 10 ("Marital Relationships: The World of Work and the World of the Home"). The former examines both "shifting" and "plowing" agricultural economies with case studies of Iran and Africa. The discussion on sex roles in "industrialized societies" focuses on Sweden with its progressive welfare system, Israel with the kibbutzim from the West, and Russia representing eastern countries. Chapter 10 investigates the advent of industrialization with the increasing dichotomization between the public and private spheres. The author contends that status and treatment have varied by involvement in the economic sphere. The family has ceased to be the economic unit of society. Women's increased participation in the labor force has found them in inferior occupational positions.

Safilios-Rothschild, Constantina
1971   "A cross-cultural examination of women's marital, educational, and occupational options." Acta Sociologica 14:96–113.

Women's options are examined in 23 countries, which are categorized into four groupings based on the gross national product as an indicator of level of development. Women's roles in family and work are investigated along such dimensions as marital status, employment status, and educational or professional preparation. The author concludes that options vary for different levels of development. Women in societies at medium levels of development appear to have greater options to remain single, work, work after marriage, enroll in college, and work at masculine occupations than women in societies at low or high levels of development.

United Nations Department of Economic and Social Affairs
  1973   Report of the Interregional Meeting of Experts on the In-
            tegration of Women in Development. United Nations Head-
            quarters 19–28 June 1972. New York: United Nations.
            Using information from studies done in five countries, this
            source reports on broad policy measures regarding wom-
            en's role in economic and social development. It is noted
            that at low levels of economic development human effort is
            absorbed mostly by two activities, homemaking and agri-
            culture. To increase women's involvement it would be nec-
            essary to tranform traditional duties and greatly expand new
            activities. Some of the topics discussed are women's role
            in rural societies, women in small-scale business, employ-
            ment of women in modern industries, employment of women
            with family responsibilities, women's education in relation
            to their participation in economic life and the development
            process, and approaches to improving the integration of
            women in development.

Societal Development and Women's Roles

Buric, Olivera, and Andjelka Zečević
  1967   "Family authority, marital satisfaction, and the social net-
            work in Yugoslavia." Journal of Marriage and the Family
            29(2):325–336.
            This study focuses on the relationship between family in-
            teractions and the social network. Data gathered in Yugo-
            slavia are compared to data from similar studies done in
            Greece, France, and the United States. Findings suggest that
            Greek and Yugoslavian men having authoritative positions
            at work (particularly those with higher education) have more
            egalitarian relations in their families. By contrast, in France
            and the United States there was a positive relationship be-
            tween the social position of the husband and his authority
            in the family. Contrary to findings on the other countries,
            the Yugoslavian data showed that the wife's marital satis-
            faction was negatively correlated with family status. The
            wife's employment, education, and family ideology affect
            this relationship.

Collver, Andrew, and Eleanor Langlois
  1962   "The female labor force in metropolitan areas: An inter-

national comparison.'' Economic Development and Cultural Changes 10:367–385.

In a study covering 38 developed and underdeveloped countries, census data are used to analyze the relationship of female metropolitan labor-force activity and economic development. General trends of development of a modern women's labor force, some effects of this development, and some sources of resistance to it are considered. The results suggest that some seemingly obvious relationships between female metropolitan labor-force participation and the level of economic development do not hold up under scrutiny. Of concern to family and work studies is the conclusion that the indirect effects of the increased size and productivity of the female labor force, such as reduced fertility, may be as important as benefits from the increase in gross national product.

Cromwell, R. E., R. Corrales, and P. M. Torsiello
1973   ''Normative patterns of marital decision-making power and influence in Mexico and the United States: A partial test of resource and ideology theory.'' International Journal of Comparative Family Studies 4:177–196.

Utilizing self-reports from selected cross-cultural interviews, this study examines normative patterns of marital decision-making power and influence across and within cultures. Findings suggest that there is a trend toward egalitarianism in both Mexico and the United States. In both societies the impact of resources and ideology toward greater wife power is most evident among white-collar groups. For Mexican blue-collar and campesino groups, the trend toward egalitarianism is clear but less pronounced. Role ambiguity, marital dissatisfaction, and higher divorce rates are predicted as possible outcomes (especially in Mexico) in the difficult transition stage when sex roles are changing.

Cunningham, Isabella C.M., and Robert T. Green
1979   ''Working wives in the United States and Venezuela: A cross-national study of decision-making.'' International Journal of Comparative Family Studies 10(1):67–80.

This article compares samples from Houston, Texas, and Valencia, Venezuela. Purchasing decisions and husband-and-wife decision-making roles in middle-class families with employed and nonemployed wives are compared. Findings suggest that the wife's employment has a pronounced effect on family roles. While there were few differences between middle-class U.S. and Venezuelan working wives, differences exist between nonworking wives in the two countries, e.g., nonworking U.S. wives exhibited more participation in purchasing decisions than the Venezuelan nonworking wives. The decision-making role of the Venezuelan working wife was similar to her U.S. counterpart. The authors conclude that a wife's employment appears to produce a significant change in the family structure of middle-class Venezuelans.

Das, Man Singh, and Clinton J. Jesser (eds.)
  1980   The Family in Latin American. New Delhi: Vikas Publishing House.
          This collection of original papers does not treat the work system systematically, but it merits some consideration because it includes the papers on Uruguay, Brazil, Costa Rica, and Ecuador. Nine countries are presented. For the most part, labor-force characteristics (e.g., occupation of household head, percent economically active, industrial sector), economic evolution, and types of agricultural activities are examined in light of family characteristics. The reader must make most cross-societal comparisons, although the introductory and summary chapters make a modest attempt.

Haavio-Mannila, Elina
  1969   "The position of Finnish women: Regional and cross-national comparison." Journal of Marriage and the Family 3l(May):339–347.
          Utilizing census and interview data, sex-role attitudes and behavior in Finland are compared with the countries of Sweden, Norway, Denmark, and the Soviet Union. Finnish women are found to be more economically active than women in nonsocialist countries. They also have high educational achievement and are well represented in parliament. Although in formal respects Finnish women are more independent and emancipated in their behavior than women in other Scandinavian countries, informal behavior and attitudes toward women's power in society and the family are more traditional.

Kandel, Denise B., and Gerald S. Lesser
1972   "Marital decision-making in America and Danish urban families: A research note."Journal of Marriage and the Family 34 (February):134–138.
        Utilizing data from a larger cross-cultural study, this research tests resource theory on American and Danish urban families. The authors conclude that while socioeconomic resources are important, they provide not only financial and status rewards but also the opportunity to learn interpersonal and decision-making skills outside the family. These skills may be more relevant to the exercise of family power than the socioeconomic resources themselves.

Kurian, George, and Ratna Ghosh (eds.)
1981   Women in the Family and the Economy: An International Comparative Survey. Westport, Conn.: Greenwood Press.
        The purpose of this volume is to explore appropriate indicators and identify similarities and differences related to the effects of family and employment patterns. Although the burden of comparative integration is left to the reader, generalizations concerning women in the family and the economy emerge from the chapters. These generalizations include: sex-segregation in the work force is a universal phenomenon; economic strength is related to increased power in the home for women and is therefore related to women's status; women's employment means double work for them; ideology makes a difference, yet countries with egalitarian philosophies have not prevented sex segregation and overwork for women; social and structural changes produced by modernization and egalitarian ideologies have not been accompanied by parallel changes in values and attitudes in all aspects.

Lupri, Eugen
1969   "Contemporary authority patterns in the West German family: A study in cross-national validation."Journal of Marriage and the Family 3l(1):134–144.
        The author tests the cross-national validity of the resource theory of marital power and reports a series of tests of the comparative participation by husband and wife in the external system (work force) to determine the balance of power in the internal system (home). Data from samples of urban

and rural West German families yielded results similar to previous cross-cultural studies, that is, comparative participation in the external system significantly affects a spouse's internal power position.

Michel, Andrée
    1970   "Working wives and family interaction in French and American families."International Journal of Comparative Sociology 11(June):157–165.

    Sample data of French couples are compared to American survey data in order to examine the interrelationships between wife's employment, the decision-making process, household-task performance, and family-planning. Findings support resource theory in which the wife's employment increases her familial power and decreases household task performance. The employed wife shares more in family decisions and succeeds more often than nonemployed wives in having the desired number of children.

Rainwater, Lee
    1979   "Mother's contribution to the family money economy in Europe and the United States."Journal of Family History 4(2):198–211.

    This article discusses the contribution of mothers, both as wives and as single heads of household, to family income in Europe and the United States. Questions central to this study are whether women are becoming full partners in marriage through the production of family income and whether the increased viability of women's labor-market roles portends a sharp increase in the number of mother-headed families. Conclusions vary according to the society and the type and class of families involved. Two major transformations in women's roles are suggested by the data; one involves the simultaneous participation by most women in both childrearing and work roles, the other suggests the deepening and intensification of work roles and identities.

Rodman, Hyman
    1967   "Marital power in France, Greece, Yugoslavia, and the United States: A cross-national discussion." Journal of Marriage and the Family 29:320–324.

    Utilizing data from previous studies, the author examines the power structure in the marital relationship for four countries. Findings suggest that in the United States and France there are positive relationships between a husband's authority score and his education, occupation, and income. In Greece and Yugoslavia this relationship is negatively correlated. The theory of resources in cultural context is discussed as a possible explanation for the contradictory findings.

1972   "Marital power and the theory of resources in cultural context." In E. Lupri and G. Luschen (eds.), Comparative Perspectives on Marriage and the Family. Special Issue, International Journal of Comparative Family Studies (3):50–69.

This article is an extension of an earlier study (Rodman, 1967) on the topic of marital power in cross-cultural context. The author summarizes several methodological issues and data on marital power and formulates a general theoretical explanation. Data from several cultures measuring education, occupation, and income, as these variables relate to power structure, suggest that normative definitions about who should have power probably influences who actually has power. They also influence the effect that resources have on power. Two conflicting tendencies lead Rodman to develop and test the "theory of resources in cultural context" to account for the cross-cultural differences in the distribution of marital power.

Safilios-Rothschild, Constantina
1967   "A comparison of power structure and marital satisfaction in urban Greek and French families." Journal of Marriage and the Family 29(2):345–352.

The responses of Greek and French wives provide the data base for this study of the relationship between the power structure and marital satisfaction. Findings indicate that in Greece, in contrast to France and other highly industrialized countries, a husband's familial authority is increased when he has a high education, a prestigious occupation, and a high salary. Marital satisfaction results show that Greek trends are similar to more industrialized countries.

Schlegel, Alice (ed.)
1977   Sexual Stratification: A Cross-cultural View. New York: Columbia University Press.

This book contains a collection of articles that examine sexual equality or inequality and the conditions under which they arise. Sexual stratification and sex roles in the home, workplace, and religion are discussed. Each author has chosen a different society in which to study sex roles. Cross-cultural comparison must therefore be done by the reader.

Semyonov, Moshe
  1980   "The social context of women's labor force participation: A comparative analysis."American Journal of Sociology 86(3):534–550.
  Literature pertaining to the relationship between the social system and women's labor-force participation is discussed. The article also examines whether women's labor-force participation is related to and can be viewed as an aspect of social stratification. Finally, it analyses the social consequences of female work-force participation. Labor-force statistics from 61 societies yielded the following conclusions: female labor-force participation is positively related to the level of economic development and divorce rate; it is negatively related to fertility and income inequality. The shape of the stratification system influences the integration of women into the labor market, and this integration results in occupational discrimination. Stratification is found to have the most significant effect on women's labor-force participation.

Silverman, William, and Reuben Hill
  1967   "Task allocation in marriage in the United States and Belgium." Journal of Marriage and the Family 29(May):353–360.
  This investigation compares urban family task allocation in America and Belgium to determine whether explanations for family behavior derived from a Detroit-based study are valid when compared to data from Louvain, Belgium. It is concluded that while task performance of husbands and wives is quite similar in the two samples, the explanation for variation in the task-allocation structure differs sharply. Of the three theories examined, the best theory for explaining the variations is found to be family development theory. This theory puts availability theory into time perspective by showing how husband and wife availability for task assign-

ments may vary according to the stage in the family cycle and whether one or both spouses are employed.

Dual Careers: Role Compatibility

Berent, Jerzy
1970   "Some demographic aspects of female employment in Eastern Europe and the USSR." International Labour Review 101(2):175–192.

Using 1950 and 1960 census data, this author examines the economic significance of female employment in Eastern Europe and the Soviet Union since the Second World War. Demographic factors considered are: age, marital status, rural or urban residence, and the number of dependent children. He concludes that it may be difficult to sustain the high level of female employment in Eastern Europe because of the effect of urbanization and the falling birth rate. However, future policies governing the employment of women in these countries may become more flexible.

Birdsall,Nancy
1976   "Women and population studies." Signs: Journal of Women in Culture and Society 1(3):699–712.

This article examines the effect of changes in women's roles, status, employment, and education on fertility and the use of contraception. These issues are discussed and illustrated by examples taken from several different societies. One major conclusion is that female employment is not the sole factor that determines fertility differentials; there is evidence to suggest that the higher the wife's work status, the greater her interest in limiting her fertility.

Boyd, Monica
1973   "Occupational mobility and fertility in metropolitan Latin America." Demography 10(February):1–18.

Using data obtained from fertility surveys conducted in five cities in Latin America, the relationship between fertility and husband's occupational mobility is examined. With the exception of Mexico City, it is concluded that career mobility does not account for differential fertility. Economic development appears to stimulate real and perceived opportunities for advancement, as well as a rationalistic value structure stressing the individual's control over the environment, including fertility and mobility. In addition to the study results, there is a discussion concerning the problems with social mobility-fertility research, including a critique of the theory and methodology and suggestions for future research.

Concepción, Mercedes B.
  1974   "Female labor force participation and fertility." International Labour Review 109(5–6):503–517.
          This article presents census and survey data to analyze the relationship between labor-force participation and fertility in a number of Asian countries. Rural and urban as well as traditional and modern comparisons are examined. It also explores the extent to which the roles of mother and worker are incompatible and how this incompatibility affects fertility. The author concludes that because there is a wider separation of work and family roles among employed women in the urban metropolis, this group experiences lower fertility. A greater compatibility of work and family roles in the rural areas results in labor-force participation having little effect on fertility.

Elizaga, Juan C.
  1974   "The participation of women in the labor force of Latin America: Fertility and other factors." International Labour Review 109(5–6):519–538.
          Factors such as marital status, education, level of development, and fertility are examined in order to account for the low rate of female labor-force participation in Latin America. Conclusions, derived from census data, are that female participation rates would increase with improved educational standards, structural and economic modernization, and a reduction in family size.

Hass, Paula H.
  1972   "Maternal role incompatibility and fertility in urban Latin America." Journal of Social Issues 28(2):111–127.
          Based on fertility surveys conducted in seven Latin American cities, this study examines the proposition that the crucial variable determining the relationship between maternal employment and fertility may be the extent of incompatibility between joint occupancy of the roles of mother and

worker. Although inconsistent findings prevented a firm conclusion on the relationship between role incompatibility and fertility, there are recurring patterns. It is argued that longitudinal data on employment histories, general domestic and nondomestic activities, reproductive histories, and clinical information on husbands' and wives' fecundity are necessary to give a more accurate picture of underlying causal relationships.

Horna, Jarmila L. A.
1977   "Women in East European socialist countries." Pp. 137–150 in Patricia Marchak (ed.), The Working Sexes. Vancouver: Institute of Industrial Relations.
Utilizing both official statistical and survey data from studies of Czechoslovakia, Poland, and the Soviet Union, this author examines the theoretical concept of women's triple role (i.e., mother-worker-citizen) as defined by sociologists and ideologues in European socialist countries. Comparison yields differences both within and between countries, especially in terms of overall labor-force participation, occupational segregation, decision-making power, division of housework, and childrearing practices.

Kasadara, John D.
1971   "Economic structure and fertility: A comparative analysis." Demography 8(August):307–317.
Using census data from 50 countries, this study focuses on the relationship between the economic structure of populations and fertility levels. The structural components examined for their effect on the nation's population, the crude birth rate, and the child-women ratio include the percentage of females active in the nonagricultural labor force and the percentage of the population under age 15 who are active in the labor force. Some of the inferences derived from the study are that fertility rates are influenced by the degree to which females are employed for a wage or salary and the degree to which children are economically active in the population. These factors are found to vary closely with levels of urbanization, industrialization, and education. Governments wishing lower fertility rates should make employment opportunities available to women and limit the economic contribution that children can make.

Kronick, Jane C., and Jane Lieberthal
    1976   "Predictors of cross-cultural variation in the percentage of
                women employed in Europe." International Journal of
                Comparative Sociology 17(1–2):92–96.
                This study utilizes data from 26 countries obtained from the
                1972 Statistical Yearbook of the United Nations and the 1972
                Yearbook of Labor Statistics. It examines the cross-cultural
                variation in the employment of women in relation to differ-
                ences in the occupational structure, the growth rate of the
                economy, unemployment, urbanization, density, level of
                living, fertility, and divorce rates. Conclusions derived from
                the study suggest that when clear normative support for fe-
                male employment (as in Eastern European nations) is pre-
                sent, economic variables account for variation in employ-
                ment among nations. Without clear normative support for
                employment (as in Western European nations), variables
                measuring individual life conditions and decisions, in par-
                ticular levels of living and fertility, become important in
                accounting for variation in employment among nations.
                Considerable attention needs to be directed toward the gen-
                eral normative values underlying the culture as a determi-
                nant of the explanatory power of individual behavior as op-
                posed to structural differences in the societies.

Lupri, Eugen, and Gladys Symons
    1982   "The emerging symmetrical family: Fact or fiction? A cross-
                national analysis." International Journal of Comparative
                Sociology 23(3–4):221–236.
                Utilizing cross-national data on occupational segregation and
                income differences by sex, the authors review and chal-
                lenge Young and Willmott's (1975) thesis, which predicts
                the symmetrical family as a future modal type. They con-
                clude that the Young and Willmott research ignored the
                present family organization as a locus of gender inequality
                and that until structural changes occur in the division of la-
                bor, both in the home and in the economy, the symmetrical
                family is unlikely to evolve in either capitalist or socialist
                countries.

Musgrove, Philip
    1980   "Household size and composition, employment, and pov-
                erty in urban Latin America." Economic Development and
                Cultural Change 28(2):249–266.

This study seeks to separate the effects of household size, family composition, and the employment status of household members on relative poverty in ten cities in five Andean countries. Results from the household budget surveys suggest that the relationship between low wages, unemployment, and poverty is not as strong as expected. Instead, poverty is more strongly related to large household size and low overall employment rates, both of which reflect large numbers of children per adult member. Slower population growth could improve welfare and also make it easier to concentrate on raising labor productivity.

Solien, N. L.
1963   "Family organization in five types of migratory wage labor." American Anthropologist 63:1264–1280.
Utilizing examples from various societies, this study examines the type of migration (where members regularly leave home to obtain money or goods) and the effects it has on the family institution. The main conclusion is that migrancy will be reflected in the social organization in different ways, depending on the nature of the sociocultural system affected, as well as on the type of migrancy itself.

Stycos, J. M., and R. H. Weller
1967   "Female working roles and fertility." Demography 4:210–217.
This study examines the relationship between female employment status and fertility utilizing survey data gathered in Turkey in 1963. Literature concerned with female employment and fertility in both developed and developing societies is discussed. The authors conclude that only as the female-working role approaches incompatibility with the wife-and-mother role does the relation between fertility and employment emerge. Whether fertility is primarily a cause or effect of employment may depend eventually on the availability of birth control technology.

Sussman, Marvin B., and Betty E. Cogswell (eds.)
1972   Cross-national Family Research. Leiden: E. J. Brill.
This book contains 12 chapters plus an introductory and concluding chapter by the editors. Although mainly concerned with comparative family research, selected chapters treat the relationships of the family and work systems, for

example, Kabsegyere's contribution "Family Life and Economic Change in Uganda." By and large, family and not work is the focus of most chapters. All the papers reported are comparative when broadly defined, that is, some are one-shot case studies making implicit comparisons with other societies, while others present data collected from more than one society. The concluding chapter delineates selected problems associated with cross-national research and its outcomes.

United Nations Department of Economic and Social Affairs
    1975   Status of Women and Family Planning: Report of the Special Rapporteur, Appointed by the Economic and Social Councils Under Resolution 1326. New York: United Nations.

Utilizing data from many sources and countries, this study examines the relationship between reproductive behavior and the exercise of women's rights in the family and in society. It concludes with the following suggestions: (1) Family planning offers obvious benefits to women as individuals, especially with regard to their health, education, or employment and their roles in family and public life. Women must be made aware of alternative roles. (2) The status of women (especially their educational level, the extent to which they are employed and the nature of their employment or occupation, and their participation in family, community, and national life) has an influence on family size and on the success of family-planning programs. High fertility is especially prevalent in the world's rural areas and urban slums. (3) Current and future population growth, structure, and distribution have serious implications both for development and for the advancement of women in a great number of countries. Family-planning programs themselves cannot fully succeed without improvements in the condition of women.

Vigderhous, Gideon, and Gideon Fishman
    1977   "Socioeconomic determinants of female suicide rates: A cross-national comparison."International Review of Modern Sociology 7(2):199–211.

This study focuses on the relationship of female suicide rates and various structural changes in women's roles in modern society. An analysis of cross-cultural data resulted in the conclusion that there is no significant relationship between women's changing occupational status and the increase in female suicide rates. Instead professional or occupational incompatibility, which produces a high level of divorce and therefore familial disintegration, is the most significant factor in suicide rates. A lower birth rate, resulting in smaller nuclear families, is also found to contribute to a higher divorce rate.

Weller, R. H.
   1971   "The impact of employment upon fertility," in Andrée Michel (ed.), Family Issues of Employed Women in Europe and America. Leiden: E. J. Brill.
   In this article a lengthy review of the research literature, including cross-cultural studies on female labor-force participation and fertility, is presented. Conclusions derived from these studies are that the relationship between female labor-force participation and fertility is produced by several causal relationships that will vary according to the predominant nature of female employment, the social, psychological, and economic conditions surrounding this employment, and whether we are considering desired, cumulative, or completed fertility. The overall goal of programs designed to lower fertility should stress certain features and minimize others and thus create alternative modes of behavior in such a way that the worker is motivated to restrict her fertility to a lower level than would otherwise be the case.

Youssef, Nadia H.
   1972   "Differential labor force participation of women in Latin America and Middle Eastern countries: The influence of family characteristics." Social Forces 51(2):135–153.
   Utilizing national census data from Chile, Egypt, Morocco, and Pakistan, the author examines the influence of marital and fertility characteristics on the female labor-force rates and tests their relative importance in explaining the significant differential that has been shown to exist in women's nonagricultural employment rates between Latin American and Middle Eastern countries. She concludes that women's labor-force participation is not merely a function of a society's marital and fertility conditions but an interaction of these variables with the social organization. She found that struc-

tures of control and institutional mechanisms strongly affect women's labor-force participation.

Policies and Services: Their Relationships to Women's Roles in Family and Work

Cook, Alice H.
1975   "The working mother: A survey of problems and programs in nine countries." Ithaca, N.Y.: New York State School of Industrial and Labor Relations, Cornell University.

Utilizing data collected in nine countries, the author examines (1) the working conditions of employed mothers, (2) national policies that might encourage or discourage their working, and (3) voluntary and state programs organized to offer them support. The most fundamental difference in the approach to the problems of working women was found to exist between communist and noncommunist countries because of their distinct policies and values. It is suggested that since women carry the double burden of home and child care, society could provide accommodations that may pay off in productive terms and in reward to women as individuals.

International Labour Office
1962a   "Discrimination in employment or occupation on the basis of marital status." International Labour Review 85:262–282.

The subject of marital status as a basis for discrimination in employment and occupation is examined by survey data from 60 countries. Findings suggest that although there is a general tendency toward nondiscrimination, the problem of discrimination against women in the world of work requires continued attention. Discrimination appears to be rare in societies where equality between the sexes has been achieved in all spheres of public and private life. Political and social ideology, as well as national custom, play an important part in the pattern of discrimination.

1962b   "Discrimination in employment or occupation on the basis of marital status, II." International Labour Review 85:368–389.

The problem of maternity in relation to the employment of

married women is cited as an important issue in many countries. Other issues discussed in this article are the nature of the work as far as suitability for married women is concerned, the efficiency and availability of married women as workers, and safety and health considerations. Measures that have been used to combat discrimination and promote the employment of married women are also described. It is suggested that the problems for both the employed mothers and their families must be confronted and that an educational effort to ensure a social climate and attitudes that will be conducive to nondiscriminatory policies and practices is necessary.

1980   Work and Family Life: The Role of the Social Infrastructure in Eastern European Countries. Geneva.

Based on national monographs on Czechoslovakia, the German Democratic Republic, Hungary, Poland, and the Soviet Union, this study examines the extent to which the social infrastructure (i.e., measures in accordance with the principles laid down in the Recommendation on the Employment of Women with Family Responsibilities, 1965 [No.123]) actually existed in Eastern European countries. The monographs contain information on the equality of the sexes and women's right to work, female occupational activity in these countries, child-care services and facilities and special employment conditions for parents of young children, and measures taken to create social attitudes that are favorable to working women and that provide workers with information designed to enable them to reconcile their occupational family responsibilities.

Kamerman, Sheila B.

1979   "Work and family in industrialized societies." Signs: Journal of Women in Culture and Society 4:632–650.

Developments that have led to various public policy initiatives to integrate work and family more closely in five European countries are described. A variety of developments and adaptations to increase the female labor-force participation are discussed, including child-care programs, maternal or parent-care benefits, and work-sharing.

1980   "Child-care and family benefits: Policies of six industrialized countries." Monthly Labour Review 103(11):23–28.

This article discusses the nature of the lifestyle of families with working parents and analyses the different types of benefits that the United States and several European countries have provided to help working parents cope. The author concludes, "The European experience clearly suggests the need for a policy strategy that includes income transfers, child-care services and employment policies as central elements even if the specifics may vary as they are modified to fit the ideology, demography and needs of each country."

Land, Hilary
    1979   "The changing place of women in Europe." Daedalus 108(2):73–94.
    This essay has two goals: (1) to describe changes that have occurred in the employment patterns of men and women in some European countries and to relate them to changes affecting men and women within the family, noting particularly the conflicts and contradictions that arise; and (2) to examine some countries' attempts to bring the demands of production in the economic sphere and the needs of human reproduction into equilibrium, and also to examine how far these policies are likely to hinder, or even reverse, the moves women have been making toward achieving greater mobility. The conclusion is that the struggle for sexual equality requires the challenging of societal circumstances that structure women's lives, such as public politics and customs, in the economic system.

Paoli, Chantal
    1982   "Women workers and maternity: Some examples from Western Europe." International Labour Review 121(1):1–16.
    The author studies measures adopted in some European market economy countries to improve maternity protection and to enable women workers to reconcile the dual function of maternity and economic activity without undermining equality. After discussing maternity as a social function, the author examines the following subjects: women workers who are protected, job security and health protection, and the arrangements made to enable mothers to look after their children for a variable period following the expiry of maternity

leave through the introduction of parental leave, to which fathers are also sometimes entitled. The study shows that maternity protection, founded first of all on the principle of safeguarding the health of women workers and the social need to protect children, now occupies a growing place in aspirations to reconcile work more harmoniously with family life.

Rueschemeyer, Marilyn
  1977   "The demands of work and the human quality of marriage: An exploratory study of professionals in two socialist societies." International Journal of Comparative Family Studies 8:243–255.

  This article focuses on the way work conditions affect personal relations outside of work, especially in marriage. Data from an exploratory study of professionals in socialist and capitalist societies are reported. The study investigates whether serious attempts to reduce discrimination against women in the world of work and changes in some of the conditions of alienation result in changed personal relations for socialist-society marriages. Conclusions derived from the study suggest that the possibilities for incorporating working wife and personal relationships are limited, despite the many supports working men and women are given in socialist societies. Other measures to reduce the tension between work and personal life are required.

Séguret, M. C.
  1981   "Child-care services for working parents." International Labour Review 120(6):711–725.

  Attitudes adopted by various governments concerning the problem of caring for the children of working parents are considered. Advantages and disadvantages of different approaches are also discussed. Women's employment trends, children's needs, the attitude of the authorities, and the systems of child-care in industrialized and developing countries are reviewed and illustrated with examples from various societies. Subregional cooperation, nongovernmental organization, use of local resources, and freedom of parental choice, as well as research into child psychology, are deemed to be important to this issue.

Smirnov, S.A.
>   1979   "Maternity protection: National law and practice in se-
>   lected European countries." International Social Security
>   Review 4:420–444.
>
>   The purpose of this study is to describe the salient features
>   and tendencies of maternity protection in two areas (1) that
>   relating to conditions of employment and (2) that relating
>   to maternity benefits provided by social security schemes and
>   labor legislation in 14 countries. There is also some infor-
>   mation on child-care facilities. The conclusion is that al-
>   though maternity protection has become an important part
>   of labor and social security legislation in Eastern and West-
>   ern European countries, it can still be improved. For ex-
>   ample, all working women should have the right to mater-
>   nity benefits; increased sick pay in the case of illness due
>   to pregnancy or confinement is needed; extension of paid
>   leave in the case of illness of the child, and the granting of
>   paid leave after statutory maternity leave, require exami-
>   nation.

Family Influences on Work Aspirations and Involvement

Artz, Reta D., and Lionel A. Maldonado
>   1978   "Social class and occupational values: Argentine and United
>   States students." International Journal of Comparative Family
>   Studies 9(3):355–366.
>
>   This study is concerned with the nonhierarchical dimension
>   of occupational aspirations. It compares both the occupa-
>   tional values for Argentine and United States youth and the
>   effects of social-class background on occupational values.
>   Research data were collected in Eugene, Oregon, and Bue-
>   nos Aires, Argentina. Results suggested that, overall, fam-
>   ily effects are greater in the United States than in Argen-
>   tina. They also present evidence to support the view that
>   family may be partly responsible for the prevention of rapid
>   social change in Latin American.

Brinkerhoff, Merlin B.
>   1982   "Familial constraints on women's work: A comparative
>   analysis." International Journal of Comparative Family
>   Studies. 13:307–328.

Survey data confirm that social factors such as education, socioeconomic status, and stage in the family life-cycle are more strongly correlated with wives' labor-force participation in a Mexican city than in a Canadian one. It was concluded that the less-educated women from the lower socioeconomic statuses of Mexico encounter greater impediments to the work world than their North American sisters. Furthermore, unlike Canadian women, Mexican wives do not exit the work world at critical life-cycle stages such as childbearing.

Cutright, Phillips
1968   "Occupational inheritance: A cross-national analysis." American Journal of Sociology 73:400–416.
Utilizing mobility data from previous studies, this author measures the openness of the occupational structure to movement across the manual-nonmanual divide and explains differences in the amount of such movement among 13 nations. Findings suggest that occupational inheritance and the level of total mobility are largely a function of demographic, economic, and social factors. The conclusion is that "if nations differ in their levels of development, we can be fairly confident that their levels of occupational inheritance and total mobility will also vary."

Davids, Leo
1972   "Fatherhood and comparative social research." International Journal of Comparative Sociology 13(3–4):217–222.
The author suggests that we must move beyond the cross-cultural work on motherhood and begin to study fatherhood in order to illuminate similarities and differences in family life and also to examine the relationships between family life and other social institutions. Important aspects of education, economic life, and religion can be clarified by considering fatherhood as the gateway to these spheres for children, especially sons.

Galenson, Marjorie
1973   Women and Work: An International Comparison. Ithaca, N.Y.: Publications Division, New York State School of Industrial and Labour Relations, Cornell University.
Through the analysis of labor-market data, the author examines and compares female employment rates, occupa-

tional distribution, familial burden, income, education, aspirations, and the general attitude of women toward their jobs in several societies. Study results suggest that because women indicate satisfaction with the status quo, it is unlikely that there will be a sudden change in their relative status in the labor market. The dual burden of work with home and child care will probably remain women's responsibility by choice. It is up to women themselves to change the status quo and break the pattern that restricts them to conventional women's work.

Horna, Jarmila
1978   Women in the Family and Employment: A Cross-cultural View. Journal of Comparative Family Studies (Special Issue) 9(1).

This multidisciplinary and cross-cultural collection of articles presents writings for the purpose of promoting understanding of the family and family change. Although the burden of comparison is left to the reader, common themes concerning women's position in the work force and the family are prevalent.

Laska, Shirley Bradway, and Michael Micklin
1981   "Modernization, the family and work socialization: A comparative study of United States and Colombian youth." International Journal of Comparative Family Studies 12(2):187–204.

Using data from Colombia and the United States, this study investigates the following themes: the role played by occupational socialization experiences; the influence of the family, relative to other socialization agents, on labor-force entry; and whether socialization for work varies significantly in societies with divergent cultural backgrounds and different levels of socioeconomic development. Findings regarding the relationship between modernization and sources of work socialization for youth entering the labor force include: parents and family members hold the important position of role models in traditional societies; peers hold that position in the transitional/traditional society; in the transitional/modern stage there is a deconcentration and expansion of the individuals selected as role models and as sources of occupational information; and at the modern stage there is general diffusion of role-model selection with parents included as models.

Rosenthal, Marilynn M.

1979   "Perspectives on women physicians in the USA through cross-cultural comparison: England, Sweden, USSR." International Journal of Women's Studies 2:528–540.

This study focuses on how the experiences of women physicians in America compare and contrast with the experiences of women in other health-care systems that organized in significantly different ways and exist within different political economies. Two central issues that emerge in this article involve sex-role choices and professional status. One important conclusion is that the decision to have children causes women physicians to have career patterns and sensitivities different from their male colleagues.

Youssef, Nadia

1973   "Cultural ideals, feminine behavior, and family control." Comparative Studies in Society and History 15,3(June):326–347.

Latin America is contrasted to Middle Eastern countries in an examination of the interdependence between cultural values and actual conditions of family behavior by application of the situational perspective. The conclusion is that "situational circumstances have created a wider range of alternative patterns of behavior for women to supersede the single traditional role circumscribed by culture and sustained by family ideals." Of interest to the study of family and work is the reference to the relatively high educational standard of women and their participation in the upgraded occupations in Latin America.

1976   Women and Work in Developing Societies. Population Monograph Series No. 15. Institute of International Studies, University of California, Berkeley.

Utilizing data on Latin American and Middle Eastern countries provided by official censuses, the United Nations Demographic Yearbook, and the International Labour Office, this study seeks to identify some of the critical independent variables that influence women's participation in nonagricultural employment. Data findings suggest that female labor-force participation is not merely a function of family characteristics such as age at marriage, extent of marriage, prevalence of marital disruption, and fertility rates; rather it is the interaction of such variables with the social organization. For example, in Middle Eastern countries, female employment rates are low because all women are restricted regardless of age, marital condition, or motherhood state. The extent to which women will be motivated to work will ultimately depend on the degree to which changing social conditions bring acceptance and recognition of women's worth for the contributions they can make outside of traditional family roles.

References

Blake, Judith
  1974   "The changing status of women in developed countries." Scientific American 231(3):136–147.
Boulding, Elise
  1976   "Familial constraints on women's work roles." Signs: Journal of Women in Culture and Society 1(3):95–117.
Cancian, Francesca M., Louis Wolf Goodman, and Peter H. Smith
  1978   "Capitalism, industrialization, and kinship in Latin America: Major issues." Journal of Family History 3(4):319–336.
Cogswell, Betty E., and Marvin B. Sussman (eds.)
  1972   Cross-national Family Research. Leiden: E. J. Brill.
Fogarty, M. P., R. Rapoport, and R. Rapoport
  1971   "Early and later experiences as determinants of adult behavior: Married women's family and career patterns." British Journal of Sociology 22(March):16–30.
Guteck, Barbara A., Charles Y. Nakamura, and Veronica F. Nieva
  1981   "The interdependence of work and family roles." Journal of Occupational Behavior 2(1):1–16.
Hoffman, Lois Wladis, and F. Ivan Nye (eds.)
  1974   "Effects on child." Chapter 6 in Working Mothers. Jossey-Bass Publishers.
Mortimer, Jaylan, Richard Hall, and Rueben Hill
  1978   "Husbands' occupational attributes as constraints on wives' employment." Sociology of Work and Occupations 5:285–313.
Nimkoff, M. F.
  1965   Comparative Family Systems. Boston: Houghton Mifflin.
Oppenheimer, Valerie Kincade
  1979   "Structural sources of economic pressure for wives to work: An analytical framework." Journal of Family History 4(Summer):177–197.

Osmond, Marie Withers
  1981   "Comparative marriage and the family." International Journal of
          Comparative Sociology 22(3–4):169–196.
Pleck, Elizabeth H.
  1976   "2 worlds in 1: Work and family."Journal of Social History
          10(2):178–195.
Rodgers, Gerry, and Guy Standing
  1981   "Economic roles of children in low-income countries." Interna-
          tional Labour Review 120(1):31–47.
Rodman, Hyman
  1967   "Marital power in France, Greece, Yugoslavia, and the United
          States: A cross-national discussion." Journal of Marriage and the
          Family 29:320–324.
Safilios-Rothschild, Constantina
  1976   "Dual linkages between the occupational and family systems: A
          macrosociological analysis." Signs: Journal of Women in Culture
          and Society 1:51–60.
Sawhill, Isabel V.
  1977   "Economic perspectives on the family." Daedalus 106(2):115–125.
United Nations Educational, Scientific, and Cultural Organization
  1978   "Comparative report on the role of working mothers in early
          childhood education in five countries." Paris Doc. ED–78/WS/71.
Young, Michael, and Peter Willmott
  1975   The symmetrical family: A study of work and leisure in the Lon-
          don region. Harmondsworth, Middlesex, England. Penguin Books.

Index

The Contributors

Ronald Angel, Rutgers University

Augustine Brannigan, University of Calgary

Merlin B. Brinkerhoff, University of Calgary

Joseph E. DiSanto, University of Calgary

James S. Frideres, University of Calgary

Eugen Lupri, University of Calgary

Margaret I. Price, University of Calgary

Hyman Rodman, University of North Carolina at Greensboro

Constantina Safilios-Rothschild, Population Council, New York

Marta Tienda, University of Wisconsin at Madison

Pierre L. Van den Berghe, University of Washington

Richard Wanner, University of Calgary

About the Editor

MERLIN B. BRINKERHOFF is Professor of Sociology and Associate Dean of Social Sciences at the University of Calgary, Canada. His previous books include *Utah in Numbers: Comparisons, Trends and Descriptions* and *Complex Organizations and Their Environments*, both written with P. R. Kunz.